His Road Trip

An Aspiring Adventure

Across America

By Lugene Hessler Hammond

Published by WebPowerPros, Inc., POBox 51654, Myrtle Beach, SC 29579

Copyright 2017 by Lugene Hessler Hammond

HIS ROAD TRIP

www.HisRoadTrip.com

Thanks for purchasing our little book. Funds from this sale will enable us to continue our ministry and keep us on the road for Him.

www.MotorHomeMinistry.com, a ministry for connecting the Bible to kids and parents.

Printed in the United States of America

ISBN 978-0-692-82910-3

All rights reserved solely by the author. The author guarantees all contents are original and do not infringe upon the legal rights of any other person or work. No part of this book may be reproduced in any form without the permission of the author, including being stored in a retrieval system, or transmitted (electronic, mechanical, photocopying, recording, or otherwise, except for brief quotations in reviews) without prior permission from the publisher. The views expressed in this book are not necessarily those of the publisher(s).

Unless otherwise indicated. Bible quotations are taken from:

Most Bible quotations are taken from the New International Version (NIV) Holy Bible, New International Version®, NIV® Copyright ©1973, 1978, 1984, 2011 by Biblica, Inc.® Used by permission. All rights reserved worldwide.

Introduction Bible quotations are taken from the Holman Christian Standard Bible (HCSB) Copyright © 1999, 2000, 2002, 2003, 2009 by Holman Bible Publishers, Nashville Tennessee. All rights reserved.

Edited by Jana Lewis

This book is dedicated to my husband of nearly 44 years,

Larry Hammond,

without whose tender care, knowledge, leadership,

prodding, encouragement, and downright bullying,

I would have never written this book.

To my good friends everywhere, whose kind words

have encouraged me.

And especially to the Lord, who makes All Things Possible.

Contents

PREFACE	6
FROM THE BEGINNING	9
MAYHEM	12
GRIEF	15
CHRISTMAS, 1986	17
GOD'S PLAN	19
BIG CHANGES	20
MISSIONS	22
CEF	27
OCC	29
TROUBLE	32
HEAVEN	35
DOWNSIZE	37
CRASH	41
MOTORHOME MINISTRY	48
GOODBYES	50
ODYSSEY	54
THE PLAN	55
JOURNAL ENTRIES	59
JUST ONE MORE THING…	288
MY FAVORITE RECIPES	291
EASY KNITTING PATTERN FOR A WINTER CAP	303
	303
BACK OF THE BOOK STUFF	305
CAMPGROUND RECAP	317

Romans 5:1-5

Therefore, since we have been declared righteous by faith,
we have peace with God through our Lord Jesus Christ.
2 We have also obtained access through Him by faith
into this grace in which we stand,
and we rejoice in the hope of the glory of God.
3 And not only that, but we also rejoice in our afflictions,
because we know that affliction produces endurance,
4 endurance produces proven character,
and proven character produces hope.
5 This hope will not disappoint us,
because God's love has been poured out in our hearts
through the Holy Spirit who was given to us.

Jeremiah 29:11

11 For I know the plans I have for you"
—this is the Lord's declaration—
"plans for your welfare, not for disaster,
to give you a future and a hope."

Proverbs 3:5-6

5 Trust in the Lord with all your heart,
and do not rely on your own understanding;
6 think about Him in all your ways,
and He will guide you on the right paths.

PREFACE

By the time, I finished writing this book, we had already traveled through 26 of our glorious United States in the past eleven months, with 4 more states to go before we arrive home next month. We have had so many amazing experiences on this adventure!

But, I feel that no one could fully appreciate our delight in being able to make this trip—this Motorhome Ministry—without knowing something about the life events that brought us here, to this point. That life was complicated, full of blessings as well as tragedy.

I will apologize in advance for the number of times I will use the words *wow, amazing, beautiful, breathtaking, awesome, terrific, spectacular, remarkable, stupendous*, and other such superlatives. Even these words do not do justice to God's beautiful creations. There are Bible verses throughout this book. The Bible is our instruction book and I feel these scriptures bring our story to life.

Joshua 1:8

8 Keep this Book of the Law always on your lips;
meditate on it day and night,
so that you may be careful to do everything written in it.
Then you will be prosperous and successful.

Before we started this adventure, Larry was given some pastoral encouragement by our youth pastor. Brandon is a Purple Heart recipient, who was shot in the chest during the Iraq war. He said, "Keep on keeping on, Brother. Where one door closes, another one opens. The devil will fight when he feels threatened. You are raising awareness of this nation's apathy and persecution. Everywhere Paul went, he faced persecution; Jesus did as well. You are following in their footsteps. Carrying the cross of Christ is never easy, but it's what we are called to do. My prayers are with you both. Don't quit what God has called you to, even if you have to relocate or adjust your game plan. God, bless you."

We cherish those words. Each time the devil would rear his ugly head, we were once again encouraged by his warning words to expect times such as these. We did have to change our game plan several times to accommodate others, but we never, ever wanted to quit.

We have often been given the look of disgust and disapproval, mocked, yelled at, told to remove our banner, told, "your kind is not welcomed here", and even banned from campgrounds for life! We didn't waiver on our mission for Him. We did what Jesus did:

Matthew 10:14

14 If anyone will not welcome you or listen to your words, leave that home or town and shake the dust off your feet.

One important note as you read this book, when I refer to Him with a capital "H", I'm referring to my Holy Father God above. Anybody else, is just a plain him.

To bring this book to life, we have uploaded thousands of beautiful photos, in date order, on our web site www.HisRoadTrip.com. You will find some of the most amazing scenery, architecture, historic landmarks, flowers and plants, and wildlife across North America. There are some blurry ones, many of which were taken through a windshield at highway speeds. We chose not to delete these, because they still help to tell our story.

I pray this book will encourage you to not only go out and see this beautiful land that we have the freedom to roam without restraint, but to also encourage you to seek His amazing grace and enjoy a greater personal relationship with our Lord and Savior, Jesus Christ.

FROM THE BEGINNING

First there was me.

Next, there was Larry.

In 1973, the two became Husband and Wife.

Some might say that we were unequally yoked from the beginning. I had been raised in church with an awareness that Jesus was always walking by my side. My husband had been to church only occasionally as a child. He knew the basics, but could not understand the inner faith that I held. If I said, "Trust God to handle this", it would just make him mad. He felt the need to micromanage every little bit of our lives.

I am a child of God. I was baptized as an infant and raised in the Lutheran Church. The Bible defines an Age of Accountability for our sins, and at that time, I was confirmed in the church and made my public Affirmation of Faith. As an older adult, I made a public confession of faith and baptized as an adult. I ask God daily to use me as He will and always for His glory.

Larry: *After we were married, we always went to church but I didn't understand why. Maybe to be seen? All Christians were supposed to go to church, weren't they? I told myself I was being a good Christian because I went to church. I, for one, felt bored. I was just a seat warmer who spent the time planning my upcoming week. I just wanted to get out and get on with my day. There, I showed up!*

In 1976, baby Diana made three.

In 1979, baby Bobby made four. Perfect!

After the kids were born, Larry began to advance his career in designing and implementing oil company convenience stores. He traveled a lot, was paged to leave the house all hours of the night, and constantly interrupted by company problems that were always more important at that moment than his family. He was climbing the all-important corporate ladder. Families do often suffer while the head of the household is pursuing a better financial future for them. I went to work, picked up the kids from school, fed and bathed them, loved on them bunches. They understood Daddy loved them, but was busy with his job.

Then word came in August, 1984, that we were being transferred from our little hometown in Ohio to Louisville, KY. We quickly arranged new schools and met a couple of the neighbors. Diana attended Girl Scouts and Bobby started T-ball. I even became Girl Scout Cookie Mom.

I decorated the house to make it beautiful, then got a job. But it just never felt like home. The church we'd found was a long drive away and after the terrific church we had long attended in Ohio, this one fell flat. We didn't make many friends there in the neighborhood. Only ten months later, in August, 1985, word came that we were now being transferred to his company's home office in Indianapolis, Indiana.

We immediately fell in love with the city. It was the first neighborhood we'd lived in with paved streets and sidewalks! The neighbors were often out walking and biking, and always waved as they passed by. Diana and Bobby were wheeling their bikes all over this cozy neighborhood, introducing themselves to everyone they met. They even told one neighbor, "My mom needs a job!" I did, and I got that job on my own merits, working downtown for the largest law firm in the state of Indiana.

We both made friends quickly, at home and at work. And the church was just down the road. God had covered everything.

Both kids were in the church Christmas play that year, about little creatures who witnessed the Savior's birth: angels, lambs, lady bugs and fireflies. It was a precious low-budget production. Diana was a firefly and Bobby was a lamb, complete with his paper-plate-and-cotton-balls costume. Right after he delivered his line, "Those were angels, weren't they?" he promptly knocked over the mic stand and everybody laughed. Precious moments we will never forget.

So here we were, living life in a nice little home in a great neighborhood. Our lives were full of church, two kids, two great careers, lots of friends, Girl Scout cookies and homework. We even had a camping trailer. Life seemed perfect. But only in hindsight would we see that God was setting the stage for a huge upheaval.

MAYHEM

After moving to Indianapolis, New Year's Eve seemed to come all too quickly. We made plans to spend the evening with a neighboring family, Jim and Jill, and their kids, Beth and Danny. Instead of going out into the dangers of traffic and partiers, we agreed that they would cut through our backyards to our house. We would play games and watch videos and eat lots of snacks until midnight. I had cleaned house and made lots of food. After working all day, there wasn't much time until they would arrive.

I sent both kids to their rooms to be sure they were ready for our company. I remember joking, "I don't want our new friends to think we live like heathens!" Excited about the upcoming evening, they scooted off quickly. Diana skipped her way back to the kitchen after about 5 minutes, proud that her room didn't need much work. I sent her back to check on her brother. Larry and I will never forget her words, as she ran back, "Bobby had an accident and I think he's dead."

Why on earth would she say such a thing?

Larry and I rushed back to Bobby's bedroom. Bobby had received a bicycle lock chain from Santa and had been "locking up" all sorts of things earlier that week. We found him hanging from the chain on his bunkbed, not breathing. I ran to call 911.

Larry, alone then with Bobby: *I ran into the room, carefully removed him from the chain and started to give him CPR and mouth to mouth. As I was desperately trying to bring him back to life, God spoke to me for the very first time in my life and I heard Him clearly, "He's okay. He's with Me. Let him go." I didn't hear this through my ears or* *thought it through my mind it was just there. Loud and clear. A strong presence was with me. But I just kept on going. I couldn't stop! I had to be in control! I stopped only when the first responders poured into the room to take over. I felt emotionally broken, almost to the point of collapsing.*

I phoned for our new friends to come quickly, as something terrible had happened. Without question, they came. The ambulance and police had already arrived. Other neighbors were out on the street, wondering what could be happening to the new folks in their quiet little neighborhood.

The paramedics quickly got Bobby into the ambulance and, leaving Diana with our friends, we were quickly whisked away in the police car. The officer driving was male; his partner a woman. I was sitting right behind her in the patrol car, with Larry to my left. As uncomfortable as it must have been, she reached over the high bench seat to hold my hand the entire ride downtown. My other hand was holding onto Larry's. No one spoke.

Traffic was horrible, as expected. There is no easy way to the hospital district in downtown Indianapolis. The ambulance eventually radioed the cruiser and asked that we run ahead of them with lights and sirens, to cut a path in the traffic. Both sets of blue and red lights pulsated against the close buildings. There were sirens, white lights, and traffic lights. We would race up the block, screech to a stop in the middle of the intersection, wait for the ambulance to catch up, then speed ahead to the next light repeatedly. Total and complete mayhem.

So, while sitting and holding hands, my mind is racing, shooting questions one after another: "Where are my Mom and Dad? I've got to call them. Oh, they're in Florida, at a campground. What campground? It's late and the campground office might be closed. Maybe I can call the local police. Where are they in Florida? I need to call Larry's Mom and Dad to tell them. No. I'll call my sister-in-law and let her and her husband drive over to tell my in-laws. What if he dies? What if he lives and needs special care? OH, MY GOD, WHAT IF?"

And my world stopped. All the flashing lights, all the sirens, all the traffic and holiday lights, all the mayhem. My mind was completely still. Then God explained that this was no one's fault, no accident. Everything was going according to His plan. I had indeed called upon the Lord with a question and He had immediately answered. That was different.

> Jeremiah 29:11
>
> 11 For I know the plans I have for you," declares the Lord, "plans to prosper you and not to harm you, plans to give you hope and a future."

Larry didn't share with me his experience with God's words until years later, but I knew at that moment God had already called Bobby home to be with Him. I knew the doctors would not be able to revive him. At the hospital, they worked on him for another hour or so, to no avail.

Sweet Bobby, full of smiles and giggles, who had been stealing Baby Jesus out of the manger scene just a few days ago, was gone. He was only six years old.

GRIEF

Larry: *In the days, weeks, and months after this tragic time, we were all struggling to get on with daily life, whatever that meant. I went through all kinds of emotions, but most of all I was mad. I was downright angry with God. I often asked why He just had to do this to our family?*

Diana and Bobby had always been close. When we moved, we changed neighbors and friends and schools, and everything was new. But they knew without a doubt that they always had each other. Because of this, I insisted that Diana see a youth psychologist to help her through these confusing times; I met with one, too. I suggested that Larry seek assistance but he is a man. Men don't talk about touchy-feely emotions with other men. Nope. Nada. Period.

Diana was trying desperately to understand this whole thing, at the precious age of nine. She understood that Bobby was in Heaven with Jesus. OK. She gets that. What she pressed to understand was HOW he got to Heaven from his bedroom. We tried to explain, "Well, God told an angel that it was time to bring Bobby to Heaven. His job on earth was done. So, the angel came and took him Home."

She thought about that for a while, and she didn't like it one bit. She absolutely refused to go down our front hall alone and that hall was the only way to get to her bedroom and bathroom (and passing Bobby's room). "Mommy come with me, daddy come with me." Why? We kept asking. "You're big enough to go yourself!" She finally got fed up with our refusals to go with her and one day spouted off loudly, "Well if that angel flew in here to take Bobby away, what's going to keep her from swooping in here and taking me away, too!?"

Hmmm. Good point. We couldn't explain that one. She would often end up in our bed at night, scared that the angel would try to take her in her sleep. But she made darn sure that angel would have to make it past her mom and dad first!

We finally got her a dog named Brandi, that followed her around everywhere. The dog would scare the angels away, if they came, we said. She finally began to settle down. But, life and our family was never the same after Bobby left us.

Larry continued to climb his corporate ladder, and I continued in my job. Coworkers were nervous around me, not knowing just what to say. I tried to put them at ease, but even I didn't know, day to day, how I would feel. Diana continued to go to school. Life went on.

Larry: *Church was still the same to me. We were all still numb; I was depressed and angry.*

Statistics show that divorce following a child's death is very high. We can certainly understand why. Months had passed since Bobby's death. I had heard God's plan, sought counseling, and was feeling better for it. Occasionally, something would come up that would actually make me laugh. One day I laughed over something small and it made Larry really mad. "How can you laugh when our son just died?" We were not handling our grief at the same rate and there was a great deal of resentment between us because of that. We both see Bobby in each of us and everything we did reminded us of him.

Then Christmas arrived.

CHRISTMAS, 1986

Larry: *"Christmas is almost here again Dad, get out the decorations," my 10-year-old daughter, Diana, insisted. When I'd put away the Christmas things last year, we'd just buried Bobby. My wife had carefully packed each item in its labeled box and I'd lugged everything out to the storage shed. I didn't want to face those sad memories again. But Diana wanted Christmas as usual, with the tree and all the trimmings. She was absolutely right. Life goes on. I steeled myself and headed out to the shed. It was a crisp, clear, windless day, with the sun high in the sky, but the beauty was lost on me. I thought I would never again enjoy Christmas.*

How can I, without all of us here together?

I yanked open the shed door and a cold wind swooshed out. A sheet of paper floated toward me, slowly coming to rest at my feet. Then the air was still once more. I bent down to pick up the paper--a handmade Christmas card. How did this get here? I wondered. We had a special box for cards we'd saved, cards whose messages were worth reading year after year. We cherished those. Especially this one from last year, the one I held in my hands. As I reread his penciled message, I could hear Bobby's voice, see his face on Christmas morning.

His card read .... from first grade 1986:

"Have a Merry Christmas Mommy and Daddy. Happy New Year."

Love, Bobby.

Bobby would always be with us, and one day we'd be with him.

HE would always be with us, too."[1]

I was pale and white as I went inside and recounted this incident to Lugene. I started to question in my mind. What? Why did this happen? I believed but did I REALLY believe? This would be the second encounter and a turning point in my faith.

Psalm 91:11
11 For he will command his angels concerning you to guard you in all your ways

---

[1] This story was submitted by Larry Hammond to: Angels on Earth A Guidepost Publication, Printed in Nov/Dec 2000 Christmas Issue

GOD'S PLAN

Amazing things began happening after Bobby's death. Amazing things within our family. We had been the only members of our extended families that regularly attended church. Over the next few years, one by one, family members began to attend church, accept Christ, and were baptized. A marriage was saved. New children were born. One began singing praise in churches. A few played in praise bands. One became a minister. One is a church secretary, another works for the church. One is studying to become a missionary. A couple created and ran ministries for the poor, the elderly and those with special needs.

God had assured me that He had a plan, and that Bobby's death was part of the plan. I had accepted His assurance and although I grieved, I sat back and waited for His plan to be revealed.

I am happy to say that, as this story continues, you will learn of many other lives that continue to be changed to this very day. And, God willing, every tomorrow ahead.

Every day of every one of our lives is spent in service of Jesus and bringing new souls to Christ.

> John 16:20
>
> Very truly I tell you, you will weep and mourn while the world rejoices.
> You will grieve, but your grief will turn to joy.

BIG CHANGES

Larry: *Corporate life just didn't fulfill me the way it had before. I could see the writing on the wall and changes in corporate structure that were coming. I needed to take control and change my career under my own terms. Two years after Bobby's death, I moved my family to Gatlinburg, Tennessee, and opened a little business with his life insurance money. We named it Pop'N Stuff, and spent the next 7 years in Gatlinburg, serving candy, popcorn, and sodas to tourists. We enjoyed our little church in the Smoky Mountains and Lugene loved serving as treasurer for our church and singing in the Community Chorale.*

Diana was doing well. She was all in favor of moving to Gatlinburg. We had come together with my extended family several times to rent a big house over Labor Day weekend. I suppose she had figured this move would be one long, extended vacation. She cried long and hard when Lugene announced that we needed to get her registered for school. "What do you mean, I have to go to school?" We laugh each time we remember.

The move to Gatlinburg had done her well, as the constant daily memories of life with Bobby in Indianapolis were now faraway. She joined us in church and was confirmed in her faith.

In 1995, we opened a second store in Myrtle Beach, SC. The bank who sponsored our loan required us to move to Myrtle Beach to supervise day-to-day operations of the shop. Move to the beach? No problem!

Although we had been commuting to oversee the construction of the store for months, we finally all moved to Myrtle Beach the same week that Diana graduated from high school. She would begin classes at Coastal Carolina University in the fall, studying art.

In 1997, we closed the shop in Gatlinburg—the one in Myrtle Beach was so busy that it was all we could keep up with. The store operated for eleven years in Myrtle Beach. And that, as some say, was that.

MISSIONS

Larry: *While in Myrtle Beach, we joined a church, Langston Baptist Church in nearby Conway, South Carolina. With over 700 souls in attendance each week, it was the largest church we'd ever attended and were initially concerned about how to become involved.*

"Just start in a Sunday School class," we were told. It all starts there. We hadn't attended Sunday School class since grade school, so the name "Sunday School" seemed so juvenile ... I think it should be something like "Adult Bible Fellowship". Anyway, we did just that and immediately started making friends. By the time we hit the road in 2016, we had been members of that same Sunday School class for over 10 years. We had hugged, prayed, mourned, and rejoiced with them. What a wonderful group of supportive, loving friends.

Lugene loves to sing in choir (she claims to be a back-row Alto) and Langston had a big one that sang every Sunday. Over the years, we both participated in numerous outreach programs, including choir, dramas, and mission trips.

My first mission trip was to Guatemala with a team from Langston. It was organized through Medical Missions Ministry. How hard could this be? I thought of it as a vacation and an opportunity to see a different part of the world. While on the flight, it finally started getting real. I thought, "What in the world am I going to say to the Guatemalan people about Him?" This had just never occurred to me—until that very moment.

I wasn't a Bible scholar, and admittedly, a so-so Christian at best. I did believe but leading foreign-speaking strangers to Christ was way beyond my comfort zone. I broke out in a cold sweat. I was nervous. What was I thinking? Whether I was ready or not, the plane landed and my team reported for duty.

It was strange that when it was time for me to speak to the people in the remote villages about God and His grace, the words and thoughts came easily to me. I knew that God was with me. Through my assigned interpreter, I told them of Jesus and how He died on the cross for each of us. If we confess our sins, believe that Jesus died and came back to life for us, and ask Him into our hearts, He will live inside of us forever. I told them of Heaven and spending eternity in the presence of God Himself.

> Deuteronomy 18:18
>
> 18 I will raise up for them a prophet like you
> from among their fellow Israelites, and
> I will put my words in his mouth.
> He will tell them everything I command him.

I shared the Gospel with people that were living in standards so poor that the poorest of poor in the United States would be considered rich. I had the blessing of talking to men and women, old and young...everyone that would come and listen.

I went home that year a very changed man. My heart had been touched by the people of Guatemala, and I went with that same medical mission group for six years running. They are amazing people. I keep in contact with them on social media—we celebrate together, we mourn together, we pray together. To this day, I consider each of them friends for life.

During my second trip, I remember clearly a man who sat down next to me. He looked very old to me. He was probably close to my age, but his deeply sun-dried skin made him look so much older. He had worked in the fields of Guatemala all his life. And he looked so sad.

Through my interpreter, I asked him, "If you died today, where would you go?" He looked at me and shrugged his shoulders and replied in Spanish, "Nowhere. I'd be dead."

I then proceeded to tell him about Jesus's free gift of grace. God provided all the words I needed.

Romans 10:9-10

9 If you declare with your mouth, "Jesus is Lord," and believe in your heart that God raised him from the dead, you will be saved. 10 For it is with your heart that you believe and are justified, and it is with your mouth that you profess your faith and are saved."

Tears began running down his cheeks. When I finished talking, he asked, "Why hasn't anyone ever told me this?" I was shocked. In America, we have churches open on every street corner, yet people choose to stay home on Sundays and go hunting, fishing, playing golf or any number of activities - except church. Plus, some feel that being a Christian just isn't politically correct nowadays. It dawned on me that I was sitting in front of someone who had never, ever had the opportunity to hear this story of Jesus. What a huge responsibility for me, as a Christian, to be called upon to spread the word to all nations. And here I was, doing just that.

> Matthew 28:19-20
>
> 19 Therefore go and make disciples of all nations, baptizing them in the name of the Father and of the Son and of the Holy Spirit, 20 and teaching them to obey everything I have commanded you. And surely, I am with you always, to the very end of the age."

Wow. God was speaking to me again. This was the moment my faith in Him really began to flourish.

My third trip to Guatemala, I again enjoyed witnessing many glorious salvations, but God provided one special encounter.

My assigned interpreter that day was Maqui, a young woman from Argentina, and she had been working with me all day. It was late in the afternoon and we were all hot and tired. An old woman came into view. We saw her approaching our station and she was acting a bit odd. She appeared to be talking to herself and swatting the air as though she was being tormented by a pesky bug. Maqui and I exchanged glances as if to say, "What's up with her?"

Then the woman began to speak. Let me make it clear that I speak English and understand only a handful of words in Spanish. The words she spoke were Gibberish to my ears, but my mind knew exactly what she'd said. Stunned, I looked at Maqui. I could tell that she'd heard the same Gibberish that I had. But she knew, too. The woman had said, "He says to Follow Him."

The woman looked up to the sky and said in Spanish, "There. I did it. I told them. Now leave me alone." She quickly stomped out the door and into the street.

Maqui and I were both speechless. I wanted to know more. I ran out the door but to my amazement, but she was gone. I went back to where I had left Maqui, and we began to excitedly discuss the miracle that we had just witnessed.

Well, Maqui did follow Him. She went on from being an interpreter to becoming a CEO of her own company that produces a women's magazine named Revista Entre Nosotras, or Magazine Between Us. She also speaks to women in large groups regarding women's issues and more importantly, salvation through Jesus Christ.

Whether in her magazine, seminars, on talk radio or television, she shares the Good News to everyone she can. She did follow His plan for her.

He tells us that He has a plan for each of us. I followed Him, too. It just took me a whole lot longer to get on board with the program.

CEF

Larry: *For the first time in my life, after my experiences in Guatemala, I began to read the Bible. Yes, I actually picked up that dusty book left on the coffee table in the living room. I read it cover to cover three times and continue to read it daily. It comes to life right before your eyes. It is life's instruction manual. It explains the history of your ancestors, your present life and what the future holds for everyone.*

I continued to grow by teaching kids in an after-school program called Good News Club. Organized by the Child Evangelism Fellowship (CEF), the club taught Bible stories, sang songs, and other activities. The kids loved it! Then we offered a quiet time in smaller groups where the kids could ask questions one-on-one with their counselor. They also had the opportunity to accept Christ as their Lord and Savior.

When I started with CEF, back in 2009, I was shocked to learn that so many of the elementary school kids had never heard of Adam and Eve, Noah, Jonah, or Moses. Even the fourth and fifth graders had never heard!!

Proverbs 22:6

6 Start children off on the way they should go, and even when they are old they will not turn from it.

In these times of a church on every corner, I was amazed that 28 million kids in America had never set foot in a church. We have sadly taken Him out of so much in our country: out of our government, out of our schools, out of our homes. We have forsaken God. And we wonder aloud why He seems to have forsaken us.

> Psalm 33:12
>
> 12 Blessed is the nation whose God is the Lord,
> the people he chose for his inheritance.

I taught in CEF for seven years. Each week, all week long, I looked forward to 3:00 on Thursday afternoon. I enjoyed this time so very much! The kids taught me more than I taught them. You could easily tell which kids didn't get love or attention at home. They were always hovering near the counselors, asking for us to tie their shoes, or compliment their pretty dress or hair bow. It was wonderful to be able to demonstrate God's love for them.

I understand that working with children or leading a Bible Study class may not be for everyone. The Bible explains that there are 27 Spiritual Gifts or Attributes that are given to individuals with which to serve Him. Your talents are different than mine; your Spiritual Gifts are different than mine. I had discovered that Evangelism is my primary gift.

> 1 Corinthians 12:1-6
>
> 12 Now about the gifts of the Spirit, brothers and sisters, I do not want you to be uninformed. 2 You know that when you were pagans, somehow or other you were influenced and led astray to mute idols. 3 Therefore I want you to know that no one who is speaking by the Spirit of God says, "Jesus be cursed," and no one can say, "Jesus is Lord," except by the Holy Spirit. 4 There are different kinds of gifts, but the same Spirit distributes them.5 There are different kinds of service, but the same Lord. 6 There are different kinds of working, but in all of them and in everyone it is the same God at work.

Okay. I found my calling, my spiritual gift, my purpose. Now, what am I supposed to do with it?

OCC

In addition to my participation in our church choir and other special projects, I began part-time work for a local Baptist Association, which led to my involvement in Operation Christmas Child (OCC). Led by The Reverend Billy Graham's son, Reverend Franklin Graham, it is a division of Samaritan's Purse, an international humanitarian aid organization. I made Shoeboxes off and on for years through our churches' involvement, but my life changed when my coworker, Diane, asked me to become a year-round volunteer with her.

I learned quickly that Operation Christmas Child is an amazing ministry. The world's largest Christmas project collects and distributes gift-filled shoeboxes for the neediest children around the world. Since 1993, more than 125 million boxes have been distributed in more than 130 countries. Shoebox gifts are collected in the US, Australia, Finland, Germany, Austria, Switzerland, Japan, New Zealand, Canada, Spain, and the U.K. Each year, the project mobilizes more than half a million volunteers worldwide— 150,000 of those in the US alone—who are involved in collecting, shipping, and distributing shoebox gifts. And I was now counted among them. I soon came to recognize the same thing Larry had seen in Guatemala: these are the people of the world that have never had the opportunity to hear about Jesus Christ.

There are year-round volunteers all over the world— some on the giving side and others on the receiving side. In the destination countries, the local volunteers arrange a date on which local children are invited to receive a gift. Now, keep in mind, most of these children are so impoverished that they have never in their lives received a gift of any kind. So the children come, probably more out of curiosity than anything. They are each given a gender- and age-appropriate box, along with a colorful book entitled, "The Greatest Gift" in their own language. They have probably never had the delight of a book to call their own, either. The volunteer explains that someone far, far away loves you so much that they made this box just for you, even though they don't know you. Why? Because someone named Jesus loved them first. And he taught them to love one another.

The OCC volunteers read the book to the kids, which details how Jesus was born, lived, died, and rose again for our sins. That is how much he loved us. Volunteers also explain how the box is a free gift to the child—undeserved, just as Jesus's gift of salvation is free—all they have to do is accept it. Only after hearing the story about the free gift of salvation are they allowed to open their boxes.

The children are amazed and squeal with delight that anyone could love them this much! Each box includes basic hygiene items like wash cloths and soap, toothbrushes, and combs as well as school supplies like pencils and paper. They also have a "WOW" gift, like a soccer ball or a baby doll, a sewing kit or fishing kit. The rest of the shoebox is filled with fun stuff like colorful hair barrettes, Matchbox cars, crayons, and coloring books. Many volunteers enjoying making things for the boxes like crocheted or knitted caps, beaded Salvation bracelets, or sewn backpacks.

In areas with sufficient volunteers, the children are then invited to attend a 13-week study of "The Greatest Journey". They receive a workbook that explains in much greater detail Jesus's life. When they're finished, the volunteers hold a graduation party for the students, complete with a diploma and a Bible of their own. As part of their study, the students commit to sharing this gift of salvation with at least nine other people that they know. OCC is a celebration of evangelism and discipleship.

I have met so many wonderful people with a passion for OCC. Our local team would speak for groups and churches, as well as present informational programs throughout the year. We would invite everyone we could to encourage them to implement OCC into their church programs.

Now, while Larry knew what his Spiritual Gift was, I knew that mine was not the same. So, I attended a workshop on Spiritual Gifts and confirmed what I already knew: my primary gift is Service. I have always been the happiest when I am able to serve others. With OCC, I was making a difference in people's lives. And my participation was making a big difference in mine.

TROUBLE

By this time, we were facing some dark times. While our spiritual lives were blossoming, other areas were not. Larry was not doing well. He was sick and nobody knew why. We saw different local doctors, who sent us to specialists, who sent us to other specialists in other cities. They ran tests, and more tests. He was weak, sick, exhausted, and frustrated that his body was fighting against him. He could no longer help at the store, which was getting busier all the time. It was way too much for me to oversee all on my own.

As the lease for the store was coming to its end in May, 2005 we learned a year earlier that the developers refused to give us a new lease. We would have to close our doors.

We frantically looked for an alternative and decided to relocate to another place nearby. We went tens of thousands of dollars in debt for the upfit, and there's no doubt that it was a beautiful store. But the foot traffic was just not there to support it. It died a slow and painful death and we closed it 15 months later, in September 2006.

Now we were up to our ears in debt we couldn't pay, Larry was unable to work, and full-time permanent jobs are very hard to find in a seasonal market like Myrtle Beach. Especially for a 53-year-old like me, who had been self-employed for the last eighteen years.

Larry: *We continued to grow in our faith and I started to follow what He wanted me to do. I just didn't know exactly what that was. But I continued to pray to Him each day and ask Him to guide me in the direction He wanted me to go. I started to talk to Him in my thoughts each day and communicate to Him. I discovered that the more I did this,* the more my life started to proceed in a positive direction. Life still got in the way of His plan—more of those valleys and mountains.

Isaiah 54:10

10 Though the mountains be shaken
and the hills be removed,
yet my unfailing love for you will not be shaken
nor my covenant of peace be removed," says the Lord,
who has compassion on you.

In 2008, we created an import business and named it Oyster & Pearls. We started it in our garage, and imported one specific product from China, a small pearl gift box, perfect for gifts. Each box contained a pop-top can with an oyster inside, a necklace chain and a pendant. The recipient opens the can, pries open the oyster and finds a pearl inside. They insert the pearl into the pendant and now has a beautiful necklace to wear. In time, Diana began designing new boxes and pendants for us. They were so much better than the standard boxes, and they were beautiful. Our friend Reggie traveled with Larry to wholesale shows to sell them. Retailers loved them! They ordered plenty and when their customers cleaned them out, they wanted more.

But manufacturing in China is a cash business. We had to wire them money before they would lift a finger in production. It usually took four weeks to manufacture and fill the order and another four weeks to receive them here, in the US. I have a whole new respect for the term "...on a slow boat from China."

But then our accounts wanted another thirty to sixty days to pay.

We had a factoring company for a while, but the fees were killing us. Eventually, the line was in such demand that there was no way we had the up-front cash to keep up with the demand.

We didn't want Oyster & Pearls to die entirely, so we sold it to one of our customers who's also in a manufacturing business. As far as we know, it continues to do well.

Larry: *Although we had no choice, I was upset with God about this, too.*

HEAVEN

Larry: *Aside from the mysterious afflictions I was feeling, I had other health concerns. I was a big man. I had many issues with my health, including diabetes and dangerously high blood pressure. A sleep study revealed that I was losing nine full minutes of oxygen a night, so I was prescribed a C-Pap machine to remedy that situation.*

One night, I awoke in Heaven. Yes, Heaven. I know this sounds crazy but it's true. There was a bright light and the most beautiful landscape you could ever see. The colors were so bright and vivid—I'd never seen anything like it! This physical world pales in comparison. This wasn't a dream. I was there. I know the difference between a dream and reality. I felt so at peace. My body wasn't in pain as it had been for so many years. I felt like I did in my youth. Free. I was free. It was the most wonderful feeling and I wasn't going to leave. Or so I thought.

I was met in this paradise by a woman named Anastasia. She had long, red hair and was dressed in brilliant white. I didn't know who she was or why she had come to meet me. In my life, I had never heard that name before. She didn't actually speak to me in words that I could hear with my ears, but she was communicating with me. I just understood somehow, just as when God has spoken to me before. After what seemed like a long time, with a brilliant blue sky above, He appeared in the clouds, as a bright light. I understood that He was motioning "go back." I wanted to go toward Him, but Anastasia also motioned me to go back.

I didn't want to go back. I wanted to stay...forever.

> ### Revelation 21:3-4
>
> 3 And I heard a loud voice from the throne saying, "Look! God's dwelling place is now among the people, and he will dwell with them. They will be his people, and God himself will be with them and be their God. 4 'He will wipe every tear from their eyes. There will be no more death'[a] or mourning or crying or pain, for the old order of things has passed away."

I woke up choking. I must have literally choked to death. I was gasping for air and it took a while to finally catch my breath. My mind was finding it difficult to process what had just happened. What HAD just happened?

I was back in the world. The peace was gone and my pain was back. But now I had a reason to live. Now I had a mission. I didn't know the mission was, but I was sent back for a reason. I did finally understand that He does want us to be in a church with other believers. But it's not about the church or religion.

It's about each person's personal relationship with God.

We continued to struggle for the next few years. Lugene went through a couple of jobs and finally realized we were going backwards in life. Something had to give. So, we decided to downsize. My plan was to get a motorhome and it would be our home.

I needed to give my life to God in service. That service would be helping others with their personal relationships with God.

DOWNSIZE

Larry: *It turns out that we had to sell everything we owned and follow Him. How did I know this? I just knew. Without a doubt. Just like the first time I encountered Him when Bobby died. I just knew that I had to sell everything I owned and follow Him.*

But the hard part wasn't the decision... It was how to tell my wife.

So, I sat down with her and explained that we needed to sell everything we had. She knew that we were losing our home anyway, because of the business debts and the loss of income.

She looked at me and asked, "And do what?" I explained my plan to purchase a used motorhome, travel this beautiful USA, and tell kids about Jesus.

Ephesians 5:22-33

22 Wives, submit yourselves to your own husbands as you do to the Lord. 23 For the husband is the head of the wife as Christ is the head of the church, his body, of which he is the Savior. 24 Now as the church submits to Christ, so also wives should submit to their husbands in everything.

25 Husbands, love your wives, just as Christ loved the church and gave himself up for her 26 to make her holy, cleansing her by the washing with water through the word, 27 and to present her to himself as a radiant church, without stain or wrinkle or any other blemish, but holy and blameless.

As the wife, I am always the "other side of the coin" person in this relationship. Larry was confirmed to have ADHD and OCD and always assumes that if he thought it up, then it's a great idea. Then he's off and running! I have the job of grounding him--slowing him down and bringing other pros and cons into the picture that he may not have considered. We are the Ying and Yang.

I cautiously said it's an admirable plan. It would be an honorable thing to do with our lives. But I was still working. We had absolutely no money saved, and all the bills from the business were still looming overhead.

Larry simply said we need to follow Him and trust Him beyond our own understanding.

Well, yeah, I do, but…

> Proverbs 3:5
>
> 5 Trust in the Lord with all your heart
> and lean not on your own understanding;

I said that I would not simply hit the road without knowing where our next meal or tank of diesel would come from. I trust God with every day of my life, but this plan was just asking for trouble, in my opinion. He was trying to convince me that all I needed to do is trust Him. But what if this plan really wasn't sanctioned by God? I didn't want to be 1,000 miles from home when I found out.

Back in October, 2014, The first earthly enabler for God's plan was Tom. He lives in Massachusetts, near Boston, and he had listed his motorhome for sale by owner with owner financing. This was imperative for us, as our failed business had turned our credit report upside-down. After Larry had spoken to him a few times, we grabbed a red-eye, flew to Boston, rented a car, and drove to Tom's home.

The motorhome was parked out front, among the trees. It was washed and waxed, and the extensions were all out. We introduced ourselves and took the grand tour. It was perfect. It's a peaceful, neutral tan inside. There are cornices above all the windows, cloth shades for privacy, and a second layer of shades to control hot/cold. The floor is patterned stone. The cabinets are cherry, and the stove had never been used. The shower is roomy and the front seats comfortable. As a side note, I have always hated RV toilets, but I could get used to this! There was even a place for both computers. And it had plenty of storage beneath. It had been used very little and well cared for. It could most certainly become home. So, we began to talk details.

It is a great act of service that Tom trusted us to drive away in his beautiful motorhome. I'd say that transaction was definitely a God-thing. We drove it away with a notarized five-year agreement for monthly payments. After five years, we will meet again to discuss the balance.

Motorhome? Check.

Larry: *So, we sold (or gave away) everything we owned. We developed a plan to travel. We created a plan for "Motorhome Ministry".*

The motorhome was the perfect place to call home. A lot of baby boomers are realizing that they want and need simpler lives, and we are no exception. They want to do what makes them happy, instead of following the consumer game by trying find happiness with bigger and bigger houses and more expensive stuff. This just makes people go into debt and become more miserable in trying to pay for all of it. But, they want more! They try to find meaning with meaningless things. Things from the material world will never satisfy the soul long term. As we have gotten older we understand this more. It becomes a vicious circle.

We are trying to go back to a simpler lifestyle and live a more meaningful life. This means downsizing, getting rid of the stuff that no longer holds any meaning to us or we can't use any more. With a smaller "world", we can more easily focus our energy on the things that really do matter: God, family, friends, making new friends and memories, focusing on life passions and dreams.

This way of life is much easier to achieve when we don't have the large bills to pay from a house mortgage plus all the expenses that go along with that.

We lived in the motorhome for a year before we planned to hit the road. We still had no money, but I felt even more secure in my faith. I knew that He would be with us. Jesus tells us that He takes care of even the small birds. I knew He would take care of us.

Matthew 6:26

Look at the birds of the air;
they do not sow or reap or store away in barns,
and yet your heavenly Father feeds them.
Are you not much more valuable than they?

CRASH

I was still working full time when we set out on our first real trip in the motorhome. We had been the promoters of a Spyder motorcycle rally the previous October in Fontana, North Carolina, in the beautiful Smoky Mountains. A Spyder is a reverse 3-wheeled motorcycle manufactured by Cam-Am, a division of Bombardier Recreational Products (BRP). The air had been crisp that weekend and the leaves were absolutely stunning. We had had motorcycle rides, a train ride, banquets, campfires, and marshmallows. We enjoyed meeting new friends, country music, and dancing. We were heading back to lead our second rally where more than one thousand were registered to attend. We hadn't even gotten out of the county when disaster struck.

We were on a stretch of Highway 501 just outside of Conway, South Carolina. We were very familiar with this area—a four-lane divided highway with a large grass median. There wouldn't be another traffic light for miles and traffic was very light. Larry was annoyed by the banging of the bathroom door, which I had forgotten to secure. Let me say here firmly that I am a seatbelt advocate. My car doesn't move without mine on. But I knew it would just take a few seconds to run back and latch the door, so I threw the seatbelt aside and moved quickly.

I had already returned to the front of the motorhome and had my hand on the back of my seat when Larry yelled something (I heard it but it didn't have time to register) and slammed on the brakes, throwing me headfirst into the windshield. The windshield cracked into all directions where my head hit it.

The motorhome stopped. Larry was out of his seat, above me, screaming to keep me conscious. As he helped me get up off the floor, we could both see the moped driver that had cut us off. If Larry had not slammed on the brakes, the driver would have been crushed like roadkill on the highway. Squished like a bug.

We saw him looking at us and the damage he'd done, and then we watched him drive away.

My God, this hurt.

I remember Larry yelling, "Are you all right?"

As if in a bubble, I heard myself speaking slowly and replied, "One thing I am very sure of: I am NOT all right."

Larry was shaking so badly that he couldn't punch 9-1-1 on his phone. I asked for the phone and instantly connected. I was calmly reporting the accident to the dispatcher, hoping that police could intercept and apprehend the driver who had left the scene. Then I said, "Oh. There are injuries and I need an ambulance dispatched, too."

Per my symptoms, they stuck me in a neck brace and strapped me to a backboard. Larry would have to turn the rig around himself and navigate it to the nearest hospital, which was no simple task. This was not an easy task at all. This wasn't just the 36-foot motorhome, but the tow dolly loaded with my Ford Escape, as well.

Conway Medical Center was just a few miles back. They quickly x-rayed me. When the doctor came back in with the results, he told the support staff to get me reset on the backboard. I had a fractured C-2 and required a neurosurgeon, which they did not have on staff. One false move and I could be paralyzed for life. They dispatched special transport that took me to Grand Strand Regional Medical Center, which was equipped and staffed to handle any Level 1 Trauma.

A quick lesson in anatomy: there are seven cervical bones in your neck. The top is C-1 and they continue down to C-7. If you fracture a bone badly enough, it can sever your spinal cord. The higher the break of the spinal cord, the higher the paralysis. For example, we all knew Superman Christopher Reeve. When he fell from that horse, he broke his C-1 and C-2, which severed his spinal cord very near the top. He couldn't move anything; he couldn't even breathe on his own. The neurosurgeon asked me if I had felt any tingling or numbness in my arms at the time of the accident. Yes, in both arms, but it lasted only about thirty seconds. That, he explained, was when my C-2 rubbed against my spinal cord, but didn't damage it. Thank you, Jesus.

Poor Larry now he had to move the big rig once again and find somewhere to park it in the crowded hospital lot.

I called my daughter, Diana, on my cell. She had been working at her new job for just a few months. I explained the collision and what the ER doctor had said. I knew Larry could not handle the activities of the Rally by himself—not 1,000+ people! And I wasn't going anywhere for a while. Within hours, Larry and Diana were on their way to the Spyder Rally with a taped-up windshield and I was left alone in the hospital. But I wasn't alone for long.

I remember clearly when my work supervisor, Ashlynn, appeared at the hospital, within hours of the wreck. She had taken the liberty to bring me paperwork to sign for what would obviously be an extended absence, so that I wouldn't lose my job. She was so worried and it was so sweet. She knew from work that I was a Christian, and there I was, giving God all the glory that I hadn't cracked my head open like an egg, ended up paralyzed, or dead. And I meant every word of it. I was very, very blessed. I remember the look on her concerned face while I was chattering on and on. I'm sure she was thinking, "My, my. This girl has really hit her head!"

Within days, Ashlynn had set up a Go Fund Me account and the funds raised were a great help in paying some expenses that month. What a blessing.

Other coworkers came—including Brent and Jess, as well as friends from church, including my choir friend, Tony. He admitted he really hadn't known what to expect when he came. A broken neck is no small thing. We praised the Lord together that the damage seemed minimal.

They didn't let me eat for days, but no one would fully explain why. They occasionally let me chew on ice, but everything else came through my IV. Days later, I learned that they considered the fracture to be unstable when I arrived. They were doing x-rays frequently, and could see it moving. If the fracture had moved closer to my spinal cord, surgery would be immediate. Hence, no food. Amazingly, the fracture stabilized after the first 24 hours and after a couple of days of stability, they finally let me eat. They then released me to go home in a cervical collar. Only problem was, my "home" was in another state – at the Spyder Rally! My terrific mother-in-law, Lois, and sister-in-law, Lisa, took me into their home and babysat me for the next few days, until Larry and Diana returned.

The pain was constant. Any movement at all made it worse. Getting up from a chair was difficult; getting up from laying down was excruciating. After a few weeks—desperate for a paycheck—I asked the neurosurgeon to allow me to return to my job in a call center. I sat in a chair, wore a headset, and answered questions—how difficult could that be? Much to my surprise, I could only handle a few hours a day for weeks. The pain was so bad! It's amazing how much effort it takes just to hold up the weight of your head.

Three months passed and an MRI was done. The fracture was supposed to have knit together over the course of 90 days. I should be healed and I should be able to take off the collar. But the pain was still so bad, and I returned to the neurosurgeon for evaluation.

The news was not good. Not only has the bone not come together to heal, there is now a gap of space where the fracture line was. Surgery was required - and as soon as possible. I was scared. I went to church that Sunday and asked to be anointed with oil.

> James 5:14-15
>
> 14 Is anyone among you sick?
> Let them call the elders of the church to pray over them and anoint them with oil in the name of the Lord.
> And the prayer of faith shall save the sick,
> And the Lord shall raise him up…

Everyone was called to come to the front and lay their hands on me while they prayed. As I sat on the front pew, surrounded by prayer warriors, I could hear their prayers going up for me. I could feel their tears on my arms, my shoulders, my face. I could feel the strength of God through them.

> **2 Chronicles 6:40**
>
> 40 "Now, my God, may your eyes be open
> and your ears attentive
> to the prayers offered in this place.

Thursday, February 11, 2016, was my first surgery. Pastor Jonathan, my choir director, had come early and kept the conversation light until it was time for me to go. Then he prayed. Oh, what a prayer it was! I was definitely covered in the prayer department.

After surgery, the pain upon waking up was unbelievable. Again, any movement at all made it worse. Larry told me that I had been gone a lot longer than planned. He shared that he suspected that all did not go well. I was only hours out of recovery when the neurosurgeon came in, not at all happy.

"I don't like the angle of the screws," he told me. They had installed two long screws that should have been straight and parallel, secured with wire. One was at a slight angle. We need to operate again.

What???

So, early Sunday morning, Valentine's Day, they put me under once again. I can only remember one thing on that day post-surgery: I could hear myself moaning in pain and I refused to open my eyes. The nurse was explaining that she couldn't give me more pain meds unless I would rate my pain from one to ten. Through the pain, I loudly replied TWELVE and the lights went out again.

Larry: *I was feeling helpless and devastated. Watching her go through months of pain only to have to endure even more* *after the surgeries was unbearable. It was as hard as when Bobby had died.*

I had done what I thought He had wanted me to do. Why had God thrown us into yet another valley? And such a deep valley! Lugene had been off work so much and we were falling further and further behind.

But, once again, what I didn't realize was that God had a plan. What an amazing God we serve.

Psalm 20:4

4 May He give you the desire of your heart
and make all your plans succeed.

Shortly after I returned home from surgery, an attorney in Charleston called me; he wanted to meet with me regarding the accident. He made the nearly three-hour trip to explain that I might have settlement options available to me that I may not be aware of. He went on to explain them in detail that, even though the moped driver wasn't found, I could still receive something to help cover the medical expenses. In closing our meeting, I asked how he'd learned about my accident. "I saw your Go Fund Me Account."

In short, God had turned that ten-second trip to the door latch into something life-changing in more than one way. Though I suffered terribly, He had indeed used the event to provide for all our needs. There was insurance money readily available, even though the responsible party was never found. My one and only concern had been addressed in a mighty way!

My recovery from the dual surgeries was painful and slow. With no end to the pain in sight, and my 62nd birthday quickly approaching, I conceded to retire from my job and apply for my Social Security early. We were going on the road for His Motorhome Ministry.

Ephesians 3:7

I became a servant of this gospel by the gift of God's grace given me through the working of his power.

Exodus 3:14

God said to Moses, "I am who I am.
This is what you are to say to the Israelites:
'I am has sent me to you.'"

MOTORHOME MINISTRY

Larry: *Motorhome Ministry is our traveling ministry that planned to meet with groups of children in campgrounds, parks, schools, churches, apartment complexes—just about anywhere the children can easily and safely meet with parental permission.*

Through our ministry, we teach kids wherever we go and give out packets full of books and color sheets, seeds, and wrist bands ... anything to teach kids about Him. We are trying to reach kids and their parents where they are. If we can't get them in church, we reach out to them while they're camping, traveling, fishing or biking.

We planned to present an exciting Bible lesson using colorful materials from CEF. This action-packed time would include songs, scripture memory, crafts, missions story and review games or other activities focused on the lesson's theme. We planned to teach outside on picnic tables, under shelters or around a campfire—just about anywhere.

Unchurched kids total about 28,000,000 (yes, 28 MILLION), and some have never even heard the basic Bible stories. Some have never even been inside a church or do not even know what Sunday School is. We are going to try to meet them where they are. If we can change one life, we have succeeded!

An estimated 73 million adults are presently unchurched. When teens and children are added, the total swells to roughly 100 million Americans. Since 1991, the adult population in the United States has grown by 15%. During that same period, the number of adults who do not attend church has nearly doubled, rising from 39 million to 75 million—a 92% increase!

People are falling out of church and so are their kids. Our society is crumbling because of this. We have a generation that is being forgotten and lost.

We wanted adult/parent participation and encouraged it. The main purpose is to evangelize to boys and girls with the Gospel of the Lord Jesus Christ and establish (disciple) them in the Word of God and get them in a local church for Christian living. We hope we can help them grow into God-loving adults.

Matthew 18:20

For where two or three gather in my name,
there am I with them."

GOODBYES

We were approaching our last days at our beloved Langston Baptist Church. There were hugs all around Sunday School class as we asked everyone to keep us in their prayers.

But what some call "Big Church" was my concern. I had lots of friends in that church, many of which I didn't see every week. They might sit in the balcony, work in the Media Room, work the sound or video booth or work in the children's departments. But I wanted them to know our journey and mission. I wanted them to know why we wouldn't be attending there anymore. I wanted them to pray for us.

I had written my farewell—I had it in my purse. I knew that Dr. Drum ran a tight ship, but I was going to do this. Larry stayed in his seat and wished me luck.

The service was ending. I approached Dr. Drum during the altar call and explained I had something to say. He requested I keep it short. Sorry, Dr. Drum, I just had too much to say to my friends.

My message is for all, so I include it here:

"It is with joy mixed with sadness that we stand here to say our goodbyes to our beloved Langston Family. These past ten years have been absolutely amazing! Having been raised in a small northern Lutheran church, my initial reaction was definitely, 'ya'll do things a lot different than we do!'" (Everyone laughed.) "But we liked it!

"We have been in Ron's Sunday School Class for all of these ten years. We have become a close-knit group of older brothers and sisters in Christ who learn together, pray for one another, we've cried together, we've rejoiced in God's mercies.

"As music is my passion, it has been my joy and honor to sing with the adult choir, for weekly worship for the past several years. Then the Coastal Evangelism Conference, our dramas: The Gift, and Jesus, the Resurrection. And there was the Children's Choir, where Pastor Jonathan and I were on our hands and aching knees teaching music to the first and second graders. What a hoot! And the older kids' choir? I have witnessed amazing things that Miss Shelley can do with those first- to fifth-graders.

"For four years, Larry had the honor of being a Deacon; that helped us to grow further in our faiths as we assisted others in growing in theirs. Larry is not well, but he volunteered whenever he could—his favorite jobs were being all decked out in the dramas and driving golf carts for special events.

"We want to encourage each and every one of you to seek out some way to serve. We learned the importance of delivering a benevolence meal, sewing for the dramas and the mission field, knitting caps for Mariners and making boxes for Operation Christmas Child. There are mission trips, Vacation Bible School, Awana, The One Ministry, In As Much Ministry…and dozens of other ways to serve.

"Recently, I asked to be anointed in preparation for some very serious surgery. The tears of the women standing closest to me dropped onto my arms and face. I could feel their hands on my shoulders, my head, my back, and knees. I could hear snippets of their fervent prayers for me. My strength comes from the Lord—but I believe that that strength is magnified through the intercessory prayers of others. I cannot thank you enough for all those prayers.

> Mark 6:13
>
> They drove out many demons and
> anointed many sick people with oil and healed them.

"But about the Goodbyes...Larry has felt for some time that God has called him to missions for children. After seven years in Good News Club at Waccamaw Elementary and nearly that many mission trips to Guatemala, he knows that his heart is in sharing the Good News of Jesus with kids.

"Well, a couple of years ago, we got rid of the house, leased a motorhome and created Motorhome Ministry. Our plans are to depart on a three-year Odyssey to travel the forty-nine continental United States, parts of Mexico and Canada, to share the Gospel. My injuries from last October and subsequent surgeries in February really delayed things, but the Lord has accomplished mighty things with these delays and everything happens in His perfect timing. We give Him all the praise and glory.

"So, I'm officially RETIRED! (laughter) I'm all signed up for early Social Security benefits and we will trust that the Lord will provide the rest for all that we will need. Keep us in your prayers, please. Those of you with computers can keep up with our journey by checking out Facebook or our website at www.motorhomeministry.com.

"Our last Sunday here will be next Sunday—Easter Sunday, March 27. Please be sure to hunt us down and give us lots of hugs 'for the road.'

"May God bless each of your lives as your lives bless others."

When I finished, much to my surprise, our preacher's wife, Janice, quickly came up and encouraged Larry to the front, so that everyone would have the opportunity to say goodbyes today. We got so many hugs we lost count.

Our Friends in Christ are great huggers. The church brings Christians together for fellowship, encouragement and to help one another. Without the church, Christianity could not have spread around the world. All persons need to belong to a church for these things, and accomplish this one goal to spread the Word, which we are all commanded to do.

As Dr. Drum is known for saying, "God is good, all the time. All the time, God is good."

Amen to that.

Hebrews 10:25

25 not giving up meeting together,
as some are in the habit of doing,
but encouraging one another—and all the more
as you see the Day approaching.

ODYSSEY

Larry: *I had been spending all my spare time planning a road trip I called "Odyssey." It is a plan to travel across this beautiful country of ours, spreading the Gospel to kids as we go. I wanted to connect kids to the Bible. I wanted us to see as many national parks as we could. I wanted to see museums, presidential libraries, points of interest and historical landmarks. I wanted to learn more about the places that our history books speak of; places I see on the news.*

We saw Hawaii years ago, and we've flown to different places across the country on business. But I wanted to see this land up close. I carefully laid out a three-year travel plan that would cover over 30,000 miles in 49 states, as well as some parts of Canada and Mexico. We flew to Alaska, because we heard that the roads are poor and there were a lot of miles to drive to get up there. And we just can't seem to find a route to drive to Hawaii.

Job 12:7-10

7 "But ask the animals, and they will teach you,
or the birds in the sky, and they will tell you;
8 or speak to the earth, and it will teach you,
or let the fish in the sea inform you.

9 Which of all these does not know
that the hand of the Lord has done this?
10 In his hand is the life of every creature
and the breath of all mankind.

THE PLAN

Larry: *Let me begin by saying that it sure hasn't been easy as I thought it would be. We have been banned from campgrounds, told to leave, and yelled out because of our faith, our beliefs, and our attempts to teach. But, just as Jesus was persecuted, He dusted His feet and moved on, so we would learn to do so as well.*

> Luke 9:5
>
> 5 If people do not welcome you,
> leave their town and shake the dust off your feet
> as a testimony against them."

From the beginning, campgrounds protested our desire to hold activities on our site. Larry's sister Sherri and her husband, Ron—who are in ministry—suggested we take a less direct approach. In this age and time, it was a good idea to make the materials available, without requiring face-to-face contact. It wasn't what we planned, but as long as we could get the Word out, it would work.

Each time we stop in a campground, we make sure to hang our Motorhome Ministry banner from the front of the motor home. We also hang free kid's packets from the mirrors that are full of Bible stories, crayons, and color sheets, CEF, and OCC materials. Everyone reads the banner as they walk by. Some smile, some take the packets and others get an angry expression and stomp off with disgust. The stomping ones are the ones we are truly trying to reach. They're so lost, they don't even know it. We pray for all of them.

Larry: *Even this book is a test in faith and trust. The Lord impressed it on my heart to write it. I didn't want to and I had* *to convince Lugene to do it with me. I admit being challenged at such things and couldn't accomplish this without her. It comes from that feeling again, that push again, that presence again. I still get up every day and ask Him to guide me in the direction He wants me to go. He pushes - hard. We just have to pay attention and listen.*

We try to give out a packet of Motor Home Ministry seed packets and a brochure about our ministry to everyone we can, such as kids, waitresses, waiters, and service cashiers. It's a packet of wild flower seeds with Matthew 13 printed on them.

Matthew 13   The Parable of the Sower

6 That same day Jesus went out of the house and sat by the lake.2 Such large crowds gathered around him that he got into a boat and sat in it, while all the people stood on the shore. 3 Then he told them many things in parables, saying: "A farmer went out to sow his seed. 4 As he was scattering the seed, some fell along the path, and the birds came and ate it up. 5 Some fell on rocky places, where it did not have much soil. It sprang up quickly, because the soil was shallow. 6 But when the sun came up, the plants were scorched, and they withered because they had no root. 7 Other seed fell among thorns, which grew up and choked the plants. 8 Still other seed fell on good soil, where it produced a crop—a hundred, sixty or thirty times what was sown. 9 Whoever has ears, let them hear."

While there is no guarantee that anyone who receives these packets will visit on Sunday morning, our hope is that it will ignite a spark that will let them explore the Word of God and bring them into a church somewhere. But for those afraid to take that first step, our goal is to help them along by coming to them.

Larry: *The rest of this book chronicles our Odyssey across America in our little motorhome. We are amazed at all the things we've witnessed from sea to shining sea! We are so blessed to be citizens in such an amazing land, with the freedom to travel it however and whenever we like. And we are personally blessed that God has given us this opportunity to minister to others along the way.*

I know I'm guilty of sticking my nose into my cell phone to the extreme. Driving this motorhome has forced me to put down the phone and look around me. It forces me to set aside the things that fill so many lives. Sadly, people are all missing the today, the now, the at-the-moment. My one huge regret in life is while I worked hard and long I failed to stop and live life in the moment. Even though I was there, I missed my kids growing up. That's why losing Bobby was especially hard for me. Lugene had been there for all his special moments and I had missed them. I was always busy planning for the tomorrow, and never in today.

We hope you enjoy our tour through this great land. Through these writings, may God open the opportunity for YOU to see it, too…this beautiful country called America.

THE

JOURNEY

BEGINS

JOURNAL ENTRIES

MARCH 30, 2016

This morning, we got up with the sun, ready to set off to see America. We are now both officially retired and God has put everything in place for us to make this journey for Him.

This was really happening! We had seen all our doctors. We had kissed and hugged family and friends, all our friends at church. We had said countless goodbyes. The tanks were filled, and Larry had made reservations months in advance.

We set the tripometer to -0-. The big Caterpillar engine came to life as Larry turned the key, the Allison transmission engaged as Larry pushed the button on the left of his console, the 36-foot Tropical motorhome was roaring to go. We pulled out of Pirateland Campground in Myrtle Beach where we had stayed over the winter, waiting for me to heal. I still had a long way to go in my recovery, but it was time to embark on this journey. I had been sitting too long and needed the challenge to work my way back physically.

Going right over the place of our accident the previous October, we were heading out Route 501 toward Gaffney, SC, to have periodic maintenance completed before we set off across America. The day is clear. The wisteria was everywhere you looked, and many of the dogwood trees were in full bloom.

The day went well, right up until the last 10 minutes of driving when the GPS and the Google map disagreed and tempers flared.

Larry and I cooled down during a delicious dinner at Outback, but left the arguing electronics in the motorhome.

Freightliner made a place for us in the parking lot to setup. They had electric service, so we enjoyed an evening of watching NCIS on the DVD player, thanks to my best friend Deb for the early birthday present.

This is really happening! Tomorrow is a free day, as our maintenance appointment isn't until Friday.

The morning of the crash, I had prayed a very specific prayer that I had learned from my coworker, OCC leader and friend, Diane. I had prayed that "God would send His angels to form a hedge of protection around us, to keep us safe." As I believe He did that day, He continues to do so. I include that prayer every single morning, every single night, and every time we leave the motorhome behind to spend a day of adventure in the car.

God be with us.

MARCH 31

We drove the short distance in our car to get to the Freightliner Factory to take the tour. It was a fantastic tour, walking right out on the floor, next to the men and women assembling these massive chassis.

They were manufacturing school buses, FedEx and UPS trucks and motorhomes. There were hundreds of folks there, taking pride in being a part of a product that remains American made. It gave us a whole new appreciation for the talents that had been used to assemble our home. They even gave us a cool keychain as a gift.

We decided to try Popeye's for the first time and really enjoyed it. We had always assumed that it was New Orleans' spicy, but it wasn't. We will do that again.

We went back to the motorhome and thought I'd get some paperwork done. I do keep the books for my daughter's small business and it was the end of the month. I took a nap instead.

APRIL 1

We were up at 6am to ready the rig for our maintenance appointment. We ate breakfast at McDonald's (with a mandatory large coffee for me).

We went to see a movie, "Miracle from Heaven." What an amazing movie! God does work in mysterious and miraculous ways. If you missed it, be sure to get the DVD or watch it on Netflix.

Now, let me tell you that Larry despises shopping. And when he does shop, he shops just like a man: in the door, pick up the item you came for, pay for it and out the door. Sometimes I just like to wander. I don't need or want anything, I just want to see what's out there. It clears my head. Since we had all day to kill, he stayed in the car playing with his iPhone while allowing me to roam Hamricks, then Crabtree & Evelyn. I spent an outrageous $7.00—on sale. I was so proud of my self-restraint.

We'd been having problems with the used tow dolly we had purchased before the trip and it's continued to be quite frustrating. God sent some terrific angels to Camping World, with whom we had the opportunity to share MHM, CEF (and OCC, while they helped us the best they could.

We paid the bill for the motorhome, then drove a while to get a head start on tomorrow. We parked in a Walmart in Hendersonville. I was bushed from a long day of activity so it was early to bed for me. Walmarts across the nation allow RVrs to "boondoggle" (park overnight in their parking lots for free). It makes a nice spot to rest overnight when you are on the road. Plus, we always need something or another on the road.

There are some exceptions though, due to local ordinances. Be sure to check AllStays/Walmart app for comments from previous RVrs, or check with someone at the store when you arrive. There are some locations that don't care that you stay, but they care where you stay.

There's just no sense getting waken up by local police in the middle of the night.

Dear Lord, I'm praying for that hedge of protection again...

APRIL 2

Now that the maintenance is done, we're heading toward Cincinnati to see family and friends. We continue to have problems with the tow dolly. I-75 is always a busy mess, but today it's worse than ever. A couple of months ago, there was a big landslide that covered a large area of the interstate, and it's still down to one lane over the mountain at Jellico, Tennessee.

The high wind advisories didn't help poor Larry at all. We stopped to camp at a beautiful site overlooking the rolling hills at the Kentucky Horse Park. Even off the interstate, we are still rockin!

On a side note, Larry figures he might as well help readers with his own personal rating system. Rating as a total: park personnel, site access, utilities, and general frustration, he would rate this a 7, with 10 being awesomely amazing. (The 10 we will describe is where we stayed in Las Vegas. They are rare, indeed).

I rushed to get the laundry done. It's going down to 29 degrees tonight and we must disconnect the water so that it doesn't freeze in the line. There's no cable here, and satellite is crappy because of the wind.

Now I need to take a moment to share another important thing about my husband: he is addicted to FOX News. It is the background noise of every waking hour of his life. I like FOX News, but to the extent of about Bill O'Reilly. So, understand me when I say, "Oh, no. Larry just found FOX News on his iPhone. Where are his earphones?"

APRIL 3

We spent hours at the Kentucky Horse Park. It was frigidly cold and spitting snow, but we enjoyed it nonetheless. The landscape coming to life in spring, the blue sky, the white fences, and rolling hills all show God's glory. And it's quiet.

The majestic horses were scattered on the hills grazing. The Park's tribute to the great horses throughout time was very educational. Larry enjoyed learning more about his favorite horse, Secretariat.

When we were entering the park, there were two young ladies, each on beautiful mounts, poised to greet us. The red one rubbed cheeks with me twice. It was so sweet.

I've never spent much time around horses, so maybe he felt some compassion for me and my neck brace. Larry said the horse probably thought I came bearing food.

Larry and I grew up in the Cincinnati area. One thing the area is famous for is Skyline Chili. It's not the type of chili they cook in Texas. It is a unique secret blend of spices, but my personal guess is the distinct flavor has something to do with cocoa and cumin. It is served plain, or on top of spaghetti, or as a 3-Way, which is chili, spaghetti, and cheese. There is also a 4-Way: chili, spaghetti, cheese, and beans or onions, or as an all-the-way 5-Way, which is chili, spaghetti, cheese, beans, and onions. When you're raised eating Skyline on a regular basis, you really miss it when you can't find it anywhere.

We're heading toward "home", and as we pass the first Skyline Chili restaurant, we just have to stop. The perfect lunch for me: a 5-way, a cheese coney (hot dog on a warm bun, chili, onions, finely shredded cheddar cheese but mine without mustard, thank you very much) and a Diet Dr. Pepper. A York Peppermint Patty at the register finishes the meal as dessert. Oh, and a couple of Tums.

We finally make it out to the boonies of Blanchester, Ohio, where my best friend, Deb, and her husband, Don, have lived on their farm for years. It is a special place to me. Unlike my own life over the years, this place is quiet. The back porch is really the "center" of life here, regardless of the weather. You see corn and soybean fields, and cattle in the back field. You can see traffic on the highway and hear the brakes on the big rigs, as they slow down for the curve in the road. The train tracks run just on the other side of the highway and their whistles are soothing to hear.

And the sunsets! They have the most beautiful sunsets, and the front-row seats are, of course, on the back porch.

My poor friend's knee had given out on her recently and she was in a leg brace. I was still in my neck brace. Weren't we a motley pair of gimps? We had to laugh.

We parked the motorhome back by the pond but near the barn, so we had electric. Beautiful, beautiful.

I was totally done in by the cold and wind and travel today. Early to bed—we could catch up on the old times tomorrow.

APRIL 4

We spent part of the day hanging out at the farm.

On Don's recommendation, Larry and I drove to the far side of Wilmington, Ohio, to buy a new tow dolly. We certainly weren't prepared for such an expense this early in the trip, but it was the wise thing to do. Now we have one less thing to worry about.

Larry spent the afternoon working on his computer, having difficulties the whole time. Deb and I relaxed in her lovely home and had a wonderful visit. A mutual friend, Marcella, had dropped off a prayer shawl for me. It had been buried in prayer by its maker and my friends. Deb also blessed me with a small quilt that she and other ladies at her church had made and prayed over for me. For months to come, when I lay down in pain and exhaustion, I wrapped myself in both, feeling their healing power.

Deb's son, Jason, brought his son, Hank, over for a short visit. Jason was born the same year that Bobby was, so I could always see how old Bobby would have been and how he would have grown as Jason grew up into a young man.

It was a wonderfully blessed day!

APRIL 5

Today's is Bobby's birthday; he would have been 37 today. Of course, I still picture him as a grinning six-year-old. I find myself quietly working on month-end financials on my computer. Out this window is a beautiful view of the lake, while the silos can be seen out the window behind me.

Deb had not yet seen the motorhome and wanted desperately to see inside. I have lived in many places over the years and it always helped her understand my activities if she could see the inside of my world. It was really a strategic exercise to get her from the house (in their John Deere Gator), up the steps and up into the motorhome. But now she had a feeling for my home.

We chatted part of the afternoon, but Deb was beat, so I left her to rest. I drove to the cemetery where my son, mom, dad, father-in-law, and Deb's mom and dad are buried. Due to some recent flooding, the markers were a mess, but despite my neck brace, I did get them cleaned up some.

I drove down to Old Milford, the downtown area of the suburb where Larry and I grew up. There's an eclectic shop there that was the subject of a fiction book written recently by another Milford graduate. I stopped in, explored, and was amazed, then purchased the last book she had on hand. It was a very interesting read.

Then I headed, once again, for Skyline Chili. This time it was to enjoy a two-hour dinner with my sister, Beve, her daughter, Jana, son-in-law, Craig, and their two kids, Allison and Nick. We had a wonderful time, everyone sharing stories, and everyone laughing at them.

In addition to paying for my dinner, Beve brought me two precious gifts. Daddy died 26 years ago, and some of his most prized things were bolo ties and several hand-made leather belts. She brought me two of his belts! I will cherish them always.

Despite what could have been a dismal day of mourning turned out to be a day of love and hugs, good memories, and laughter.

And Skyline Chili! It was a wonderful day.

APRIL 6

The devil showed up today. Larry's computer has completely destroyed itself. When Larry's not watching FOX News, he's on the computer. Sometimes both at the same time. After spending hours on the phone with tech people, they concluded that the only solution was to wipe it clean, then start all over.

I visited in the house with Deb while Larry vented in the motorhome. This would mean days of downloading programs and data backups online. We have mobile internet service and it's quite expensive. If we had to depend on that access alone, it would have cost us at least a couple thousands of dollars to do all of the necessary downloads.

Somehow, while venting to others, he learned that his sister had unlimited Wi-Fi. Her home was our next destination before leaving Cincinnati. Out of necessity, we left the farm a day early so Larry could begin repairs. It was a difficult afternoon getting the rig to the other side of downtown Cincinnati. The route was tight and Larry was not in his best form, to say the least.

The highlight of the day was to grab lunch at another Cincinnati landmark, White Castle. Yum.

Larry's gastric sleeve surgery back in November, 2014 sure dampens moments like today at White Castle. He used to be able to east seven or eight of those little gut busters, but he had to limit his lunch today to only two hamburgers and a couple of onion rings. I, however, made a pig out of myself. I suffered for the indulgence later, but it was worth it.

APRIL 7

Larry began his downloads. Getting everything on his computer back to normal totally possessed every waking moment. God most definitely provided the way and the means to reconstruct his computer through my sister-in-law Sherri, and her family.

We all had lunch at a nearby Skyline. My niece, Lydia, joined us along with her new husband, Aaron. We hadn't been able to attend their wedding, so it was the first time I'd met the groom. He's a delightful, light-hearted young man. I treated myself by purchasing a hot pink Skyline Chili t-shirt.

Sherri shared a story with us at lunch, and it was the first time I'd ever heard it. I'd known that Bobby's death had certainly affected her in those early days. What I didn't know was that it was the day after what would have been Bobby's next birthday, that she had come to Christ. She resolved that she got saved because of Bobby. That was exactly 30 years ago, today. I suspected, but I never knew.

By the end of the day, I concluded that most of our family is a mess right now. I am still in my collar, Lydia had messed up her shoulder and had it in a sling. My niece, Maria had what I call "the greenies" and couldn't join us for lunch. My niece Kelly's husband, Scott, showed up for a few minutes to say hello but he was also ill. My nephew Matt's wife, Erika, had experienced an accident at work and had a full arm brace and her foot in a walking boot. We are a mess, indeed.

My sister-in-law is a terrific cook, whether it be for 2 or for 50. With it cold and pouring down rain outside, we all enjoyed a homemade dinner of potato soup and biscuits. It was delicious.

I mentioned earlier the sound of trains at Deb's. I love the sound of trains. It's a treat when I hear their sad whistles and the rhythm of the cars on the tracks. But there are no trains that run into Myrtle Beach, where I've spent the last two decades. Well, Sherri's home is in a place where the trains are heard from all directions! What a beautiful sound!

Christians do believe that the more you are out there for Jesus, the more of a threat you are to the devil. And the devil doesn't like it one bit. In retaliation, the devil picks away at you, trying to frustrate you so much that you lose your faith in God. If the devil is rearing its ugly head in your life, you can figure that you're doing something right in your faith.

Boy, oh boy, all of us around here must be doing something right.

> 1 Peter 5:8: NIV
>
> 8 Be alert and of sober mind. Your enemy the devil prowls around like a roaring lion looking for someone to devour.

APRIL 8

We tried to finish the computer at Sherri's, but we have reservations in place and have fallen a bit behind schedule. Ready or not, it's time to go.

We hug everyone and Sherri's husband, Ron—who is a pastor—prayed over us and our ministry. We finally pull out in the motorhome, but seconds later I ask Larry to stop. I need to go back and speak to Erica alone. My voice was urgent; he didn't bother to question why.

I texted Sherri and requested that Erica meet me in the kitchen and to allow us some privacy. By the time Larry turned around the motorhome and I walked inside, she was there alone, waiting for me.

You see, Marcella hadn't given me just one prayer shawl, she had given me two. Her instructions were to give the extra one to someone I felt truly needed it. Erika truly needed it. She was a broken soul, consumed by pain and the frustration that she didn't know how or if she would ever heal. I gave her the shawl and prayed for its healing prayers to be upon her.

I cried. She cried. We agreed to pray for each other in our recoveries. She struggled with her cane to stand upright and she hugged me long and hard. I quietly headed to the door to let myself out. I looked back to see her standing in the same place, but with her eyes and arms lifted heavenward.

God is good.

I returned to the motorhome and buckled in to leave. The peace I'd received lasted only a few moments. Ron called us while we were still driving the building parking lot to tell Larry the bedroom pullout was still extended. I had left it out! That could have been disastrous on the tight city streets of Cincinnati. I apologized profusely and blamed it on my pain meds. But thank God that we turned around, or we could have been on the road before it was discovered.

We spent a few hours on the road. Exhausted and cold, we pulled over and slept the night.

APRIL 9

We drove down Interstate 71 towards Louisville, KY and stayed at the KOA in Shepherdsville, Kentucky. It was a nice place; Larry rates it a 6.

We took the full tour at the Jim Beam Distillery. It's in a beautiful part of Kentucky, but it was frigidly cold today. The buildings are neat and well-maintained. You feel as though you've stepped back in time for the day. We learned about the seven generations that have been making Jim Beam and enjoyed the sweet smell of the barrels. I would recommend this to everyone in the area. We had never seen such an operation before and it was fascinating! There were thousands of these wooden barrels stored in all of the barns.

At the time, we had found an app called Easy Shift to do "shops." You go into a place that they offer to record observations about specific products, submit your report and you get paid. We learned quickly that some shops were very long and difficult. Others were easy. One month we did over $200 in shops. Today, we did a couple of shops and while we were in grocery stores anyway, we picked up some meals. We drove back to the motorhome for laundry and a nap. It's a great thing to be able to multi-task shopping with making some cash. And I sure like naps!

APRIL 10

Another day of the devil. But in the end, God always rules.

Ephesians 6:11

11 Put on the full armor of God,
so that you can take your stand
against the devil's schemes.

We were behind schedule and a major winter storm was on its way. Tensions were still high because the computer still wasn't finished but we had to keep going. Arguing began early. Yes, even Christians who have been married 40+ years argue. It was over something quite simple. He had the GPS and I had the Google Map. I had set the course for today's destination but Larry had set his for another destination— for tomorrow. They would both bark out instructions, but they differed, because mine had selected the best route to arrive at Point B, but his was focused on the best route to Point C. I couldn't convince him to shut his down, and it was mounted on the driver's window, out of reach for me.

We nearly had a collision with a semi. Scary indeed, but God had that hedge of protection all around us. But while avoiding the collision, we hit a dip in the road that threw open the one and only overhead kitchen cabinet. My Corelle Ware plates and bowls slid right out of the cabinet and went flying. One little dessert plate hit the tile floor and broke. But that tempered glass doesn't just break, it explodes!

It sounded as if a bomb had gone off. Larry's ADHD was already in overload and it was all he could do to keep control of the motorhome until we could find a place to pull over and assess the damages. The other pieces had landed in the dish strainer. We were lucky. Or so we thought.

I finally convinced him to change the destination on the GPS. We're going along just fine when we come to an intersection that his said turn left and mine said turn right— and they were both set to the same place!

I decided that moment to name them Frick and Frack. I used my best judgment to listen to Frack and we finally arrived at the Diamond Caverns RV Resort, close to Mammoth Cave, which Larry rated a 3.

We choose a site with electric and completely set up. Larry plugs in and discovers that we have no electric. We hail down this guy named Charles and he gets us going for like one minute, and it blows again. We finally agree (after the horrendous day we've already had) that we should break down and move if we want to run anything electric.

We're setting up again when I discover more damage done by the dishes. When the other pieces had fallen into the dish strainer, they had first fallen on to the pull-out sprayer faucet at the sink and put a hole in the hose. When we connected to water pressure, it sprayed everywhere!

Thank God for Google! I searched and found out there's a Camping World just 20 miles away, right on I-65. We use Google for just about everything we need to find: restaurants, post offices, urgent care and even Walmarts! My usual search, "restaurants near me" should rate a shortcut!

I've mentioned Skyline Chili. Then White Castle. There was only one more Cincinnati favorite on my check list: Frisch's Big Boy. There just happened to be one on the way and Larry even offered to take me for my favorite onion rings. They have the best onion rings on the planet (maybe I'm a bit prejudiced). Check, check, and check.

We finally get to the tiniest Camping World I'd ever seen. Yes, they have the fixture. You can't buy just the part you broke, you must buy the whole assembly. That means that WE must install the whole assembly, too. Ugh.

We returned to the motorhome to begin repairs. Charles stops by, pointing out our ministry packets. We figured, oh boy, here it comes. We assume he is knocking on the door to kick us out or shut us down. It turned out that he's all for the ministry and begged us to change our next reservations so that we could be a part of his Tuesday evening program for the homeless. We continued talking and I told him about the accident last October. Then I told him about the computer and the semi and the dishes and the kitchen sink, and I asked him to pray for us. Before he would leave us, he anointed the motorhome with oil and the three of us stood right there in the grass, holding hands, and praying that the same hedge of protection would accompany us wherever we go.

While Larry was under the kitchen sink to begin working on the plumbing, Charles came back to say—per his request—there were currently four families of campers praying for us at that very moment.

We dug into this plumbing job knowing that God answers prayer. We were both tired and hurting and had stretched this day to its limits. Larry's pain is always there, but the evening is always worst. And after the nerve-wracking events of the day, this task smelled of nuclear disaster to me. But we couldn't use any of the pressured water until it was fixed. I prayed.

In the collar with my range of vision obscured, I was really limited as to how I could help. Steps were still very difficult for me. Especially the down ones, because I can't drop my chin far enough to see where I'm stepping. And at this point, I am petrified of falling.

Every step Larry took in installing the sink, I would pray specifically for that step. And I knew from Charles that others were praying, too. God gave to Larry the gifts of strength and tenacity with which to do this job. God enabled him to get in and out of the cabinet, up and down from the floor, and up and down the steps to get tools from compartments outside. I have never seen him keep his cool like that. At one point, he had somehow managed to feed one of the water lines through the top of our LED lantern and he had to completely undo it. I had to laugh aloud because it was funny, and he calmly undid the connection and removed the lantern. I think he laughed, too.

God was definitely in control of this job!

Okay. Now was the moment of truth. With a 2-way radio in hand, I went outside to turn on the water at the source. Nothing on the radio. Moments pass. I finally say, "I don't hear any screams in there, are you okay?" He calmly asked if I'd turned the water on. Yes, like a minute ago. "Well, come on in then, because there are no leaks."

Amen. Praise the Lord in Heaven.

A miracle.

APRIL 11

Today was a day of delightful discoveries as we walked the Mammoth Cave Tour. It was totally, totally awesome! It would be the first of many National Parks that we would visit this year. In the gift shop, I purchased a Passport for the National Parks. It's divided into sections and lists the many parks available to see in that region of the US.

There are also lots of empty pages for "stamping", just like you would a real Passport—a record of your travels. I carefully stamped my first National Park. I was told that many of the parks will have at least two stamps this year, as 2016 is the Centennial Celebration of the National Park Service. Indeed, Mammoth Cave NP had both stamps.

Driving through the countryside, I could fully appreciate the beauty of God's creations. It is spring, after all and so many beautiful plants and trees are in bloom. The colors are amazing! The rolling hills of the Bluegrass State are so beautiful this time of the year.

My daughter is an artist and has taught me much. An avid photographer, her best pics are not of mountain grandeur or the mass of the Atlantic Ocean. The best pics capture the tiny things: butterflies, caterpillars, tiny flowers on bushes, the grain of a piece of wood, the veins of a leaf or the pattern on a teacup. She has one perfect photo of an itty-bitty frog, sitting inside a lily. Precious.

So everywhere we would walk, I would stop to capture photographs of the tiniest flowers, rocks, and shells. What a blessing that has been, because those tiny things are quite different in every region we would visit.

I was really tuckered out from yesterday's antics and today's exploring, so I took a nice, long nap. Larry was still neck deep into getting his computer back in shape. It was a good day.

APRIL 12

We drove to Nashville, Tennessee. It was a beautiful scenic drive and we arrived before noon at the Music City KOA. It was a great campground, but there was lots of construction going on at the time.

My neck pain was terrible! I took some meds and slept part of the afternoon—no sightseeing for me today.

We have finally hit some warmer weather. A beautifully sunny day, it hit 65 degrees today.

It was a quiet, peaceful day. And, we are still hearing trains everywhere we go!

APRIL 13

We took a shuttle this morning into Historic downtown Nashville—America's Music City. We paid for a tour of the city and it was fascinating! All the rich history of this once-small town that has now become an internationally-known metropolis.

Out on the streets, we recognized old places we had heard of, saw things we never knew existed and gawked at the architecture. We saw the Ernest Tubb Record Shop, Grand Old Opry, the Bridgestone Arena, the Parthenon, and the State Capitol building.

To our delight, when we entered the Legends Gift Shop, we discovered the custom pearl boxes and display that we had designed for them! They were so beautiful. We bought one to complete Diana's collection of every box that she personally designed for our company.

We had been to Nashville before and had enjoyed the show at Opryland and wandered the Opryland Hotel. I've heard it's especially wonderful at Christmas time.

APRIL 14

On the road to Memphis, Tennessee today.

It was a long day, at least four hours of driving. We did well until the last hour of the drive. We were both hungry and tired, I was in pain and we figured we were too close to pull over and eat now. Then Frick and Frack are at odds again, each of them telling us a different way to turn, sending us on a wild goose change through downtown.

So, if you're an RV driver, you know that any downtown is not going to be RV-friendly. At the moment, we were not happy campers. We finally arrived and are delighted to see that the campground is right next door to and across the street from Graceland, so we'll be able to walk.

Saturday's weather was forecast for 73 degrees. We figured we would tour downtown then.

APRIL 15

We were standing in line to get our Graceland tour tickets when a guy from Gibson Guitars came up and encouraged us to go on that tour today. We told him we already had plans to go tomorrow, but he explained that if we go on the weekend, none of the workers are there. Well, that would be no fun!

He'd arrived just in time. We jumped out of line, walked back to the campground and drove the car downtown.

We took the tour at the Gibson Guitar Factory. Every Gibson is handmade and many are custom made to specifications given them by famous musicians. Their employees are truly gifted in their craft. It was an amazing tour. Larry always thought that the electric guitars were plastic or fiberglass, and had no idea that each was made of wood, each one had its own paint scheme. No two are exactly alike.

We came to the Lorraine Motel, where we learned that Rev. Martin Luther King, Jr. had been assassinated. His room, 306, was never rented after that day. Other famous guests that have stayed at the motel, included Ray Charles, Otis Redding, Aretha Franklin, Louis Armstrong, and Nat

King Cole. History class in school or specials on television were never this interesting! History was coming alive, right in front of us. The motel is now home to the National Civil Rights Museum.

We wandered historic Beale Street, whose stories probably outnumber the bricks in the streets. We even saw the old Sun Studios, a recording studio opened by rock-and-roll pioneer Sam Phillips, who recorded Elvis Presley, among many other famous musicians.

I was delighted to discover "Dirty Chai" in a little coffee shop. It was a great combination of chai with a shot of espresso; exactly what I needed. Yum.

We also discovered the largest Bass Pro Shop in America, in the form of a giant pyramid. They have two huge levels of amazingly marketed retail. We paid the fee to ride the elevator up 28 stories to view the city from the observation deck/restaurant. Wow. The view of the Mississippi River and the City of Memphis is amazing. This place is huge!

We ate a delicious dinner at Marlow's BBQ, where pigs fly! There was an Airstream parked out front that had been painted bright pink and disguised as a giant pig. You can't miss it!

APRIL 16

Today in one word: Graceland.

Elvis Presley's estate was simply amazing. In a small tour group, we were guided through the mansion and grounds. Elvis certainly had eclectic tastes and it was shown in the themes and decorations of each room. There are large panels with stained glass peacocks to welcome you to the piano room. His Safari Room was of green carpet, large plants and rustic, carved wooden furniture. The room where he played pool was entirely decorated in wild fabric—pinched and pleated over the walls and ceiling, to match the upholstered furniture. It wasn't a huge place, but it was certainly eclectic. It was like nothing we had ever seen.

Even his plane, the Lisa Marie, was there.

The rose gardens and grounds are beautifully maintained and those of us who stopped to see his grave were solemn. He is buried there with his grandmother, mom, and dad. His stillborn twin brother is also nearby. What a gifted young man he was, who had served his country, loved his mamma, and touched the lives of so many, but was so troubled that he died young. You can tell by Graceland's grounds that he loved his momma and he loved God. Viewing their graves left us with an unbelievable somber feeling. People leave flowers as they pass by all day long, every day.

> 1 Chronicles 23:5
>
> 5 Four thousand are to be gatekeepers and four thousand are to praise the Lord with the musical instruments I have provided for that purpose."

This morning, I had walked right off and forgotten my cervical collar and refused to walk back to the campground to get it. I made it four hours in public without it today! There were lots of steps and I was so very careful. What a victory.

The weather was gorgeous and I finally broke out my shorts. When we returned to the motorhome after a wonderful day, we discovered we had brought a visitor with us from the farm—a mouse. Oh, no.

This little mouse was a smart little one and he knew how to bypass the traps we set for him. It would be several weeks on the road before we got him. For all he ate, he was sure to be a chubby little stowaway.

APRIL 17

We took our time driving toward St. Louis. We left Memphis, drove through Arkansas on I-55 North, and wound up boondoggling at a Walmart in Perryville, south of St. Louis.

We stopped to do quite a few shops for extra cash today. Larry did the shops for cash and I shopped to spend it. He'd get so aggravated that I was spending it as quickly as he'd earned it. Well, the way I see it, we needed the stuff anyway, we were multi-tasking and in the end, all the stuff I bought was pretty much "free." Don't you agree?

APRIL 18

After using only, the auxiliary batteries the previous night, it became clear that we needed new ones immediately. Larry had already priced the batteries and installation through Camping World and it was pricey! Instead, we arrived in St. Louis around 1pm, and went straight to Costco to purchase 4 deep cycle batteries. Larry saved us $600+ by installing them himself. Then he fixed the wiper mount. He had a busy day.

And we noticed from the tripometer that we had completed 1,700 miles so far. That was fast.

We were camped in an area at the Casino Queen, so it was time to go check out the slots. Don't fear—I never play big. I play penny or nickel slots and usually don't ever power them up. But when I walked away with nearly 150% of my startup funds that evening, I figured that wasn't all too bad.

APRIL 19

I learned something very important as we dashed around the city, sightseeing: St. Louis isn't just one city—it's actually two.

I first knew that something was amiss when Larry drove the car across the bridge over the Mississippi River. I admit openly that I'm directionally challenged, but even I realized the importance of crossing the Mississippi River. The view of the Arch from the Casino looked so close, so where were we going?

Well, it turned out that the Casino Queen is in East St. Louis and we were camped in the state of Illinois.

St. Louis, Missouri is the one you know that's famous for the Arch, Budweiser, and Busch Stadium.

East St. Louis, Illinois, is the one you've probably never heard of. I Googled it as I wrote this—months after we stayed there—to find out that it's not only one of the most violent cities in the US, but it continuously ranks among the world's most dangerous cities. I did not see any evidence of that during our stay. We were just fine staying at the Casino Queen and would do it again. Thank you, Jesus!

It does have a claim to fame though, in the Gateway Geyser, a manmade fountain directly across the Mississippi River from the Gateway Arch. Three times a day (in season and weather permitting), the Geyser shoots water to the same height as the Arch, about 630 feet. What a beautiful pair of monuments to view at once.

Now on to the Arch. It was built in the 1960's to honor the early 19th-century explorations of Lewis and Clark and America's westward expansion in general. It is 630 feet tall and built of stainless steel. It's the world's tallest arch, the tallest man-made monument in the Western Hemisphere, and Missouri's tallest accessible building. I collected four Passport stamps from this area, one of them celebrating the 50th Anniversary of the Arch in 2015.

Once downtown, you really can't miss the Arch. Many places on the sidewalk are stamped: "This way to the Arch"—with the shape of the Arch pointing the way. There was massive construction going on for blocks around it, and the Arch Ground Project will be beautiful when complete. We must have walked more than a mile each way to view it.

We bought tickets so that we could ride to the top. To anyone with acute claustrophobia, I would not recommend this. There are lights inside, of course, but no windows to view out during the trip. If you can make the 4-minute trip with your eyes closed, DO IT! Because the view from the top is spectacular. We could actually see our motorhome parked across the river in the campground!

For a laugh, I took a photograph downtown of a very complicated road sign. On the same pole, there were indicators for I-44 East and West. And I-55 North and South. Another to get to I-64 and another to I-70. The last one was for US Route 40, turn left please. Wow.

And trains! Everywhere we were, day and night, was the sound of trains.

We traveled on to take the Anheuser Busch factory tour. There are several different options to choose from, but the complimentary (no charge) tour was great enough for us. We walked the beautiful grounds and observed their 7-Step Brewing Process. We saw some of the Brew Kettles and the Beechwood Aging Cellars. The highlight to us was to visit the historic stables built in 1885 that houses the world-famous Clydesdales. What amazing humongous animals!

The tour lasted about an hour and it ended with free beer. Can't beat that. And I received a double portion, as Larry doesn't like beer at all.

APRIL 20

Today was another travel day that served up more confusing realizations.

We left St. Louis, Missouri, to go to Kansas City. Once again, this directionally challenged person learned that Kansas City also has dual personalities. We came first to Kansas City, Missouri, to stay at the East Kansas City KOA, which Larry rated a 7. It was the first time I'd encountered highway signs for Supplemental Routes. We drove past Exit 203 for Foristell, indicated with large letters, each in a box, T and W. What in the world?

Google on the road is great. I quickly learned that Missouri set up a Supplemental Route system in 1952, designed to place state-maintained roads within 2 miles of more than 95% of all farm houses, schools, church, cemeteries, and stores. There are four types of such roads:

- Farm to market roads
- Roads to state parks
- Former alignments of US or state highways, and
- Short routes connecting state highways from other states to routes in Missouri.

Minor branch routes and farm-to-market roads, which often end at county roads or are former alignments of the other highways, are typically assigned with two-letter designations consisting of two of the same letter (e.g. "KK")[2]

The best such highway sign I photographed was at an intersection that showed that US 63 goes left and right. But, if you want to go PP, it goes only to the right. PP. No kidding.

We did a few shops on the way, so I probably chalked up another mile of walking today. I really need to get my strength back after all of this laying around.

Other than Frick rearing his stupid head several times during the drive, it was a pretty quiet day. And once again, there are trains everywhere.

APRIL 21

Today was a whirlwind day.

[2] https://en.wikipedia.org/wiki/Missouri_supplemental_route

We drove first to the Truman Library in Independence, Missouri. It is a grand, clean-cut building on beautifully manicured grounds. It would be only the first of many Presidential Libraries we would visit.

If you have plans to visit at least two libraries, buy a membership. For the price of less than two admissions for a couple, you can buy a single membership. Then, all subsequent visits of that member and a guest will be free in most of the Presidential Libraries. What a bargain.

They have their own stamp program, too. I chose not to purchase a separate Passport for just Presidential Libraries, but asked them to put the stamp in my National Park Passport.

My preconception of a Presidential Library was totally, completely wrong. There was a library, of course, which contained all the records during that President's term. But it was also full of large, life-sized exhibits of Harry Truman, his childhood, his early years, and his rise to the presidency. It has exhibits of equipment used at that time, timelines of events and the effect his presidency had on the US and the world.

Let me first say that I am not a history person. I simply cannot correlate dates and places and times and people. It's just not my talent. I can sight-sing music, but I cannot remember history. But this was fascinating! Larry and I kept saying, "I didn't know that", or "I didn't know that was President Truman." Of course, Truman became president in 1945 and we weren't born until 1954, so our knowledge would not be abundant. But I don't even remember learning much about him in Government class.

We spent a couple of hours exploring the displays and watching the videos.

We also learned that each and every modern President has decorated his own Oval Office to taste. We got to walk right into Truman's. The green carpet and drapes, his massive desk, his television set, all of his personal trinkets on tables and shelves—just as it was then.

It was an amazing and solemn experience.

When we finally dragged ourselves away from Truman's Library, we drove downtown to Hallmark. We were hoping to get a first-hand look at artists at work, perhaps even the production and manufacturing of those beautiful greeting cards. But that wasn't possible. They do have a self-guided tour but it was very limited and I was so disappointed that they didn't have a manufacturing tour. It was okay, and I did get to make a small bow. We didn't stay long.

The Lego Store right down the sidewalk, however was quite busy, with kids running around everywhere. We quickly decided to pass on that.

We walked to the Money Museum at the Federal Reserve. Be sure to take your Driver's License or Passport for entry, because you can't get it without one. Now this was a cool self-guided tour that I would highly recommend!

There are all sorts id exhibits and displays that show the "history of the Fed, historic coins, and a framed $100,000 bill, everyone can find something of compounding interest here…Finally there's the cash processing and vault area: a nine-story room filled with bills, where real Fed employees sort and examine money, disposing of the ones unfit for circulation and storing the rest in the vault. Three robots—named Huey, Dewey, and Louie after the animated nephews of Donald Duck—lift large piles of money."[3]

We spent a bit of time there, because there was so much to see. When we left, we each received a free bag of money! It was micro-shredded and worthless, but it was fun, walking out of the Fed with free cash.

In comparison to the busy day, the evening was beautiful and quiet.

APRIL 22

We drove today to Deer Creek Valley RV Resort in Topeka, Kansas, which Larry rated a wonderful 9. Nice, neat, concrete slabs and lots of great amenities.

We decided to go to Wamego to see the little town of "Oz", per Diana's request. It was a beautiful drive. All along I-70, many farmers were burning their fields for the upcoming planting of crops. We went wine tasting at the Oz Winery and through texting, she requested a bottle of "Emerald City Lights." I finally decided on a bottle of "Fraidy Cat" after disliking the "Squished Witch". I admit to being a very wussy wine drinker who prefers only the really sweet stuff like Moscato. None of that dry stuff for me.

There's a little Oz Museum down the street and I had Larry take a photo of me alongside a large Tin Man, but we didn't pay admission to go through the entire museum. We also saw the Yellow Brick Road, which, in fact, was simply a

---

[3] http://www.missourilife.com/travel/the-money-museum/

yellow-painted alleyway shortcut to the town's park. It was a delightful diversion.

We did lots of shops to and from Wamego, which made us some money.

We ate a quiet meal in the motorhome. Or at least it was quiet until I spilled my entire Diet Coke down Larry's keyboard. Oops. I guess we'll be buying a new keyboard tomorrow.

To this point, can you stop to count the states and cities we have been to in past three weeks? This was the day I actually wrote "Topeka" on my left hand because it was difficult to remember where on earth I was! I even took a picture of it. You may laugh, but if you travel a lot, you may just have to do that someday, too.

I am pleased to say that my pain is finally beginning to abate. I still need some afternoon naps, but that too will end at some point.

Praise the Lord.

APRIL 23

We were planning to go to the Eisenhower Library today, but nixed the idea when we realized it would involve over three hours of driving to get to St. Abilene, KS.

It turned out to be a lazy day instead. We went to Walmart to buy a new keyboard, then we drove to Goodwill to donate our bikes. Both of us also got badly-needed haircuts.

We went to see the new Kevin Costner movie *Criminal*, and I must say it sure was good to sit for a while. And the movie was great!

We enjoyed chicken and dumplings at the Cracker Barrel then drove back to the motorhome.

Then it was bedtime. It had been a wonderful day.

APRIL 24

Today began as a travel day.

We stopped at Strataca, the Kansas Underground Salt Museum. If you're ever anywhere in the area, be sure to plan some time there. We paid the admission for the descent, including the Train Ride and the Dark Ride. Everyone who made the descent was required to wear a hard hat.

The descent is 650 feet down into the mine, and takes a few minutes by elevator. Wow.

It's impossible to describe this place in words. Go to www.underkansas.org. Even the website doesn't do the enormous mine any type of justice. The mine was active for salt mining in the 1940's and 1950's, bringing salt to your table. There are all sorts of relics that the guide explained as he took our moving tour through the mine. Amazing.

We also learned that the specifics of the mine make it a great place on earth to store movie film. I can't repeat all of those details today, but beginning in 1963, they began doing a great business with Hollywood in the storage of movies. They were long known for keeping the original of *The Wizard of Oz*.

A side story here: My daughter and I both love the Movie *Twister*. We watch it every year. Unfortunately, fate has it that usually after we watch it, we have a clip of bad weather that includes a tornado. Strange but true. *Twister* is among the movies stored at the salt mine as well as one of the "Dorothy" props from the movie. Between *Twister* AND *The Wizard of Oz*, fate would have it that only hours from now, we would personally encounter such a phenomenon.

Back in the motorhome shortly after leaving the mine, the weather alerts on both of our phones went off. There was a tornado warning right where we were! We scanned the horizon. There were lots of nasty looking clouds, but we did not see a tornado. We were on our way to I-70, and figured we had better stay put here. There, on US 281, was a closed convenience store parking lot. Larry pulled in and yelled, "Hold on!"

Now let me stop right here to say that I am a person who has always been fascinated by weather. I did some research while writing this page, because I wanted to be sure my details were correct. The scary beast that shook the motorhome was not your typical cloud-to-ground tornado. I termed it as a funnel cloud at the time, but in research, it didn't fit the description of a funnel cloud, either. In layman's terms (which I most definitely am), I would say it swirled around near the ground like a giant dust devil, barely visible to the naked eye, except for the debris it held. But we could definitely feel its power.

Later, on the website for the National Severe Storms Laboratories, I found the term "gustnado: a whirl of dust or debris at or near the ground with no condensation funnel, which forms along the gust-front of a storm."[4] Yep, it was a gustnado.

It was hailing like crazy all around us, creating a huge noise on the roof of the motorhome and covering the ground in white. We watched helplessly as the gustnado approached, and it shook us like a rag doll.

Then, as quickly, it went on its merry way Phew.

---

1 Kings 19:11

11 The Lord said, "Go out and stand on the mountain in the presence of the Lord,
for the Lord is about to pass by."
Then a great and powerful wind tore the mountains apart and shattered the rocks before the Lord.

After the excitement of the day, we parked at a Walmart in Hays, Kansas to spent the night. We walked to a nearby Applebee's to eat supper, then we decided to call it a day. And what a day it had been!

APRIL 25

Today was a travel day into Colorado. We were traveling west on I-70 towards Denver, and there they were, in all their glory. It was the first time we had seen the majestic Rocky Mountains with our own eyes. They were all snow-topped and beautiful. The pictures we had seen had done them no justice at all.

Deuteronomy 33:15

with the choicest gifts of the ancient mountains
and the fruitfulness of the everlasting hills;

---

[4] http://www.nssl.noaa.gov/education/svrwx101/tornadoes/types/

We made it to Denver, but not without Frick and Frack having yet another argument.

Most of the day was perfection. It was in the 70's and sunny. But the further we drove, the windier it got. The weather had something cooking. The 13-foot-high, 35-foot-long rectangle motorhome is considered a "high profile vehicle", and does not do very well in high winds. Trying to keep this massive machinery in a tight lane of its own is hard work. Your arms begin to feel the pain by the day's end.

We pulled in to stay at Cherry Creek State Park in Denver, which Larry rated an 8. The first thing we saw was a herd of 20 animals. We later learned from a ranger that they were the resident mule deer of the park. We had never seen mule deer before, only white-tail deer. But I could tell you that they were still carrying very heavy winter coats. Winter was not yet over here in Colorado.

APRIL 26

True to form, the weather that came throughout the night brought severe thunderstorms. The temperature was dropping quickly and the forecasters say there might be snow. Snow? Yes, snow in the spring! A rare event indeed in Myrtle Beach, where we'd driven from. The whole week is full of either rain or snow, depending on the temperatures.

We got up early because we have lots of places to visit today. We drove to North Denver to get my neck x-ray done. It was the only way that the neurosurgeon would release me to travel. I had my instructions in hand and the procedure went quickly.

Then we drove on to Hammond's Candies. They have complimentary factory tours so we watched in awe of all the specialty candies they make, some in the same old-fashioned ways they hand-made them back in 1920. We visited their retail store last, where everything was on sale. We just had to buy some to eat on the road…and some more…and some more.

Hammond's is a fabulous place, even though I'm a bit prejudiced because my married name is Hammond. It is definitely worth the time to stop. We bought a bag full of different chocolates and candy—lots of "manufacturing mistakes". We didn't need them, of course, but they were delicious. It took us several weeks to eat it all.

We drove out to Golden, Colorado, Camping World to buy some new folding bikes that we could fit in our tow vehicle. I explained my neck situation to the salesman and politely asked if I could give one a test drive in the parking lot. It was drizzling and I was wet when I finally came back inside. Yes, I should be able to do this, considering I could do it when I was like, six. Nice little bikes. Now if I can just remember how to ride one!

We finished the afternoon touring the Denver U. S. Mint. Again, it was fascinating to learn so much about the development of our currencies and watching coins in various stages of minting.

APRIL 27

We stayed in Denver longer than we'd planned to. There is just too much bad weather forecast for us to be driving our big rig and tow vehicle through the mountains.

We left to go wandering in the car, but we didn't get far before I'd asked Larry to go back to the motorhome so that I could get the iPad. Thank God that we went back! A valve had been moved and the toilet had been overflowing the few minutes that we had been gone. There was water over the flooring and pouring outside, some of it fresh water and some backing up from the black tank. We got to it just in time, before any real damage could be done. I cannot begin to imagine what kind of a mess we would have come back to if it had run all day long.

We drove all the way to Vail, via I-70 west, but there was really nothing going on this end of April. We passed through lots of snow squalls and enjoyed a great lunch at a little place called The Happy Moose. Supper was at Casa Vallarta Mexican Restaurant, just a little place in a strip center nearby. It was so good that we ate there two nights in a row. Yum.

APRIL 28

We woke up to forecasts of a winter storm. We had been looking forward to taking the COG Railway up to Pike's Peak today. We called them to learn that the trains would not be running today because of the poor weather and visibility. It's just as well; we rescheduled for next week.

We ran out long enough to pick up some grocery essentials, and had supper again at Casa Vallarta Mexican Restaurant. It was so close and so good, why not?. Our poor heat pumps were giving their all, but it just wasn't enough against the cold temperatures and wind. We turned on the furnaces for the night.

Let's see just how much snow accumulation we get.

APRIL 29

I stayed tucked in my warm bed later than usual, as I figured we weren't going anywhere anyway.

As predicted, we stayed inside all day. I caught up on laundry and bookkeeping.

I noted that around 1pm, it was raining more than it was snowing. It looked like snow out the window, but the noise on the top of the motorhome sure sounded like rain. It was just enough ugly weather to make the grass all crusty.

My pain is pretty much gone now, even with the cold temperatures. I haven't heard from the neurosurgeon's office about my x-rays. I will have to call them next week.

APRIL 30

Because of extending our stay, today we would have to move our motorhome to another site. We got everything packed up and were ready to go, when another problem occurred. The front levelers wouldn't retract.

We tried over and over again. Larry crawled under the rig to see if there was something to fix. He sprayed them with lots of lubricant. Nothing. We couldn't move. But we had to move. What would we do?

So, while Larry's still working, I went up to the park office to explain the whole mess. I certainly respected the fact that we had to move, but we physically could not. They weren't happy, but they were accommodating. They would change the newcomers to another site.

I go back and tell Larry. I go back inside and set everything back up to stay another couple of days. THEN, the levelers come to life. Well, we could now move, so pack up again and move we did.

After that circus, we decided to go see a movie. Larry tells me that is one of the few places that he can sit and not be distracted by anything else in the world; with ADHD, that's really saying something. That's why we go to the movies often. We saw *Mother's Day*. I really enjoyed it, but Larry summed up his review in two words: "Chick Flick." By the time the movie was over, all seemed better in the world.

Thank you, Jesus.

But when would the levelers choose to act up again?

MAY 1

Yesterday was just too much stress and tension for me and I'd been forced to take a pain pill to sleep last night.

As much as Larry hates to shop, he kindly offered to take me to the local Mall, since we'd been cooped up so much this past week. (You see, I'm still not cleared to drive—that will come after the doctor reviews my x-rays and Larry feels comfortable with my range of motion.) It was a huge mall compared to South Carolina standards and it was packed. I guess everybody else had the same idea that we did on this cold, bleary day. It's not like I needed to buy anything, it just felt good to be up, walking and watching people, instead of sitting and watching the TV.

We spent more time than usual cleaning up the motorhome, due to that stinkin' mouse. He seems to like chewing paper from packages and moves from bread, cookies, noodles, crackers. Plus, the fact he is a smart little mouse, he's managed to go from lower cabinets to the overheads.

I tried to get some bookwork done, because the next 3 days are jammed full of activities. But I wasn't quite in the mood for that, so I watched NCIS instead.

MAY 2

In the car, we headed down I-25 south to Colorado Springs, ninety minutes away. We first went to the Garden of the Gods, where we drove through a "garden" of huge, beautiful rock formations. It's a public park and it was designated a National Natural Landmark in 1971.with free admission to the public. You can drive through (as we did), bike, walk, hike—the possibilities are endless. What an awesome way to spend a day. If we had been thirty years younger, it would have been an amazing hiking experience. The huge red rocks and boulders are absolutely beautiful.

We finally took our ride up the Pike's Peak COG Railway. We learned all about COG Railways and why it's the only way you could get up to a place like Pike's Peak. "A cog, or rack, railroad uses a gear, or cog wheel, to mesh into a special center rack rail to climb much steeper grades than those possible with a standard adhesion railroad. An adhesion railroad can only climb grades of four to six percent, with very short sections of up to nine percent. A "rack" railroad can climb grades of up to forty-eight percent, depending upon the type of rack system employed."[5] Because of the increased elevation, they had received several feet of snow in last weekend's storm and personnel were doing their best to clear it. We saw a huge snow-blower rail car that moves the snow off the tracks. But they can only do so much, so fast. We weren't able to go all the way to the Peak at 14,500 feet to see the magnificent panoramas that inspired the song, *America the Beautiful*. We made it to 12,600 feet before going back. We were bundled to the hilt, but were still mighty cold on the ride. But none of us on the train seemed to mind.

Who can view such amazing creations and feel there is no God? You can even see the curvature of the earth on the horizon.

---

[5] cograilway.com

MAY 3

We drove US 36 north to Boulder to take the factory tour at Celestial Seasonings. This was a great factory tour! They guided the groups through the actual work floor, explaining each step on the way.

We learned in great detail the working relationships they have with growers of these pristine teas and spices all around the world. We saw the crops in their natural forms, stored there and awaiting processing.

One fascinating aspect of the tour is The Mint Room. At the end of the tour, we found all sorts of mugs and t-shirts reading, "I survived the Mint Room." They are careful to keep the spices apart, to keep them from sharing tastes and scents. Hence, the need for The Mint Room.

When our group arrived, they opened the garage-type door to The Mint Room. The outpouring scent of mint nearly knocked you down where you stood! Larry tried to go in, but quickly backed out of the room, along with several others. It was sheer will that I stood in the room, drawing deep breaths and could feel the mint sear the very bottoms of my lungs.

The factory's automation is second to none. We watched robots move and stack pallets. There were other machines packaging the tea in little boxes, then shrink wrap them. Those boxes then get packed into shipping cases that will soon make it to your grocery shelves. What a manmade marvel. The employees smiled and welcomed us to their little great-smelling world, working under the Sleepy Bear logo.

Back home, I found some very interesting information about Celestial Seasoning Tea:

"...Did you know that green, black, and white tea all come from the same plant? It's true—they're all from the *Camellia sinensis* bush, but how they're processed after harvest produces their very different aromas and flavors.

"Here's another one: what we call "herbal teas" are technically not 'teas' at all. Herbal tea contains no Camellia sinensis leaves; rather, it is made from many plants, using not just the leaves, but also the flowers, roots, bark, and seeds. These brews typically contain flavorful, beneficial ingredients like chamomile, lemongrass, and mint, and naturally contain no caffeine at all."[6]

I have always loved flavored teas and could have gone crazy in their terrific gift shop. They combine some of the most amazing blends on the market today. Sleepytime is their favored classic. This is an experience that everyone should enjoy. And the tour was free. If you've never tried their offerings, you should check out celestialseasonings.com, or your local grocery store.

But we had another assigned mission to go to Boulder: Diana wanted us to take a photo of the house used to film outside scenes of *Mork & Mindy*.

With the help of Google maps, we found the pretty, well-maintained, but unassuming house located at 1619 Pine Street. It's a beautiful quiet neighborhood. If a texted photo will delight my daughter, well then…

It was indeed yet another amazing day of seeing new things and learning so much. There were many college students here, all walking and biking around the town. We

---

[6] celestialseasonings.com

couldn't help but wonder just how many were high on marijuana at that moment. It IS legal....

MAY 4

We drove north on I-25 and arrived at the Manor RV Park in Estes Park, Colorado, at an elevation at 7,500 feet. Larry rated it at a 4. The people were nice, but they were just opening for the spring. There was no water. None. Not even in the showers or bathrooms. We sure wished they'd called to notify us of that little detail. And, it was very, very difficult to navigate our big rig through the campground.

We took a drive around town after we setup. Herds of elk were walking all around town, up and down streets and sidewalks. It was an amazing view coming down into the town from the mountains. US 35 from I-25 is a very curvy and steep mountain road from Denver, CO, as well as US 34 going north out of town.

The Stanley Hotel, a beautiful white building from 1909, overlooks the town. You have had a peek of the inside of The Stanley, as the infamous scene of the twins in the hallway from The Shining was filmed there. Estes Park was a perfect little place for folks to come for a day trip—lots of little unique shops, but not too many hotels.

We enjoyed a tasty dinner at Chelitos Mexican Restaurant that was located up on the second level of a shopping area. We shopped a little afterwards. I bought some expensive huckleberry preserves and a gourmet lollipop: huckleberry cheesecake. Yum.

MAY 5

What a magnificent day!

We drove to Rocky Mountain National Park for the day. Larry's Access Pass saved us the $20 entry fee. I was happy to get another two stamps in my passport, one for the park and one for the Centennial.

We drove up to about 12,000 feet, which was as far as the road had been cleared of snow. I took a picture of my 6'3" husband next to the plow bank, which was a few feet taller than him!

We came to a place called Sprague Lake and walked the half-mile hike around the lake. There wasn't one moment when the view wasn't absolutely spectacular. The lake was as smooth as glass.

We stopped for groceries on the way back and mailed a few things.

We found out that this first Saturday in May is the Estes Park Annual Duck Race. A person can sponsor as many rubber ducks as they want, for $20 each. The ducks are released into the river and compete toward the finish line. The winning ducks qualify for prizes that were donated by sponsors in the community. We learned that it's been held annually since 1989, and in that time returned more than $2 million to local charities and groups.

Everybody that attends will probably know everybody else except us. I think we'll just stay up in the campground for the next few days.

MAY 6

I finally settled down and got some bookwork done. We had gotten a Red Box at the store the day before, so we had no choice but to go out to return it.

We knew we wouldn't come down over the weekend, so we decided to go to the cinema to see *Eye in the Sky* today. It was an amazing movie. It is difficult for someone like me to believe that our military has such technology in their hands today.

I'd put a chicken breast in our mini crock pot before we left, so we enjoyed it grilled with a fresh ear of corn. Yum.

Caught up on Facebook. Watched NCIS.

Sleep came easily.

MAY 7

To my calculations, I have survived 200 days since my accident. To God be the glory! I suppose those moments of the accident will always be painted clearly in my memory. I never, ever forget for one moment how easily I could have died that day, but God's angels and His hedge of protection were there.

Eleven months before my accident, I had gone to work in a call center. I had never given much thought to the people who answer my customer service calls. I always knew that God wanted me to touch the lives of those around me. I thought early on, with such a diversified working environment, what did God want of me here, in this place? I was just 60+, white-haired, pleasingly plump me. And I went to work every day, just being me. But, when I came back to work after my accident, everyone was encouraging me, caring about me, worried about me. It blessed my heart, because, apparently, I had blessed theirs.

Today's celebration included reconciling business bank statements.

But it sure was a crazy weather day! It was 49 degrees and we were under a tornado watch. What? The thunderstorm that came through covered everything in tiny hailstones. Then came rain mixed with snow!

I wonder what time that Duck Race was?

MAY 8

Today was a blessedly peaceful Sunday. We did drive into town in the afternoon, figuring most everyone had already headed home. Larry gave me some time to shop in a small quilting/knitting shop. What a remarkable place. I'd had a long-standing childhood dream of someday owning my own yarn shop. I had cut ads out of magazines for years. Wow, to be able to knit or stitch all day and get paid to do it. That would be my dream job.

Even though I'd had fun in town, I really wasn't feeling well. I personally believe that the altitude has finally affected me. My heart's been out of rhythm all day and all I really want to do is sleep.

Hopefully, the lower elevations that we'll be heading to will help.

MAY 9

We left Colorado in the morning. We traveled the curvy and steep decent north up US 35 to I-25 toward Cheyenne, Wyoming. We turned on US 85 to Scottsbluff and Bayard, Nebraska. The scenery was so different than the mountainous hill country we had just left. It was flat and grassy. Also in contrast, there weren't many other vehicles on the rural roads. It made for a great day of driving in a motorhome.

> 2 Samuel 23:44
>
> he is like the light of morning at sunrise
> on a cloudless morning,
> like the brightness after rain
> that brings grass from the earth.'

We have traveled 12 states in 41 days!

The GPS managed to misplace us several times today, especially at the very end, as usual.

We pulled into the Chimney Rock Pioneer Campground in Bayard, Nebraska, for a few days, which Larry rated a 4. It's in an open field, on gravel and the store was still closed until summer. But the view was great.

We parked the motorhome so that Chimney Rock was right out our front windows. We learned that "Chimney Rock is a prominent geological rock formation in Morrill County in western Nebraska. Rising nearly 300 feet (91 m) above the surrounding North Platte River valley, the peak of Chimney Rock is 4,226 feet (1,288 m) above sea level. During the middle 19th century, it served as a landmark along the Oregon Trail, the California Trail, and the Mormon Trail, which ran along the north side of the rock.

It is visible for many miles from the east along US Route 26."[7]

There are ground lights on it so that it can be seen at night. I learned of a Facebook account named CR365 which means 365 days of Chimney Rock. Two people alternately came to the Rock around sunset every day for the 365 days of 2016. Actually 366, because it was Leap Year. Check it out. Every photograph is from a different angle under different weather conditions—they are breathtaking!

Deuteronomy 8:9

9 a land where bread will not be scarce and you will lack nothing; a land where the rocks are iron and you can dig copper out of the hills

---

It was a beautiful day. The sun was shining and there wasn't a cloud in the sky. I feel so much better already, at the lower altitude. Before the sun went down, we had seen two mules, a horse, and a few bunnies. I made friends with the two mules behind a fence and Larry took our picture.

And then there were the trains just across the road…

MAY 10

We drove a half-hour to get to visit the Scotts Bluff National Monument in Gering, Nebraska. Between Chimney Rock and Scotts Bluff Visitor Centers, I received nine stamps in my Passport. They included not only the monuments themselves, but the Centennial, Oregon National Historic Trail, California National Historic Trail, and the Mormon Pioneer National Historic Trail. They even had one that was

---

[7] https://en.wikipedia.org/wiki/Chimney_Rock_National_Historic_Site

just a hand-drawn picture of Chimney Rock with the sun and clouds behind it. That stamp was old and worn from many years of use.

The Visitor Centers had so much to learn about the California and Oregon trails. I just don't remember learning any of this from American history class. The national park film is always a learning experience in itself.

I went to sleep that night with all sorts of wagon train stories in my head, listening to the trains.

MAY 11

Today was another chilly day, but the skies were blue with a few clouds.

We drove into a little town nearby. When I say little, I mean a Dollar General and one gas station. Period.

I kept busy doing laundry, because tomorrow we hit the road again.

The neurosurgeon's office called today. Everything looks as it should. They released me. Praise the Lord in Heaven, and give Him all the glory! After all that pain and suffering and all these months of recovery, I am finally declared healed.

Exodus 23:25

25 Worship the Lord your God,
and his blessing will be on your food and water.
I will take away sickness from among you,

MAY 12

Today was a travel day. Our destination is Chadron State Park, Nebraska, up US 385. Larry rated it a 6.

We were held up on the way out of town by the one of the very trains I'd been enjoying. One last whistle song, for the road.

While we were driving through Alliance, Nebraska, we saw American flags everywhere. I Googled it to learn that the Patriot Ryders would be coming through here today, on the way to Denver. They were accompanying some WWII veterans who would be boarding an Honor Flight to Washington, D.C. About fifteen minutes later, we began honking our big air horns as we passed the police-escorted convoy, with vans full of vets and dozens of roaring motorcycles bearing flags, coming from the other way. What a remarkable sight!

The state park is lovely. It was 74 degrees and sunny today, but back to the 60's and 30's tomorrow.

MAY 13

Today was Friday, the 13th. There is absolutely nothing to report today. There are no FOX channels where we are, darn it. It was so lazy that Larry even took a nap.

We did finally head into town and enjoyed a meal at Helen's Restaurant. We were a little confused when we stepped up on the porch. There was a door on the right and another door on the left. It turned out the restaurant on the right served simple, plain good food in a very simple and plain atmosphere. The door on the left led to fine dining.

We chose the door on the right. We chose well. The food was great.

MAY 14

Today we drove to Custer State Park in South Dakota to stay in the Blue Belle Campground, which Larry rated a 5.

We would learn that the beasts we had always called Buffalo were actually American Bison, and there are no Buffalo in the US. It was the first time we saw one up close and personal—they were grazing right next to the road! They are huge, magnificent beasts of God's creation, grazing and snorting as we pulled the motorhome over to observe.

They were amazing to see. And then we saw more and more. Over the course of our visit, it got to be funny because we eventually saw so many, that we began saying, "Oh, look! Oh, it's just another buffalo—oops—bison."

We grabbed a quick lunch after we set up and headed for the Crazy Horse Monument. This was yet another amazing piece of history that I knew absolutely nothing about.

Crazy Horse was a Native American war leader of the Oglala Lakota American Indians. The monument is the largest mountain carving in progress since 1939, at 641 feet long. The carving is so massive, just the horse's nostrils are 26 feet in diameter. In comparison, the head of Crazy Horse alone is 27 feet taller than the six story heads of Mount Rushmore.

The sculpture was originally carved by Korczak Ziolkowski, who died in 1982. The monument is now being carved out of the mountain by his children and grandchildren. We will learn as we visit National Parks across the country that all of them celebrate the different American Indian tribes and the peoples that settled these areas of land.

We have absolutely no satellite reception and there's no cable in the state park. What will we do? Poor, poor Larry.

MAY 15

It was cloudy and cold this morning. The poor church group that was camping in tents right next to us must have frozen their toes off last night. They packed up and left early.

Just walking by, Larry noticed that the pin holding the hitch of the tow dolly to the motorhome was missing. It was only by the grace of God that he noticed it, as it's not something we check daily. Fortunately, we had extras and fixed it promptly.

But if we had been driving down the road and the dolly slipped out, the results would have been disastrous! And, we knew without a doubt that it could not have just fallen out on its own. Someone with muscle had to unclip it and remove it. If it was a prank, it was a very foolish one. It could have had deadly consequences to anyone who would have been behind us when the dolly came loose. Shaken, but thanking God again for His hedge of protection, we drove the car to spend the day at Mt. Rushmore.

I have seen pictures of Mt. Rushmore but to see it up close—wow. I guess I would say it's bigger than life, but you already knew that. I am learning so much. It makes you really wonder about the men who could bring the faces of some of our greatest presidents in US history out of the side of a mountain. Man alone could simply not do this. It's like the hand of God came down to lead their every stroke.

Larry mentioned that there seems to be room for another face or two. I wonder…

We saw some bison up close and personal again today, a few white-tailed deer, some mule deer, and something like a badger. On such a gloomy day, I would have figured they would all be tucked away in warm, small places.

When I text back and forth with Diana, I can sure tell that she wishes she was here with us. Not only for the scenery and the photographs, but this is the longest time in her whole life that she's been so far away.

I think she misses us. I sure do miss her, too.

MAY 16

It was cloudy again today. We drove the entire wildlife loop of the state park and it was delightful. We saw lots of bison and prairie dogs. The prairie dogs come up close to the road and appear to be praying that you'll give them something to eat as you drive by. They were so cute. And no, we didn't feed them.

We did see a large group of antelopes. They can run so fast!

But the funniest were the wild burros. The ranger at the campground had warned us about them. They must associate vehicles to food. The whole group was standing right in the middle of the road, so you had no choice but to stop. One walked right up to my window. I took photos of him as he approached, but I pulled away right before the greatest photo op! Imagine him coming up to the window, opening his mouth to show his big buck teeth, then smearing his upper lip on the glass like he was trying to take a bite out of it. I don't think I'll ever be able to erase that sight from my mind. It was so funny!

We later drove to the big city of Cedar Rapids, South Dakota, to stock up at Sam's and Walmart.

I am thanking God for each and every day! The pain is gone and we have the means—through this tragedy—to really enjoy this journey for Him.

Despite a fridge full of groceries, we enjoyed Buffalo Stew and cornbread at the lodge. The buffalo tasted yummy and went down well, but sat a little heavy through the evening. I never did do well with gamey meats. But it was nothing that a little Pepto Bismol couldn't fix.

MAY 17

We enjoyed another drive through the Wildlife Loop and the Needles today. On the loop, we were disappointed that we saw only one prairie dog and one small group of elk. We may go back closer to sunset tonight, if the weather holds.

The Needles of the Black Hills of South Dakota are a region of eroded granite pillars, towers, and spires within Custer State Park. There is only one road through the Needles, Route 87. It's a skinny, curvy road with switchbacks and tight turns. Do not attempt this drive with your motorhome!! It has rock tunnels—really two boulders leaning against each other where the road goes through. The overhead clearance is low and two cars cannot clear the tunnel at the same time.

Just so you know, a switchback is defined by a 180-degree bend in the road. In my experience, they are often more than a 180-degree bend. Sometimes you even bend around so tight that the road goes over or under where you just were. It's difficult to navigate a big rig that's long and doesn't bend in the middle, especially if there's someone coming the other way.

We got out of the car several times while driving the Needles. I enjoy things so much more when I experience them with the sun on my face and breathing the fresh air.

While we were traveling east on 87 in the car, we could see a sightseeing bus up ahead. We said aloud, "There is absolutely no way he can make it through the tunnels, and probably not some of the switchbacks."

Several miles up this mountain, the driver apparently realized that he had taken a very wrong turn. He was stuck. There was no way to go forward and nowhere to turn around. He would have to back down this twisty, curvy road. We didn't stay around to watch how the driver would accomplish this feat. I wonder if they took the folks off the bus and, if so, how? I would have been a nervous wreck! The sun was finally shining for us but definitely not this bus driver!

Then, we stopped at Lake Sylvan. What a beautiful body of water as smooth as glass. It dates back to 1881, when a man named Theodore Reder built a dam across Sunday Gulch. There were kayakers on the lake, out to enjoy the beautiful day. It had been yet another day of amazing discovery.

MAY 18

Today was a travel day to Badlands National Park in Interior, South Dakota, which Larry rated a 6.

We headed up Route 16A and I-90 east from Custer State Park—yes, east. It was the first time we'd headed east on this trip. What an amazing change of scenery on today's highways.

We decided when we arrived that we should get the laundry caught up first, and we didn't have facilities to do it here.

We got directions from the place next door and set out to the laundromat in the car. We started out in the direction of Hall, but somehow figured out that we were going in the wrong direction. By that time, our destination was like fifty miles away, We turned off the main highway and took a secondary road in what we thought was the right direction, and some of the trip wound up on dirt roads. It was a good thing we were in the car; I don't think the motorhome would have survived parts of this trip.

The laundromat was a tiny little place, but everything was clean and in working order. When all was done, it took us another forty minutes to get back to the campground. The Badlands are awesome but very remote.

Long ago, we traveled to Grand Cayman, where we visited a little town named "Hell." There were amazing rock formations there. The view seemed to change greatly depending on which way you were facing, and the position of the sun overhead. Well, if Satan made anything on earth which speaks of hell on earth, the Badlands would be it, in my opinion. Hell, Grand Cayman is a little place, but the

Badlands go on for miles. If you woke up in Hell, you could easily walk to water and refreshment. The name "Badlands" is pretty self-explanatory.

In every direction, there are deep canyons and crevasses. There are limestone spirals popping up with no pattern to them. The pink and purple sunsets are as spectacular as the night sky and stars that follow.

The Milky Way. Who can say there is no God?

> Genesis 1:16
>
> 16 God made two great lights—
> the greater light to govern the day and
> the lesser light to govern the night.
> He also made the stars.

MAY 19

We rose early to drive to the Minuteman Missile National Historic Site Tour, in Philip, South Dakota. Our tour guide was a retired USAF Lieutenant Colonel, who personally worked in the Minuteman Missile Delta Command Center.

It was another amazing aspect of our military at work. These men resided in the Command Centers, spending concurrent days, hundreds of feet below ground, in a little room. They were to be ready at a moment's notice—hence "minuteman"—should the word to launch come down from the President. We could view all the technology that existed in the 60's and 70's and now decommissioned. Wow.

One commander and two men would simultaneously turn a key from a safe and push the buttons for a nuclear war and surely the demise of mankind. Such power, held in the hands of these trained men and women.

After the tour, we drove to the Delta 09 missile site. It's in a dusty field out in the middle of nowhere. The lid is flush with the ground and they've installed a window so that you can view the inactive missile. I remember we had missile sites out in rural Ohio, miles from where I grew up. The Minuteman was ready in a minute. Those, if I remembered correctly, needed a lot more time to prepare to fire.

We drove back west on I-90 in our car to historic Wall, SD. We learned with a laugh the history behind this million-dollar locale.

Ted and Dorothy Hustead bought the Wall Drug Store in 1931. There were only about 300 poor folks that lived anywhere nearby and the passersby on the highway just didn't stop. They were slowly going broke.

One day, during a nap with her small son, Dorothy came up with a brilliant idea to get the travelers off the highway: Free Ice Water.

They put up billboards on the highway in both directions, advertising "Free Ice Water" and the rest, as they say, is history. It was an ingenious marketing program that actually worked! Now it's a ginormous tourist attraction, more like a small town, designed for travelers going down the highway in either direction.

They have a whole collection of odd things there at the complex. Among them was a Zoltar machine, like the one that granted Tom Hanks his wish in the movie *Big*.

And they still give out free ice water, just ask.

> John 4:14
>
> but whoever drinks the water I give them
> will never thirst.
> Indeed, the water I give them will become
> in them a spring of water welling up to eternal life."

Back at the park, there was an excellent park movie at the visitor center. The movie taught us to much about the formation of the Badlands as well as the American Indians who were there before us. And I got my Passport stamped again.

Back at the campground, I rode my bike. That probably doesn't sound like much to some of you, but to me, it was a very big deal. I was winded, but I was happy.

MAY 20

We put on our hiking boots and "hiked" the Door Trail and the Window Trail, just up the road. Both were easy treks and most of the walking was on a raised boardwalk. That's why I put the word in quotes. That's just a walk in the park—literally—to many of my friends.

But this walk was certainly amazing. The sun was shining and with temperatures in the mid 70's, the day was perfect. I was still so out of shape and it felt great to deeply breathe the dry air. There are signs "Watch for Rattlesnakes". We were on the watch for them but never did see one, thank God for that!

We spent the evening watching thunderstorms as they passed to the west. There was God-touched beauty all around.

> Zechariah 9:14
>
> 14 Then the Lord will appear over them,
> his arrow will flash like lightning.
> The Sovereign Lord will sound the trumpet;
> he will march in the storms of the south,

MAY 21

Larry spent a while working under the motorhome this morning. He finally determined that we have a fluid leak from the differential after seeing oil on the cement. This is where the axels connect with the drive shaft of the Freightliner chassis of the motorhome. It's a great blessing that we have coverage through a Good Sam extended warranty policy for stuff like this but it does have a $500 deductible. He spent time on the phone to arrange a service appointment at the freightliner dealer in Rapid City next Tuesday.

The afternoon was cloudy, chilly, and windy. We found some movies on the satellite to watch (no obstructions out here in the Badlands) in lieu of FOX News.

My nephew Nick is getting married to his girl Andrea soon. I have a special counted cross stitch pattern that I use to make personalized and embellished wedding announcements as gifts. After making them for my nieces Kelly and Lydia recently, I'd sure better make Nick one, too.

As I lay out my supplies, I am quickly reminded that these old eyes are not what they used to be. Groan.

MAY 22

We were lazy again today and watched a couple old movies on satellite.

We finally roused to go for a bike ride to the nearby lodge and I asked Larry if we could eat lunch there. I ordered buffalo stew and cornbread to share. It tasted just like beef stew, but it sat heavy just like when I ate buffalo the last time. Guess I won't eat buffalo any more. Oops, I mean Bison.

A tornado watch was posted at 3pm. It was originally set to expire at 9pm, but it was extended until 2am. I hate tornado watches in the dark, when you just can't see what's in the sky. I guess I have watched *Twister* too many times. The big ones in the movie happened at night. I prayed for God's protection. I watched storms come and go on every side, but we barely had a few sprinkles. Praise the Lord!

MAY 23

This day in my journal said very little. I mentioned that it was our last day here in the Badlands and we began to prepare for hitting the road again tomorrow. Every time we move the motorhome again Willie Nelson's song, *On The Road Again* starts to play in my mind.

I have some beautiful sunset pictures taken from the parking lot at the trails of Door and Window. I do believe they were taken on this day. We had seen so much, and some things twice.

I will have an entirely new respect for the Badlands when I see them in the movies. The National Parks are such a blessing to all Americans, protecting and preserving these natural marvels for enjoyment for generations to come.

The way that God intended for us to see them.

MAY 24

We were up at dawn to drive back to Rapid City, South Dakota, via west bound I-90 for the fluid leak repair. Once we'd dropped off the motorhome, we went all over the big city running errands. When we returned, the Freightliner dealer told us that parts had been ordered and they would arrive in the morning. We promptly made reservations at the nearby Country Inn.

The route to the dealer had taken us downtown. We were delighted to discover that on every corner of the business district there is a bronze statue of an American President. Every past president was represented, made to their height and size, and clothed to the personality of the man. I wish we'd had more time, I would have loved to stand close to each and every one. It was such a tribute to these American servants.

Instead, we were on another mission for Diana. She had Facebooked a pic of Dinosaur Park in Rapid City and wanted photos. We Googled and followed the winding directions to a large park, up on a steep hill overlooking downtown.

I groaned as I exited the car and discovered that I would have to climb like 50 steps from the parking area to actually get up to the park. Larry said there was no way he was walking all those steps, just to see a dinosaur!

The largest one was a long-necked herbivore known as Brachiosaurus (don't be impressed, I Googled that). There were six other different types of dinosaurs up there with him. I later learned that the park was dedicated on May 22, 1936. The statues are made of large pipes and wire mesh. The park was well-maintained and well-attended.

At least the steps were easier going down.

To kill time, we went to see *Money Monster* at the Carmike. Larry and I usually enjoy George Clooney movies, because he's from the greater Cincinnati area, too. We grew up watching his dad, Nick on daytime television and have watched George's rise to stardom. I may not agree with his political views, but this newest movie did not disappoint us.

We had supper at the TGIF right next door to the Country Inn. The service and food were great. Back at the hotel, we enjoyed the hot tub, but it was too hot for me. There were lots of kids playing in the pool and water slide. It was fun watching them play. Back in the room, Larry found something goofy on SyFy and fell asleep. I tried to sleep, but then came the leg cramps, from climbing all those steps.

Oh, my goodness, they were bad!

I quietly redressed, so as not to wake Larry, and went to the lobby. I explained to the night clerk that I have a problem with leg cramps and a Debbie I'd worked with had told me to drink pickle juice as a cure. When she politely "gave me a look", I laughed and told her that I'd made that same face when Debbie had told me, but it really works. I asked if she would be so kind as to call the TGIF next door to ask if they would deliver a carryout drink cup of pickle juice to me at the hotel, sort of as a medical emergency. There would be a $5 tip if they would.

It arrived within minutes. It was probably the easiest $5 the guy had earned all day.

I drank some in front of the clerk to prove that it really works within ninety seconds. Even professionals don't know why it works, but it does.

If you suffer from leg cramps, this hot tip just changed your life.

MAY 25

I slept so late. It was wonderful to have a queen-sized bed and covers all to myself.

We checked out, did some errands at Walmart and ate at McDonalds. I insisted we go shopping to buy me a new pair of New Balance shoes. Cramps usually come that bad when I've entirely worn down a pair of shoes. Larry really doesn't understand my complaint, as the outside of my shoes still looked fine. But it's not the outsides that are between me and the pavement, and I usually only get six months out of a really good pair of shoes—I never buy cheap ones. He reluctantly agreed, since I was obviously pressing the matter so hard.

Now back at the motorhome, Larry insists he has work he must do today, but the motorhome hadn't been repaired yet. The parts came in this morning, but all the bays were now filled with other rigs. They finished in the afternoon, so we proceeded to Rushmore Shadows RV Resort there in Rapid City, which Larry rated at a 6.

Sleeping back in our own queen bed: priceless.

MAY 26

Larry decided this morning that there would be times that our roof-mounted satellite just won't find the satellites, due to obstructions like trees and buildings. And since it's roof-mounted, we can't move it. We drove the car to the north side Camping World to buy a mobile satellite dish that we could set up anywhere the fifty-foot cable would reach. We may be "camping" but Larry still needs FOX News.

The afternoon was awful! One would need a PhD to set up a satellite dish. I made like six telephone calls to our satellite provider, Dish, but we finally figured it all out ourselves, piece by piece. The operators just aren't trained in providing tech service. You must contact the manufacturers directly, but they were closed for the day. Here's some basic help, just in case you ever buy a satellite.

Larry found a couple of apps that he loaded on his iPhone that really help in locating the satellites. One is called "Dish Align" and the other, "DishForMyRV".

You need three separate adjustments. You could call them up and down, left and right, around and around, but that would be too simple. The industry calls them, "azimuth, tilt, and elevation".

Azimuth

"Azimuth is your compass heading. It's what you're changing when you spin the dish around on a mast. Here, you want to have the center arm pointing to the compass heading you need. You'll need a little skill in using a compass, but it's not hard. With any compass, point the needle to North and then take a reading to correspond with the heading you want. North is -0- degrees, East is 90, South is 180, West is 270. A bubble-style compass like you can find in an auto parts store will always give you a heading, if you look at the line inscribed on it. Some of you might even have a compass app on your smartphone, that will show you degrees.

Elevation

Elevation describes how high in the sky the dish is pointing. For this, you will use the measurements inscribed on the back of the satellite mount. Zero degrees has the dish pointing straight ahead, and 90 has the dish pointing straight up.

Tilt

Tilt describes how low one side of the dish is compared to the other. In other words, if you put a marble on the top lip of the dish, would it roll one way or another. Tilt is set using the markings on the back of the mount, as well."[8]

Geesh, I would just rather read a book.

I insisted we to go the hot tub at the campground. It sure did alleviate the tension of the afternoon. It was a perfect ending to a very imperfect day.

MAY 27

Crummy weather day agenda:

Slept late. Ate breakfast. Ate lunch.

Napped. Knitted. Watched NCIS on DVD.

---

[8] http://forums.solidsignal.com/showthread.php/2980-SATELLITE-101-Basic-terms-when-aiming-a-dish

Knitted while watching NCIS. Ate supper.

Knitted some more. Watched more NCIS.

Bedtime.

MAY 28

Ditto, see May 27.

MAY 29

We sure are getting a lot of rest this week.

Finally, the sun shined, so we drove to itty bitty Hill City, South Dakota. The motorcyclists flock to this little town and you do see them everywhere. I assume it's the challenge of riding the winding roads of the Black Hills that bring them here. It's also close to Sturgis, the motorcycle rally capital of the world. 2015 was the 75th anniversary of the Sturgis Rally, and over a half-million bikers came to ride.

As we walked the city streets, we were delighted and amazed by the metal sculptures displayed. There were life-sized horses, steer, and bison, all made of metal parts. I took quite a few pictures and upon closer inspection, here's a list of many of the parts I could identify: wrenches, gears, springs, car parts, files, horseshoes, bike chains, tubing, cable, and barbed wire. I would have to say that there probably some whirligigs and thingamabobs in them too. Awesome!

We wound up walking to the historic Black Hills Central Train station. We sat outside to enjoy a sandwich while we soaked up some much-needed sunshine. They called, "All Aboard" and we watched as the train loaded with all sorts of folks.

They would ride this steam train for a twenty-mile journey, just as folks did more than a hundred years ago. The train runs several times a day between Hill City and Keystone.

We watched as the woman engineer filled the steam locomotive with water from an old wooden water tower, like we've all seen in the movies. The water rushed down a wooden flume into the engine tank. The train's steam whistle came to life as the engineer released the brake and allowed the train to move forward.

We waved to the passengers as they waved back. We lingered, then walked slowly toward the car.

We drove out Highway 385 and stopped at the Prairieberry Winery. They allowed us to choose five of their wines to sample, at no charge. We purchased a bottle of the one we liked the best, KickAss Rhubarb. The place was clean and well-merchandised, with a café that offered views of the nearby Black Hills. A fifth-generation winery, it's Hill City's only working winery, just a few steps from their tasting room.

Texas Roadhouse is always good for supper, so we enjoyed a great chopped steak dinner, while throwing peanut shells on the floor.

After being cooped up the past couple of days, we really enjoyed being able to get out and about.

MAY 30

My mother would have been 94 years old today, had she lived to see the day. She went to her glory on a hot evening in August when she was only 49. Miss, you, mom.

Because it's traditional Memorial Day (not the Monday holiday), it seems as though everything on Facebook and cable is about past wars. It is so very sad what mankind can do to a fellow man.

My father, Harlan, served in WWII in the Army Air Corps, stationed in Reykjavik, Iceland. He had to bury my mother long before our local cemetery had completed their Veterans section. So, despite complaining every year and finally putting a Veteran emblem on his grave marker, he's never gotten a flag from the Boy Scouts for Memorial Day. But over the years, my sister, Beve always makes sure he gets a flag of his very own.

> Isaiah 25:8
>
> 8 he will swallow up death forever.
> The Sovereign Lord will wipe away the tears
> from all faces;
> he will remove his people's disgrace
> from all the earth. The Lord has spoken.

We rode our bikes throughout the campground but it didn't take long to do me in. I am still so weak in the knees, and it's hilly here, hence "Black Hills." We returned to find the National Weather Service had posted yet another severe thunderstorm watch for this evening.

There was one big highlight to the day: I fixed Frogmore Stew for the holiday. Before you groan out loud, it's NOT what you think! It's not a stew and it doesn't contain frogs. It's a low country South Carolina dish. The recipe (as I make it) is in the back of the book.

The hot tub was great. Again.

MAY 31

The wind was rockin' the place today! The main storm event may have already passed through, but this wind is crazy.

Sad to say, I had to put my engagement ring away in my jewelry box today. I found a snap in the band and now both my engagement ring and my wedding band need repairs. We went to Landstrom's, the oldest Black Hills Gold manufacturing company to see if the rings could be repaired while we were in town. This place is the only true heir to the original Black Hills Gold designs, tools, and manufacturing methods made over hundreds of years ago. We watched through glass windows as artists hand-made beautiful creations of leaves, grape clusters, and vines. They make everything, including bracelets, rings, necklaces, earrings, and pendants. I was disappointed to learn that their repairs were two weeks out, so it's a good thing I had made Larry buy me a pretty anniversary band this spring, or I wouldn't have had a thing to wear —on my ring finger, that is.

We headed into town to see some movie I didn't even bother to write down. It was definitely a movie kind of day. It was in the 80's yesterday and the storm front that blew through last evening dipped it to the low 60's today. No biking or hot tub today.

We ate at a nice Mexican restaurant downtown. Can you see a pattern here? Larry may not eat much, but he sure likes Mexican food.

Then we watched Netflix and hit the hay early.

JUNE 1

Another beautiful day! The drive in the motorhome to Deadwood was scenic, sunny, and short. What more could one ask for?

We set up quickly at the Deadwood KOA, which Larry rated a 3, then drove the short trip to town.

The day began with a City of Deadwood Museum tour and ended in the Mt. Moriah Cemetery, where Wild Bill Hickok is buried. It was a very steep climb up a paved road to the gravesites. It really took your breath away! Other famous people associated with this little town in a gulch are George Custer, Calamity Jane, Jack McCall, Poker Alice Tubbs and even Potato Creek Johnny. It was certainly a town that had been full of interesting and colorful people.

The website defines Deadwood: "An Entire American City Named a National Historic Landmark!"[9] If you're curious about any of those odd folks I've listed above, just check out the website cityofdeadwood.com.

We took our time walking the streets, learning all we could about this little town that was established in 1876 during the Black Hills gold rush. The afternoon treated us to a gunfight in the streets and a shooting in a bar—both bringing history alive.

Deadwood was a very dangerous place back in the day. It was a lawless boom town due to the gold strike. HBO has used the town as a setting for a series called

---

[9] www.cityofdeadwood.com

Deadwood. Nowadays, Kevin Costner owns a saloon and casino in the middle of town called The Midnight Star, which we made sure to visit. The tin type ceilings, velvet-covered furniture, huge bar—all historically maintained, but disregards all the electronic slot machines further back in the building. He fell in love with the area when he filmed the movie *Dances with Wolves.* He also has a buffalo museum outside of town called Tatanka: Story of the Bison.

Our 43rd wedding anniversary is tomorrow and since we're already "in town", we decided to celebrate tonight. We enjoyed a curious but delicious supper at Saloon #10, upstairs at the Deadwood Social Club. We were led up a skinny staircase to the second floor to sit in a comfy booth near the 19th century bar. The floors were hardwood and creaked pleasantly when you walked on them.

We ordered the Seafood Nest from the menu. The online menu recalls that it included "white tiger shrimp, diver scallops, Chilean blue mussels, red bell pepper, basil cream sauce and fried capellini".[10]

When it arrived, it was indeed a curious presentation, and we loved it! The description fails to explain that the capellini (like spaghetti) had been fried in one large thin "pancake", taken in one big, hot piece and draped over a domed object, so that it would cool in the shape of a dome. Inside, on the plate, was the creamy stew. You had to break the dome to get to the stew and the noodles were thin and crispy. Quite the experience.

All in all, it was another informative and beautiful day.

---

[10] http://www.saloon10.com/dining.html

JUNE 2

Happy 43rd Wedding Anniversary to us! If someone had asked me many years ago where I saw myself on this date, my answer would never have resembled my reality today! I couldn't have imagined this at all.

We had absolutely no plans, but set out in the car to adventure anyway. We had a nice lunch at Cadillac Jack's Casino, a $9.95 BBQ lunch plate. We walked past the slots to leave and encountered a huge Wonder Woman machine. Well, Diana loves Wonder Woman, so I laughed and said it must be an omen. I sat down to play and promptly lost $9.49. It was time to leave.

We visited two museums in Deadwood: The Day of '76 Museum and The Adams Museum. They were both fascinating, and we learned much about the old American West. They had all sorts of interesting relics and exhibits about the heyday of the town. Their website states, "We inspire the global community by preserving and celebrating the cultural heritage of Deadwood and the Black Hills in the context of the American West through exceptional exhibits, innovative educational programs and access to extensive collections in unique settings".[11] They have most certainly done just that.

With no plans, we drove the area and one road lead us to the town of Lead (pardon the pun). In the middle of town was a big hole in the ground. Huge. Gigantic. Gargantuan. Ginormous!

It was so big you could barely see the other side of it.

---

[11] http://www.deadwoodhistory.com/about-us/deadwood-history-overview-explanation.html

We learned that it was an old strip mine, where they had pulled out various minerals like gold, copper, and silver. We stopped and walked into a building nearby, entitled the Sanford Lab Homestake Visitor Center. Upon entering, a cheerful lady promptly asked, "Are you looking for the tour?" We didn't know anything about a tour, but we replied, "Sure." She told us to hurry, because it was just starting.

We had absolutely no idea how amazing this free tour would be. They issued us bright blue hard hats and gave us an hour-plus trolley tour through the town of Lead, through the campus, and a guided visit to the Yates Shaft hoistroom. Much of the grounds were originally developed to process gold from the nearby mine.

Their website explains: "At the Sanford Underground Research Facility, we pursue unique, world-leading research that can only be done in an underground environment. We work with many institutions and organizations around the globe including the Department of Energy (DOE), National Science Foundation (NSF), NASA, Lawrence Berkeley National Laboratory (LBNL), and Fermi National Accelerator Laboratory (Fermilab). The research conducted at the lab covers everything from physics and chemistry (dark matter, neutrino oscillation and neutrinoless double-beta decay) to geology and biology (seismic observation, rock strain sensing, and astrobiology)."[12]

Well, you can bet your bottom dollar we sure didn't know any of that!

Most of the work is done in labs nearly 5,000 feet underground, away from the natural radiation found topside.

---

[12] www.Sanfordlab.org

Wow. Who knew? We had had no idea this was even here. It's amazing what you find when just driving nowhere.

We enjoyed a simple supper at the motorhome. We sat outside at the picnic table with our supper and a nice (cheap) bottle of wine. A lady stopped by to ask us about Motorhome Ministry. We invited her to sit down with us, and we had a delightful conversation, taking the opportunity to ask about her personal relationship with the Lord. This is what it's all about — meeting people and sharing our beliefs.

---

1 Thessalonians 2:8

8 so we cared for you.
Because we loved you so much,
we were delighted to share with you
not only the gospel of God but our lives as well.

JUNE 3

That devil just picks and picks and picks away.

It was a long, hard travel day on I-90 to Billings, Montana today. It was a pretty day, with blue skies and a few clouds. The scenery on the drive was beautiful. But it was so windy that Larry struggled to maintain control every moment on the road. I don't think he could enjoy much of the view.

Getting off the interstate, we traveled US 14 and then on Route 24. We enjoyed stopping at the Devils Tower National Monument Visitors Center in northeastern Wyoming to learn about the Tower and get more stamps in my book. They had three stamps: The Monument, the

Centennial, and a hand-drawn image of the rock formation itself.

Their web site describes "An astounding geologic feature that protrudes out of the rolling prairie surrounding the Black Hills, this site is considered sacred to the Northern Plains Indians and other tribes. Hundreds of parallel cracks make it one of the finest traditional crack climbing areas in North America. Devils Tower entices us to explore and define our place in the natural and cultural world."[13] It reaches out of the flat landscape to heaven. There seems to be no rhyme or reason as to its forming, but I attribute it to the hand of God.

> Genesis 7:19
>
> They rose greatly on the earth,
> and all the high mountains under the entire heavens were covered.

But the devil reared his ugly head when we arrived at the Hardin KOA in Hardin, Montana, which Larry rated a 2. He pulled in the rig, glad to have finally arrived. The wind took all his strength. Larry now feels for full-time truckers—this is hard work! I opened the door to go register and the steps will not extend. I closed the door to try again. Opened. Nothing. Tempers flared because Larry was tired from the trip and he tells me to just go to register. Easier said than done for a 61-year-old who, her mom would have said, is "short on one end." Well, maybe I could get down but I knew it was gonna be bad to get back up. It was.

Oh, and did I mention that I broke a tooth today? Out of nowhere – a broken tooth. On a piece of nice, soft

---

[13]https://www.nps.gov/deto/index.htm

delicious pizza at a joint in downtown Hardin, that was once an old wooden saloon. The pizza was great!

> Proverbs 25:19
>
> 19 Like a broken tooth or a lame foot is reliance on the unfaithful in a time of trouble.

JUNE 4

We got up early and went to the location of Custer's last stand at the Battle of Little Big Horn National Park. It is a solemn place, to reflect upon the actions of June, 1876.

"This area memorializes the US Army's 7th Cavalry and the Sioux and Cheyenne in one of the Indians' last armed efforts to preserve their way of life. Here on June 25 and 26 of 1876, 263 soldiers, including Lt. Col. George A. Custer and attached personnel of the US Army, died fighting several thousand Lakota and Cheyenne warriors."[14]

We went to the Visitor Center and viewed a National Park movie about the area. Most of the National Parks have a park-specific movie and they are well worth your time. Usually in the span of twenty minutes, they quickly encompass all you need to know about the park. I got another stamp in my Passport. We took the auto trail and drove miles around the park to witness the white grave markers of the soldiers as well as the Indians who perished during this battle in our American history.

The history books we read as kids in elementary school came to life right in front of us. Standing on the peak

---

[14] https://www.nps.gov/libi/index.htm

at the Visitor Center, looking over the hills and fields of scattered graves, brought sorrow to my soul.

To our surprise, there are wild horses that wander throughout the park, grazing peacefully, and blocking the roads. They are beautiful and majestic beasts.

We returned to the motorhome, prepared to hump the ladder up into the rig. But we opened the door and the steps worked!

Then, we headed down US 310 towards Cody, Wyoming. It was a very remote route that offered mountains, flatlands, hills, and long stretches of straight roads that seem to go beyond the horizon.

We found a truck wash. Brother, did we need that! So, while a whole group of men tediously washed the motorhome, I took a nap that was very much worth the $1.00 per foot I paid for the wash!

We ran errands at Costco and Walmart, got gas for the car and diesel for the motorhome, then ate lunch. I tried for a haircut, but no one was available.

We made it to the campground and setup at Absaroka Bay RV Park in Cody, Wyoming, which Larry rated a 5.

Larry and I have long been fans of the A&E/Netflix series *Longmire*. I was delighted to be standing in the real Absaroka County, Wyoming, where the series is said to take place. Rugged, beautiful country. The true wild west!

We ate at the Irma Hotel, which possesses an amazing history. "'Buffalo Bill' Cody helped found Cody, Wyoming, in 1895. He also established his TE Ranch in the area. He built the establishment in 1902 which he called 'just the sweetest hotel that ever was' and named it for his youngest daughter, Irma...The Irma is listed on the National Register of Historic Places by the National Park Service"[15]

The hotel was a busy, beautiful place. It reminded us of those old western movie saloons. You imagined that a gun slinger would surely enter at any moment. The food was great and when we finished, we left a tip and a Motorhome Ministry brochure with a packet of seeds. We leave these seeds wherever we go with the prayer that God would water those seeds to fruition, both physically and spiritually, for those who receive them.

We wandered around the bar and hotel before we left. The incredible bar was a gift from Queen Victoria. It's intricately carved of cherry wood and takes up the entire length and height of the wall. There are grand photos on the website.

We watched the Wild Bill gunfight. Once again, history came alive for us. This is how they should be teaching stuff in the schools.

But the best, most fantastic part of the day was the Cody Night Rodeo at Stampede Park. We had never been to a real, live rodeo before! There were cowboys and cowgirls everywhere and lots and lots of rodeo clowns. As we walked into the stadium, there was a huge live bull tied down with ropes, where people were taking selfies. Oh yeah, we were definitely at a rodeo! I hope I can remember everything they offered: bareback riding, bronco, bull riding, roping, and barrel racing. I'm sure there was more.

---

[15] http://www.irmahotel.com/

Everyone stood for the flag and sang to the Star-Spangled Banner, as the amazing color guard charged in for the opening ceremonies. This was America at its best. During one of the bull riding events, a snarling bull threw its rider and continued to buck over a high fence and into the spectator stands. The rodeo clowns then got him to jump over another fence and into the nearby corral. Thank God no one was hurt. But it was a scary illustration that the riders risk their lives each night showing the crowd their skill in taming the beasts.

We indulged in popcorn and Diet Cokes. If you go to a rodeo, be sure you bring cash, because only the alcohol bar takes anything plastic.

They even had competitions for kids under twelve. There were some mighty speedy and talented kids there. I remember one little-bitty girl (maybe 4-5) who was in the pee wee barrel "race." She was the cutest little thing, dressed to the hilt and trotting her pony around those barrels at a careful, slow speed. It was so sweet.

We laughed and oohed and awed out there in the fresh air and had a wonderful time. Now, from this point on in life, I can proudly state, "This ain't my first rodeo" and mean it. The sights and sounds were great things to take away from the rodeo. The smells, however, you can leave behind.

We made it back to the motorhome around 11pm. What a fun-filled awesome day!

JUNE 5

I needed a haircut so bad and we knew we wouldn't have utilities this week. Larry agreed to stop while I ran into the Cody Walmart and there was the nicest lady who was available to cut my hair on the spot. She told me that she had recently moved there and that she'd been a beautician for over thirty years. She certainly did a great job. I personally think she was an angel, sent there in answer to my prayer.

Today we made the trek to Yellowstone National Park, the nation's first National Park, to stay at the Canyon Village Campground, Canyon Village, Wyoming, which Larry rated a 3. The park says people have been coming to this area for 11,000 years and we are no different. We made these reservations a full year in advance to be sure we would have a place to stay. As a little side note: the park service describes the age of the parks from a scientist's point of view. But we believe our world exists according to the Bible. The Bible-based genealogy from Adam and Eve dates the universe as only about six thousand years old.

It was a long, beautiful, uneventful drive. We saw lots of bison and a few elk on the way. We entered the park from the east side on US 14. We were at a high elevation on a mountain and were treated to see snow in June. As we drove over the last of the ridge crests, we enjoyed the most spectacular view of Yellowstone Lake and the whole park valley. The scene was breathtaking! You could really see the hand of God in this place.

Of all the parks in the National Park system, Yellowstone will become our favorite spot on earth.

> **Ecclesiastes 2:24**
>
> 24 A person can do nothing better than to
> eat and drink
> and find satisfaction in their own toil.
> This too, I see, is from the hand of God.

We also saw some steam vents and mudpots. I learned from the National Park Service website, in great detail, that "a mudpot is a natural double boiler! Surface water collects in a shallow, impermeable (usually due to a lining of clay) depression that has no direct connection to an underground water flow. Thermal water beneath the depression causes steam to rise through the ground, heating the collected surface water. Hydro sulfide gas is usually present, giving mudpots their characteristic odor of rotten eggs. The result is a gooey, rainbow-colored mix through which gases gurgle and bubble."[16] They look like thick oatmeal cooking on the stove.

On the road here, we enjoyed many views of the Shahone River and it is beautiful. The sun shimmered on the rolling, clear water, and the sound was comforting, as it traveled over rocks and roots.

We pulled in to register at the campground and the stupid steps went on strike again. At least now, with some practice, I can get in and out on my own. For safety's sake, please do not attempt this at home. But it was doable.

When it started getting dark, we dragged out our little, portable "campfire", that we had bought at Camping World last year. It's a small set of ceramic fire logs that hooks up to propane. We hadn't used it in a while and it just wouldn't light. With nothing better to do, we took it

---

[16] www.nps.gov/yell/learn/nature/mudpots.htm

completely apart and cleaned it up. With both of us addressing the problem, we had it working in no time.

Then it was time to break out the marshmallows.

It is so beautiful and dark and quiet, hidden here in the trees of the primitive campground, no electric, no running water, no sewer, no cable, just our generator on standby, batteries, water tank, and holding tanks. We had all the comforts of home, including the kitchen sink, in the primitive forest of Yellowstone.

JUNE 6

Today was spent enjoying the amazing discoveries of Yellowstone National Park. Most places have easy access by car. But, summer traffic can be full of traffic and backups.

We saw three black bears up close. We drove miles through the park and saw hundreds—perhaps thousands—of bison. There were elk and pronghorns and lots of other little creatures.

We learned something about bison today: if you see a single bison off to itself, it's a male. The females were running in the herds, with all the young'uns. But over there, way away from the herd would be one single male. No parental responsibility there.

We saw rushing waterfalls and rivers. The Canyon Village Area Campground has several falls that are so mighty you can hear their roar for miles through the canyon. There were snowbanks everywhere, even though it was 81 degrees today and June.

Then we were off to see the geysers. We walked the 1.5-mile trail through the geyser beds, and they were amazing. I never knew that Yellowstone National Park was on a massive volcano. Here we were, learning something brand new again.

The combination of the heat and elevation really punched me hard today, even though I drank multiple bottles of water. Rain was forecast for tomorrow, perhaps that would cool things off a bit.

JUNE 7

We spent another day driving through the Park. We saw lots of mudpots, steam vents, and geysers. But we couldn't come to the Park without waiting around to see Old Faithful! We ate lunch at the lodge there, then found two wooden rockers outside on the porch, in the shade, sat down, and waited. The shade was such a blessing, and we could see everything perfectly. Most folks waited on the benches closer to the geyser, but there was no shade. With the heat and sun, and at that altitude, I would have fainted straight away.

Old Faithful was right on time! They forecast the next eruption based upon the time before the last one. There were little spurts of white smoke and steam. Then, all at once, an explosion of water, smoke, and steam. Just like a tea kettle on the stove when the water boils. The sound was just as intense.

We continued to drive the Park, and learned that, not too long ago, the American Bison was near extinction. Looking at today's herds, I'd say the Park's restoration project has gone very well.

It was yet another day of amazing discovery. A person could (and probably did) write a whole book on just Yellowstone. The pictures we took of the park simply don't do it justice.

JUNE 8

I Googled, then called a dentist in Helena to make an appointment to take care of my broken tooth. Larry and I agreed to leave Yellowstone early, so that I could get this tooth pulled before our Alaskan Cruise. We had a great few hours to finish seeing and re-seeing the things in this amazing park.

I went to the large laundromat to catch up the laundry. It's a big place and most folks were there right off the trails. They were washing sleeping bags and paying to take showers. Larry kept busy dumping and filling the tanks for the trip.

The motorhome steps still didn't work. Thank God, we had that small 3-step ladder, or I would have certainly broken an ankle or an arm by now.

JUNE 9

We were packed up and on the road early for the drive to Helena, Montana. We had made dozens of trips up and down that little 3-step ladder over the past few days. So, when we pulled the rig up to the registration area to hook up the tow dolly, what happens? Ta daa! The steps extended! I took a moment to do ** HAPPY DANCE**

History lesson: Going way back to the time Diana was born, we lived for a short time in Winston-Salem, North Carolina. We met two wonderful people who have become lifelong friends, John & Diane. When we posted that we were headed to Montana, they encouraged us to plan to stop to see their son, Brent, who had recently moved there. We had made the date. But this day-early drive through Bozeman, Montana left us no choice but to cancel. Brent is an air traffic controller, and I took photos as we passed the control tower to text to his mom and dad. It was as close as we would get to Brent that day. It was a great disappointment, indeed.

We drove US 89 north from Yellowstone, then to Route 90 west, then up I-15 north. At some point on US 89, going 70 miles an hour, a car tries to pass us. Larry looked out of his side of the rig to see that the passenger in the car is hanging out the window, signaling us to pull over. We pulled to the berm and Larry got out.

The man explained that he'd been traveling the opposite way and passed us a few minutes ago. Just as his car went past, one of our basement storage doors flew open and nearly hit him. The doors are hung from the top, a full three feet down. He said it was obvious we weren't aware and he turned around and sped to catch up with us.

We apologized and thanked the man profusely! This could have been a devastating accident. Larry discovered that one of the two locks on that door had broken. I'm glad Larry can fix just about anything.

God sent another one of His angels to watch out for us.

> **Psalm 1:6**
>
> 6 For the Lord watches over
> the way of the righteous,
> but the way of the wicked leads to destruction.

We arrived in Helena late in the afternoon, with reservations at Lincoln Road RV Park, Helena, Montana, which Larry rated a 6. We completed a couple of shops, then made a trial run, by car, to the dentist's office. We called Larry's mom that evening, to check in with her. She knew that we'd had no satellite reception (or electric or cellular) in Yellowstone. She told us about a story she'd heard on the news: about a young man who had died just this past Tuesday at the Norris Geyser in Yellowstone. Wait a minute, we were at the Norris Geyser on Tuesday. Then Larry recalled that, just as we were leaving the parking lot at the Geyser, there was a ranger quietly putting up barriers so that the public could no longer enter the lot to park. Drivers were upset because they couldn't go in. We thought it was curious, considering it was the middle of a beautiful afternoon and there were already tourists everywhere. We had absolutely no clue that someone has just died.

We recalled walking through the area on a long, wide boardwalk path scarcely above the beds. There had been signs everywhere, warning folks not to leave the pathway. There were signs that explained that although the crust appeared solid, it could be only inches thick. The news reported that this young man and his sister were more than 100 yards off the walkway at the time he fell through.

The brutal part of their disregard of the signage is that the young man dissolved almost instantly in the high heat of the volcano, right in front of his sister. There could be no recovery.

It continued to be an evening of sad news. Diana texted that a law enforcement officer that we'd known during our long tenure in Gatlinburg had died an early death, following a lengthy illness. Rest in peace, Tommy.

JUNE 10

I started out the morning by getting that canine tooth pulled. Dr. Johnson was fantastic. I know that God had led me to him, as he was the first and only one I called when I Googled for a dentist. He was so gentle and comforting. He reminded me of my terrific dentist back home, Dr. Billy. For both of them, it is all about alleviating the patient's anxiety and making them as comfortable as possible.

We needed to get some keys for the motorhome made, so when we drove past a little place called "Burdicks" (which is my niece's married name), the decision was made to stop there. Their service was great, too.

Now you See Me II was showing at the local cinema, so we enjoyed some down time while the Novocain in my mouth wore off. There was no popcorn for me.

There was only one local place to eat out by the campground, so we went there. Everything coming out of the kitchen seemed huge! I told the nice waitress all about Larry's gastric sleeve surgery and how he can't eat much and me having a broken tooth pulled earlier that day. I was probably whining but didn't mean to. She was so accommodating and kind. She offered me a child's spaghetti supper and Larry a cup of clam chowder. Everything was delicious and we were filled. The tab was an entire $6.90. We left her seeds and a brochure, and a $5.00 tip.

> God had been busy today.

JUNE 11

We were up early for the long drive, continuing up I-15 to US 89 to St. Mary. We had reservations for June 12 at St. Mary Campground at Glacier National Park, St. Mary, Montana, which Larry rated a 3. We arrived a day early, and we were grateful that they could accommodate us.

We set up, and I requested a brief nap. The pain was gone, but there were still some days that I was still so worn out. I suppose that strength will come in time.

We drove to the Visitor Center, got my stamps, watched their park movie, and quickly learned that this part of the Rocky Mountains was formed by glaciers, unlike the volcanoes of Yellowstone. Glacier, as are many of the national parks, is rich with American Indian history, including the Blackfoot, Salish, Pend d'Oreille, and Kootnei tribes.

We drove as far as the road allowed, due to construction. We were rewarded by waterfalls and rapids and some very awesome views of the steep mountains, lakes, and even glaciers. As in Alaska, the glaciers are a blue like no other color. When these glaciers feed into nearby lakes, they become that beautiful color, as well. The air was so clear and crisp, you could almost taste it.

Even though the calendar tells you that it's nearly summer, Glacier was just showing signs of spring and the flowers were just beginning to bloom. We learned that Beargrass is a wildflower that seemed to be everywhere we looked. It grows up to five feet fall with a large white blossom. Everywhere we looked was simply beautiful. And wild.

> **1 Peter 1:24**
>
> 24 For, "All people are like grass,
> and all their glory is like the flowers of the field;
> the grass withers and the flowers fall,

It's amazing what tasty treats we've discovered for the microwave. Tonight, we enjoyed Jack Daniel's BBQ ribs without standing outside in the cold to grill. We just microwave what we need and presto they are ready to eat.

Tomorrow we travel to the Canadian side of the Park.

JUNE 12

Our reservations required us to move to another site in the Park. Then we drove on to see Canada.

We passed through US and Canadian customs, both ways, but we never left Glacier National Park. Each side was as beautiful as the other. It was cold, but wildflowers still abound. I kept asking Larry to pull over so that I could take pictures of each different type that I saw. Sorry, Larry. There were a lot of them.

We stopped at the historic 1920's Prince of Wales Hotel. It was a beautiful hotel on a lake, in a vast valley. It was a picture postcard view for sure. "A true historic Canadian icon, the Prince of Wales Hotel offers an experience like no other. Views from the hotel lobby and lawn are magnificent panoramas of Waterton Lake and the surrounding mountains in Waterton Lakes National Park in Alberta, Canada. Located just North of Glacier National

Park, Waterton makes up the other half of the Waterton-Glacier International Peace Park and is a must-visit location on your Glacier Vacation."[17] They offered entrees like Shepherd's Pie, which we love and authentic Fish N' Chips, which we ordered and enjoyed. The tall and handsome hotel staff were all in Scottish Kilts.

We were in another country and culture, another date and time.

JUNE 13

This was our last day at magnificent Glacier National Park. We drove the dead-end highway to journey the "last" side of the Park, out to Many Glacier. They call this area the "Switzerland of America," and it is considered the heart of Glacier National Park.

We had just commented aloud that we had yet to see any Bighorn Sheep. As if on cue, a herd began to cross the road, right in front of us! There were five or six of them, up close and personal.

We were close to the Many Glacier Hotel, a Swiss Alp-looking building, on a glacier-fed lake called Swiftcurrent Lake. The main road was closed for construction, but the Hotel was open. This 1914 hotel stood majestic on a lake with views of several glaciers high above. We turned down a side road, and there are some more Big Horn Sheep!

We returned to the rig early for recharging ourselves and the batteries during restricted generator hours.

---

[17] glacierparkinc.com/lodging/prince-of-wales-hotel

This afternoon's entertainment was a Crazy Yellow Bird. A small, bright yellow bird came to sit on one of our rear-view mirrors. Look, isn't he cute? He flew away, just to come back seconds later to land on the other mirror. He repeated this escapade hundreds of times, for SIX solid hours, until it became dark.

The bird unnerved me, for some reason. It was as though he (or she) had something important to say, and desperately wanted me to understand. It's not as though he could see himself in the mirrors, because he was on top of them. Perhaps he could see himself in the windshield, and the mirror was just a place to sit, I don't know. Sometimes he would swoop down the side of the motorhome, then swoop back to the mirrors. But all the time, it appeared that he was looking straight at me, with something urgent to say.

We brought out one of the cherished cans of Skyline Chili for supper. It is indeed Cincinnati at its finest. Yum.

I went to bed still unnerved from the bird. Why did he do that?

JUNE 14

Crazy Yellow Bird came back and talked to us right up until we pulled out. Goodbye, Bird.

It proved to be a long day. We had left the Park before 7am, with poor weather reports ahead of us. We were heading toward Leavenworth, Washington, but the trip would be divided over the next two days. We traveled over the Rocky Mountains by going over US 2 to Kalispell, Montana. Route 28 then took us along Flathead Lake, a massive lake along the mountain range of Glacier National Park, then headed west on I-90.

It was gloomy when we left and the weather changed by the hour: rain, snow, rain/snow mix.

One delight of the day was when we finally came out of the mountains to see Coeur d'Alene, Idaho. The view of the lake was breathtaking. Since we were on a schedule, we couldn't stop and linger. But Larry said if we ever get in the area again, that would be a place where we would spend a few days.

We drove further than we should have and were both cranky by the time we stopped at a Walmart to camp for the night.

Larry picked up a Red Box movie, but I was pooped. I took a quick shower and tried to sleep, but there was a certain redneck with a loud muffler and way too much time on his hands who kept me awake for quite some time by driving around the parking lot. Thank God, the Walmart closed at 10pm.

Then I slept, long and hard.

JUNE 15

We left the Walmart parking lot about 8am.

Looking ahead to CVS locations and our need for prescription refills, we took a long detour to a CVS in Spokane. Tight roads in city driving makes Larry tense, considering the size of our motorhome. We never knew the eastern part of Washington State was flat and dry, much like the deserts of the southwest.

From I-90 west, we went north on Route 28 along the Columbia River. Then we took US 2 again, which eventually crossed the Cascade Mountains. Part of the drive today took us though miles and miles of orchards. This is a very fertile part of the US and it seems everyone has heard of Washington State Apples or Rainer Cherries. We saw where they are grown.

We wanted to, again, enjoy the tastes of our adventures, so I asked Larry to pull over next to a produce stand in the middle of these miles of orchards. I asked the workers which items were fresh area fruits, and ready to eat this time of the year. The Rainier Cherries and apricots were local, so I purchased some of both. They were yummy.

Genesis 1:11

11 Then God said,
"Let the land produce vegetation:
seed-bearing plants and trees on the land
that bear fruit with seed in it,
according to their various kinds." And it was so.

We finally pulled into Icicle River RV Park in Leavenworth, Washington, a former timber town, about 3pm. Larry rated this park at 8.

The town of Leavenworth proper was a delightful surprise! The entire town is in strict Bavarian style, a themed town. It was hilarious to see McDonalds and Starbucks and even the post office decked out in strict Bavarian code. There were baskets of flowers everywhere, in every type and color imaginable. There were murals painted on the sides of buildings big and small. We were blessed to witness a young woman painting a brand new one! We were taken back in time to another country far away.

It was our pleasure to be there on the very same day as the International Accordion Festival. From the white gazebo in the center of town, musician after musician entertained everyone. When was the last time I'd heard an accordion? On the Lawrence Welk Show, perhaps?

The music heralded a light and cheerful mood to everyone in town that day.

The restaurants were also Bavarian-oriented. For lunch, we agreed on a second-floor establishment that offered Bratwurst on the menu board. We were seated by an upstairs window, overlooking the street.

Larry and I were both raised around Cincinnati. My ancestors and many others were German immigrants who came down the Ohio River and settled there generations ago.

Just to name a few things, we like rye bread, bratwurst, corned beef, goetta, potato salad, pretzels, and a lot of us love sauerkraut. This town offered them all and more. I described to the waitress that I wanted "white" bratwurst, and she said that's what they call Bockwurst. Larry picked at the plate when it arrived, but I dived in and ate every bite of Bockwurst, sauerkraut and potato salad on my plate. We enjoyed a delicious apple strudel for dessert.

As we were still wandering the streets around supper time, we chose an outdoor restaurant with warming fires in the centers of the tables. Once again, I ordered the local fare and ate every bite.

Yum. Again. Gotta get it while you can.

JUNE 16

We had plans to put lots of miles between here and Leavenworth, but we were still there at 1pm.

Larry kept saying he had "fifty million things to do" and had to get them all done this morning. Because of the upcoming cruise, and despite it was only the 16th of the month, he insisted we issue statements for our business customers right now.

What should have been a 5-minute task turned out to be nearly two hours on the phone with Intuit. I won't get into all that. I will say that when QuickBooks works, it works great. But when it doesn't…Grr.

We did finally get on the road and on our way. We parked at a Walmart again, and ate at a nearby Panda Express again. I think we have found a new favorite national chain.

I spent the evening gathering little things together for the trip. The little things are what takes the most time. Gotta get it done.

JUNE 17

Another day over the mountains on US 2 west, over the Cascades this time. The road was a tedious one, full of steep climbs and descents into the greater Seattle Washington area. Another moving day to get us closer to Seattle for the Alaskan cruise.

Larry had used his All Stays app to give us directions to the next campground. But, when we "arrived", we discovered we were at the wrong place! We were tired, we were cranky, but God had once again gone ahead of us and this place had ONE space left for tonight.

It was a nice little place, thank you, Lord.

Larry gives the Lakeside RV Park in Everett, Washington a rating of 6.

JUNE 18

We were ready early to move to the correct campground this morning. Because of the small size of the slip last night, we'd had no choice but to unhitch the tow dolly and the car.

It was raining just enough to aggravate Larry and he decided that I would drive the car behind the rig, instead of putting it back up on the tow dolly. Ok with me, as it wasn't too far.

About halfway there, he blew a tire. BAM! I saw the rig jerk and heard it through the closed windows. Larry told me later that it had sounded like a bomb had gone off inside the rig.

I tried everything I could to get Larry's attention. We were on a busy thoroughfare and he was concentrating on keeping the rig in the lane, in the pouring rain.

I honked, called him on the cell phone, flashed my lights from the lane left of him.

He had the GPS, I didn't know where we were going or how much longer it would take to get there. When I finally got him to pull over, he said, "What's the big deal now? We're almost there!" He had heard the noise, but knew that even if it had been a blown tire, the rears were duals, and the other tire would bear the weight of the rig. He just needed to get to the campground.

You're welcome, Larry.

We finally arrived at Lake Pleasant RV Park, Bothell, Washington, which Larry rated a 6. Whew.

I went right to work packing—we leave on our trip tomorrow! I cleaned, washed clothes, and even defrosted the freezer. Feeling the need for some quiet space, I told Larry I was going to go shopping for a camera strap for our new camera. It required a special kind and I already had Google Maps set for a camera shop. He had called for tire repair, so I knew he couldn't go with me.

The quiet in the car was great. If you're also long-term RV'ers, go ahead and respect the fact that each of you will probably need such "time out" adventures when you're confined in such spaces for such lengths of time.

I was delighted to come back with the camera strap. It would certainly come in handy on our Alaskan journey.

Les Schwab Tires had been called by our warranty company to replace the tire, and the young man was finishing up when I returned. The tech explained that the other three back tires were not so much worn out, but they were old and needed to be replaced. Great. We would just have to deal with that when we returned.

The afternoon continued to be gloomy, but the rain had stopped. Welcome to Washington.

JUNE 19

Today was the big day!

We packed up the rig and moved it to another section of Lake Pleasant RV Park. Their "storage" section was the main reason we'd chosen to camp here. The park was nice and appropriately priced. But they had a grassy section for folks who needed to leave their rigs behind for trips like ours. They offered a space with 110v electric—so we didn't have to empty out the fridge or run propane while we were gone—all for just $3 a day. Wow.

We had made a few inquiries to the campground staff about the most cost-effective way to get to the Sea-Tac Airport, which is not nearby. They supplied us with the name of a limo service. I scoffed that we didn't need a limo, but she insisted we call them.

That was the second-best tip of this stop.

For a fee of $200 total, they would pick us up from the campground and deliver us to our hotel at the airport. AND, when we returned, they would pick us up from the airport and bring us back. I could pay $100/$100 if I preferred, plus tip. Again. Wow.

The driver was a pleasant woman who picked us up in a slightly extended Lincoln Towne Car. The smoothness of this ride sure beat the bumpy sway of our motorhome! She chatted with us all the way to the Hampton Inn and handled our luggage each time. She made sure we had the information to call and give them any updated airline information. It was great. And for a 40+ minute drive, you couldn't beat the price.

We checked in, then made arrangements for the hotel to get us to the airport in the middle of the night.

We went on to Pike Place Market by way of RapidRide, the public rail system into downtown Seattle from the airport. Well, being summer, it was packed and so was the Market. We had a wonderful lunch of northwest salmon, overlooking the waterfront. Being from the East coast, we have discovered a great difference between Atlantic salmon and northwest salmon. To us (just our opinion), Atlantic salmon is neutral in taste. Bland. That's why you often find it served with a fruit relish or garnish. Pacific salmon has a sweetness all its own and needs nothing on top. We love it, but you sure can't find it back east.

Even though we'd been to the Market on previous business trips, we enjoyed strolling through it again. There were huge bundles of fresh flowers, and the seafood openly displayed on ice were full of bright colors and fresh smells. We enjoyed the street entertainers performing in the sun, then walked back to the station.

On the way, we encountered one particular entertainer. She was completely covered in something white, that made her look like a dusty stone statue. She was wearing a beautiful full-hoop skirt with a ruffled blouse and a huge hat. She poised frozen as tourists walked by.

When someone would venture exceptionally close, she would gently move and quietly say, "Hello" to the passersby. Spooked, they would cry out, then laugh. We watched her do this again and again. It was so funny to watch her.

There was also a local music band performing, playing guitar, banjo, mandolin, and a wood saw. Their pudgy white dog made himself useful by keeping the guitar case warm by sleeping in it. Cute.

We took the rail back, and by 6:30 we were back at the hotel, munching on cookies and Diet Coke, waiting for the Ambien to kick in, as 2am will come very, very quickly.

JUNE 20

We were up at 2:30am to prepare for our 6am flight to Anchorage, Alaska. The Hotel was true to their word and transportation was ready.

We boarded Alaskan Airlines Jet service to Anchorage, Alaska. The sun was starting to rise over foggy Seattle. As we took off, we could see Mt. Rainier in the distance. In time, the flight had some spectacular views of the snowy mountain ranges along the coast of Canada and Alaska. Later, the Icy Straits, virgin forest and wilderness seemed to go on for eternity.

We had signed up for what Royal Caribbean calls a Cruisetour. We enjoyed five amazing days of adventure on land, then seven days at sea. The land tour was by train and bus, the sea tour was on the Royal Caribbean's ship Radiance of the Seas.

The flight was three hours long and passed quickly. A huge surprise was waiting for us when we arrived in Anchorage. We had been told that transfer transportation would not be available until noon. We arrived at 9am local time, and lo and behold, there was a Royal Caribbean rep standing right there with a sign—they had come for just for the two of us! So, instead of hanging around the terminal until noon, they took us directly to the Anchorage Marriott. Now, that was customer service!

We both took a short nap, then wandered around the streets. The weather was pleasantly spring-like and crisp, just requiring a light jacket. We were actually in ALASKA! Wow!

My Daddy had always wanted to travel to Alaska. Later in his life, he spoke often of the trains through Canada he wanted to ride to take him there. But family responsibilities always got in the way, and he never made it there. This part of the trip is for you, Dad.

We found the Alaska Museum of Science and Nature and learned that there is wildlife everywhere in Alaska, including moose, salmon, polar bears, and whales. We learned about the Eskimo, their way of life, and the art of totem poles.

We also learned about the Alaskan pipeline. The pipeline is so massive it's hard to believe man could build something like that across the frozen tundra of Alaska. They even had a big section of pipe you could see up close.

Lunch was a quick Stromboli, before returning to the Marriott for an appointment with our tour director for the week, Lisa.

When that was done, we were back on the streets, this time walking a couple of blocks to Benihana for supper. We came up to a young woman trying to fix a flat tire, and walked right past her. Well out of earshot, I quietly asked Larry why he didn't offer to help the woman. "What woman?" I turned him around. He hadn't even seen her!

I know nowadays, women are entitled to be leery of men offering assistance. But I guess, because I was white-haired and with him, she reluctantly allowed him to change it. It was a good thing, because she would have never gotten it done with the limited knowledge she had. Larry gave her a tire-changing lesson as he went along.

It was so rewarding to assist someone in need.

Benihana is a terrific place with terrific food. So much food that, even though we shared one entrée, the two of us couldn't finish it all. We left our brochure and seeds for the wait staff, hoping that God will use us in Alaska.

We turned in early, because suitcases had to be in the out in the hall by 6am. The bus would take us to the train station.

Today was Summer Solstice. There were 19 ½ hours of daylight today, here in Alaska. It is so strange to wake up at 3am to go to the bathroom and outside it's all sunny!

We couldn't wait to board the train headed for Denali National Park.

JUNE 21

Today was an amazing day spent riding the Wilderness Express train, heading for Denali National Park. I could clearly understand why Alaska is considered the Last Frontier. It's thousands upon thousands of acres of unimproved wilderness of mountains, valleys, rocks, trees, lakes, streams, plants, glaciers, and wildlife. Every mile in every direction offers something new and different to see.

The train had windows on each side of the car that curved upward to form a tinted, glassed-in ceiling, as well. There was only a small solid strip down the middle, which held light fixtures. You could see everything! The seats were comfortable and the ride passed much too quickly. The train swayed gently back and forth as the train clattered along the rail. The motion, the sounds, and the amazing scenery lulled me into a remarkable sense of peace.

Lisa, our tour guide, had lived in Alaska for many years. Her personal knowledge and side stories really highlighted the ride.

On the way, we saw about a half-dozen moose, with eagles and osprey scattered everywhere. It was quite funny when someone would yell "Moose", all the people on the train would jump up and move to that side of the train to look. Larry quietly joked to me that he wanted to yell out "Bear" just to see what would happen! I laughingly begged him not to.

As we chugged through Wasilla, Lisa was quick to say that this was Sarah Palin's hometown and pointed out the lake she had a house on.

When we arrived at Denali, after eight hours on the train, through breakfast and then lunch, we were assigned one of the countless cabins and handed the keys at Denali Backcountry Lodge, which Larry rated a 5. We curiously walked to check it out. It was nothing too special to look at on the outside, but were we impressed when we opened the door.

The interior was all done in wood planks, like the inside of a log cabin. There was a huge king bed with a rustic wooden headboard, a big television, a nice vanity sink with overhead lights and a coffee maker. The bathroom was small but certainly adequate. It was perfect. Except it was freezing in there!

Looking for a thermostat, we found none. But there was a small electric heater sitting outside of the bathroom. We plugged it in, then left for supper at the lodge.

The ceiling of the dining room was massively vaulted. The chairs were all made of whittled wood (or made to look like whittled wood). The upholstery was bright and the floor done in slate. The cheerful servers came quickly, as did the food.

Our cabin was warm and toasty when we returned. We snuggled into bed and quickly fell asleep.

We were in Alaska! What surprises will tomorrow bring?

JUNE 22

When we were ready in the morning, I bundled up and went looking for breakfast. There was a young Russian in a nearby rustic-looking shop who freshly prepared a whole bag of mini powdered donuts just for me, while I waited. I thought to myself that really Russia was not that far away. We are closer to Russia right now than we are to the lower 48 states. With the warm donuts in hand, I bought Larry a bottle of chocolate milk and made myself some coffee in the room. Yum.

All members of our tour group loaded onto the bus for a tour of Denali National Park, and we took the Denali Natural History Tour. While outdoors, an Eskimo woman stood atop a small rise and told us all about her heritage, and how her life is so much different than her ancestors. It was fascinating to hear.

We passed two orphaned moose along the side of the road. The bus driver informed us a poacher had shot and killed their mother several weeks ago. Park personnel and rangers are watching over them to help them to survive this harsh environment.

We saw a massive male moose in a creek bed within the National Park. They stopped the bus so all of us could get off to take photos. The moose gave us a sideways glance as if to say, "What is with these people?"

We were surprised to see wildflowers everywhere along the highways, in this cold. A true tourist on the bus asked the bus driver, "Did the State of Alaska plant all these flowers along the roads?" She replied cheerfully, "They sure did!"

If you believe that, I will sell you an acre of the National Park. Cheap.

You couldn't miss what was once known as Mount McKinley, which is North America's highest peak, and was buried in snow. It is, again, known simply as Denali, which means "The Great One."

There is quite a story regarding the name change which took place in 2015. Wikipedia has many details, and you can read a story that covers over 100 years of dispute at: http://www.nbcnews.com/news/us-news/mckinley-denali-how-mountains-renaming-got-tied-politics-n418811. At over 20,000 feet, it is indeed a massive mountain that seems to touch heaven.

> 1 Corinthians 13:1-8
>
> If I speak in the tongues of men or of angels,
> but do not have love,
> I am only a resounding gong or a clanging cymbal.
> 2 If I have the gift of prophecy and
> can fathom all mysteries and all knowledge,
> and if I have a faith that can move mountains,
> but do not have love, I am nothing.

The scenery was as awesome as it had been the day before. Denali National Park encompasses six million acres but there is only one road. The snow on the mountaintops, the scenery, and waterways were simply breathtaking. Even your body feels different in this fresh, unpolluted air.

My dad would have loved this!

> Job 33:4
>
> 4 The Spirit of God has made me;
> the breath of the Almighty gives me life.

We finished at the Park and began the trip to Talkeetna. Once again, the scenery was beautiful. We passed little clusters of homes along the way, often wondering how far these folks had to drive to get groceries or nails or new underwear. Where was the closest Walmart?

That evening, we stayed at the Talkeetna Alaskan Lodge. The lobby of the hotel is a high vaulted ceiling with a beautiful fireplace in the center. Now this wasn't your usual fireplace, it's the tallest stone fireplace in the state of Alaska. It was constructed of smooth river rocks and stood 46 feet from floor to ceiling.

Our room was also beautiful. We decided to eat in the Foraker Dining Room, there in the Lodge. I ordered a large bone-in pork chop served on a bed of mashed potatoes, with soybeans, radishes, tomatoes, mushrooms, and several things I couldn't identify, but I ate them anyway. It was all good. Larry ordered a shrimp appetizer, which proved to be all he could eat. I nearly licked the plate clean. Great food.

When we returned to the room, we realized there was no air conditioning. Come to think of it, I haven't noticed it anywhere in the whole hotel, as all the doors are standing wide open. I guess you don't need AC in Alaska. So, we opened the window and ran the fan for the night. Out in all this fresh air all day, we had no trouble sleeping.

JUNE 23

We hopped back on the bus and left at 10am. The scenery didn't change one bit! It was so beautiful and continued mile after mile. The tour guides dropped us off in downtown Anchorage and gave everyone a couple of hours to eat and shop on their own.

We first headed to the National Park Service Visitor Center to watch the film for Denali and get my Passport stamped again.

The Museum had invited a worker from a local zoo, who brought some baby otters for us to see up close. They were so cute! They looked like little furry puppies, all curled up with one another, asleep in a plastic tub lined with towels.

We walked into a tourist shop named, *Once Upon a Blue Moose*. It was with tremendous delight that I found some of Oyster & Pearl's boxes! One was a whale box, different than the design we had sold and the other was a Forget Me Not design. I texted Diana, sent her a couple of pics and asked if she had designed these before we sold the company. Yes, indeed she had designed them both. The new owners had expanded our line with designs we had included in the sale. How delightful!

Hunting down lunch, we decided on Chinese. Yum again.

At 2:30pm, we boarded the bus to continue to Hotel Alyeska Ski Resort. It, too was amazing. Our room did not disappoint, either. It was big and roomy with a king-size bed and an indescribable view. It was truly a 5-star resort.

Our tour included tickets for the ski tram. We took advantage of them and were rewarded with another breathtaking view. The Upper Tram Terminal is atop Mt. Alyeska, 2,300 feet above the resort!

While we were going up, a bright red bi-plane came through the valley. It was a sight to behold.

Although the weather was quite nice at the Hotel, it was literally freezing at top, with snow covering the ground. There was much to see, including the seven hanging glaciers, majestic mountains, and sparkling streams among the spruce. We decided to eat up top, buying 2 bowls of soup, which were quite delicious. We were loving everything about this trip so far!

We have been on at least a dozen cruises over the years, but never one of these land and sea adventures. We didn't know what to expect, but we simply didn't expect such world-class accommodations as these! Out of curiosity, I gave the front desk my room number and explained that I was with a group. But, if I hadn't been with the group, what would the nightly rate of my room be? $350 a night. Awesome!

Clowning around back at the gift shop, I took a photo of Larry in the clutches a huge stuffed black bear. Not stuffed with polyester—it was taxidermy stuffed.

The look on his face was priceless.

JUNE 24

Promptly at 10am, our last day on the bus began. We were heading for Seward, Alaska, where we would eventually board the ship.

Before noon, we stopped at the Alaska Sea Life Center in Resurrection Bay in Seward. It heralds as Alaska's premier public aquarium and the state's only permanent marine mammal rehabilitation facility. Once again, our admissions were prepaid, so we walked right in.

I've been to probably a half-dozen aquariums across the US and this one did not disappoint. We had a wonderful time.

But just as amazing as the inside of the Center, outside, we sighted Bald Eagles everywhere! They sat by the dozens on top of buildings in every direction. Back home, those birds would have been pigeons or sparrows, but these were all majestic Bald Eagles.

We bid farewell to our Tour Guide, Lisa, and our Bus Driver, Steve. They had treated us well and had handled our luggage for us all week. We had had a wonderful time.

Now, to the ship. We depart at 8pm.

The ship was wonderful, as Royal Caribbean ships have always been for us. Our cabin was nice, our steward attentive. We always prowl the entire ship upon arrival, to get a feel for everything. We found our supper, and walked some more. It was an early bedtime, as we were totally worn out from the magnificent fresh air. Tomorrow, we will explore some more.

JUNE 25

We've cruised enough times that we felt no need to attend all the shopping, customs, shore excursions, and ports of call lectures. That freed up lots of time.

In the afternoon, we bundled up and headed topside, to watch as the ship traveled closer and closer to the Hubbard Glacier, where we stayed for about an hour. As we approached, there were brilliant bright blue and white chunks of the glacier floating in the frigid water.

It was cold, misty, and windy, but we didn't care. Putting up with the weather was a fair price to pay for the experience of being this close to the glacier. The sights, sounds, and the crisp air felt wonderful. Occasionally we saw an Eagle or other bird perched on the chunks of ice.

The Hubbard is a calving glacier, meaning pieces of ice break off and fall into the water, creating an iceberg. From the deck, you would hear a loud crack and see huge sections of ice break away from the glacier and crash into the water. It was yet another amazing experience.

JUNE 26

We docked in Juneau for the day. We had purchased tickets for a shore excursion to the Mendenhall Glacier and the Salmon Hatchery tour.

The Mendenhall was as amazing as the Hubbard. We stayed awhile there, watching it calving. We were in awe—speechless—overcome by its beauty. Out on the water just before the glacier was a large chunk of blue ice and perched on top was a bald eagle. He stayed there on the ice for quite some time, eyeing the lake, I guess for food. An American Bald eagle in the wild is a rare treat in the lower 48. But, here in Alaska they are as plentiful as pigeons.

> Isaiah 40:31
>
> 31 but those who hope in the Lord
> will renew their strength.
> They will soar on wings like eagles;
> they will run and not grow weary,
> they will walk and not be faint.

Next, we were driven to the Hatchery Tour. Until we had visited the Pacific Northwest, and now here in Alaska, we had never knew to what extent and expense state governments would go to undergird the salmon industry. Hatcheries are everywhere along the streams in Alaska, Oregon, and Washington.

We learned that there are five types of salmon: King (or chinook), Sockeye (red), Coho (silver), Pink (humpback), and Chum (dog). I listed them in their order of richness, from most to least.

For more information about salmon, go to experienceketchikan.comwww.experienceketchikan.com. It will tell you everything about what it looks like, to how oily it is, what's best to eat, what you purchase in a can, and what type of caviar you might like.

We viewed huge tanks of new, itty bitty baby salmon. We learned that the hatchery also had 20 million young salmon they would raise to the age of two years, when they would be released into local streams. Sometime between the ages of three to five, they will swim back here, to the place where they were originally released, to spawn.

We could spot salmon in the adjoining river. The most interesting part of the hatchery tour was watching salmon released years ago actively returning to the hatchery to spawn, via a manmade water ladder of sorts. After they spawn, they die. From this vantage point, we could witness every stage of a salmon's small circle of life.

There were dozens of eagles perched all along nearby buildings, eying the jumping fish from their vantage point, hoping to get lucky.

Genesis 1:26

26 Then God said,
"Let us make mankind in our image, in our likeness,
so that they may rule over the fish in the sea
and the birds in the sky,
over the livestock and all the wild animals, and
over all the creatures that move along the ground.

JUNE 27

We were docked in Skagway for the day. We had tickets for another shore excursion, this one called the Klondike Summit and Historic City Tour. Our tour guide told us all sorts of stories of what was happening when the gold rush hit here in the 1890's. The Summit he drove us to was at high altitude and considered a high avalanche area. There were signs posted that there was no stopping anywhere in the area.

Well, despite the fact that the US/Canadian Border was marked, there were no signs of either Border Patrol, because of the avalanche risk. We had already passed through US Customs about six miles back and the driver explained that the Canadian Customs was not for another six miles.

So, there we were, all of us standing in Canada, but no one around to check us in. He turned the bus around to allow us to take photos from the Summit, then back to US Customs. The view was amazing.

Before he returned us to the old town, he drove us to a secluded cemetery in town, and filled our heads with all sorts of stories of the men and women buried there. Who owned what, who hated who, and the type of fellows they were. There were all sorts of colorful scoundrels in Skagway during that gold rush.

There are historic buildings down in town from the turn of the century and an old train that still chugs through. Looks like time stopped here a very long time ago.

When we returned, there were now two Royal Caribbean ships in port, parked end to end. What a huge, massive wall they made! We stood on deck as we prepared to leave, and marveled at a curious sight on the hillside above the wooden pier. There were names of captains and the names of their ships painted on the large rocks in the hillside, some with dates going back decades. There were some large signs, beautifully and artfully painted. Some were small, just the captain's name, and every size in between. I saw the names of cruise lines I knew like Royal Caribbean, Norwegian, Princess, Costas. I saw the names of ships I'd seen like Zaandam, Rhapsody, and Tropicale (which we have cruised on). There were other names like the Regent Star, Glacier Bay Explorer, and North Star that I didn't recognize at all.

"Alongside the Railroad Dock in Skagway is an impressive wall of solid granite that is home to one of the most unique art collections in Alaska. Since 1928, the crews of ships have been 'autographing' this wall to commemorate their first voyage to Skagway. Though access to the dock has been severely curtailed since 9/11, passengers on the cruise ships which use the dock and off-season visitors can spend hours reading the signatures, which comprise a virtual 'Who's Who' of Alaska passenger ships from the past 80-odd years."[18] What a fascinating testimony to days gone by.

JUNE 28

We docked in the small town of Hoonah, Alaska, at Icy Strait Point for a short while today. We discovered much later that this is the town they talk about on *Alaskan Bush People* on the Discovery Channel. The Brown Family travels the Icy Strait to get here, a very remote part of southeastern Alaska. There was little to see and do, so a few hours in port were just fine.

A large, crackling bonfire greeted us along the path at the town's docks, and must have been full of split cedar and pine, because the smell was heavenly. The path took us past some small, tidy, and colorful homes of the locals.

---

[18] explorenorth.com/alaska/skagway-photos.html

The warmth felt so good in the frigid air, and we lingered there awhile to get our hands warm. We strolled over toward a 1912 salmon cannery that had been remodeled with indoor local shops. A great idea to get prospective shoppers in out of the cold, willing to spend more time shopping.

We could hear screams from the moment we left the ship. Other sounds of a distinct zip and hum we heard led us to conclude there must be a zip line somewhere. Walking in the direction of the screams, we learned that this is the world's longest zip line. It's over a mile long, with a length of 5,495 feet. It claims a vertical drop of 1,320 feet at a top speed of 56 mph. There are six cables side by side, so you can race your friends to the bottom. Oh. My. Goodness! While standing there, we ran into our new dinner table friends, Lucy and Bob. I've always joked about wanting to do it, but wasn't sure my neck hardware would appreciate the thrill. The four of us stood there chatting about it, because both Bob and Lucy had ridden one before.

The price was huge to me, $139.00. But for a once-in-a-lifetime experience, I was ready to fork it out. Larry said, "Uh, uh. I'm not doing that." Lucy loves them and I finally committed to do it with her.

Sad to say, after we got all excited about it, they had already booked beyond our stay in port. We wouldn't finish before the ship left. I was so disappointed, but we all agreed we had better make the ship. Ha-ha.

Later, as the ship left port, Larry spotted an Orca whale that breeched the calm waters off in the distance of Icy Strait. It was his first time seeing a whale in the wild. It was a breathtaking moment. Everyone on board who saw it yelled out in excitement.

It had been yet another amazing day in Alaska.

JUNE 29

Today's port of call was Ketchikan. Today's excursion was the Potlatch Totem Park and City Highlights.

The day began by boarding a bus for the drive to the Park. The driver was quiet, not preparing us at all for the treasures to be discovered ahead of us.

"Totem poles are sculptures carved from large trees, such as the Western Red Cedar. In North America, totem poles are part of the cultures of many indigenous peoples of Alaska, British Columbia, and the Pacific Northwest. They tell a story.

"The carvings may symbolize or commemorate cultural beliefs that recount familiar legends, clan lineages, or notable events. The poles may also serve as functional architectural features, welcome signs for village visitors, mortuary vessels for the remains of deceased ancestors, or as a means to publicly ridicule someone. Given the complexity and symbolic meanings of totem pole carvings, their placement and importance lies in the observer's knowledge and connection to the meanings of the figures"[19].

The Park was a modern-day creation, built to represent a 19th century native village. It was located on historic Tlingit fishing grounds on the shores of the Tongass Narrows. We wandered through the village full of houses,

---

[19] https://en.wikipedia.org/wiki/Totem_pole

totems, and carved panels. They were smoothly carved and colorful.

There were five tribal homes with painted carvings both outside and inside—full wall murals! They had sod roofs on them, which I'm sure helps to insulate them in this chilly region. We were told that the largest totem in the village stood at 42 feet tall.

There was a building completely set aside for the carving of these huge totems and we were encouraged to touch and feel the creation in process. The guides translated the depictions on the totems, and explained how the paints were still made like they were 200 years ago.

This unique place was also home to an antique car collection that featured a 1934 Ford Coupe and a 1924 Stanley Steamer. Their museum and gift shop were well-stocked, too. It was amazing.

We all got back on the bus and were given the City Highlights part of the tour. I must say there wasn't much to it, because Ketchikan is such a small town. The guide zipped through much of the hilly town. The nicest part of town was the waterfront, where a stilted boardwalk had been constructed. There were dozens of tidy wooden structures there, all painted in pretty bright colors.

It was time to go back to the ship.

JUNE 30

Happy Birthday to Me! Yep, I am officially an Old Fart at the ripe old age of 62. What a way to celebrate the day!

We were at sea today. I had no idea just how many miles we've walked these past few days, but I am plum tuckered out. Today will be a day of rest.

I had been kidding our waiter every single night that I had a birthday at the end of the cruise. He brought me a big warm brownie with a candle on top, along with a group of waiters to really ham it up!

All week we had been seated at the end of a long table, and supper conversation had been pretty much limited to Lucy and Bob, a couple near our age. We had been able to discuss our motorhome ministry as well as our relationships with God, and theirs. We really enjoyed their companionship.

We exchanged names and phone numbers this last evening together. We discovered that we would be traveling through their part of Texas after the first of the year. They have horses and Lucy promised to take me riding if we stopped by. We celebrated the making of new friends.

Larry hit the hay early. I wasn't quite ready for bed yet, so I blew $20 in the casino and bought myself a glass of wine to celebrate the last hours of my birthday. I knew there would be lots of voicemails on my phone when I turned it back on in the morning. My best friend Deb always calls to sing Happy Birthday to me.

It had been a remarkable week of adventure, and brand new friends.

JULY 1

When the ship docked in Vancouver, we were in no rush to get off. Our hotel was here in town and we could show up anytime. We let the folks who had planes and trains to catch scurry off first.

We spent the quiet time catching up on a week's worth of emails and voicemails. And for Larry, that's a LOT!

Our 10am departure was flawless. We hailed a cab to the Metropolitan Hotel. Larry had chosen well, as this place was very nice.

We had assumed that the masses on the dock were due to the cruise ship arriving. As we walked back, it was like a carnival with food and music everywhere. Then we noticed that everyone was carrying little Canadian flags: grownups, kids, even babies in strollers were carrying these little flags.

We finally figured out from signage that it was "Canada Day". But what was that? I went up to a security guard to explain that I was visiting from the states. I asked, "What is Canada Day?" He apologized that he'd only lived here for a year and didn't know. I received the same reply from another person I asked. That's odd.

By now we'd walked into the convention center. There was a spectacular choir singing on stage. We stayed a few minutes, then moved on to the next large room, where the Canadian armed forces were showing off their equipment. There were kids crawling up on the stuff, encouraged by men and women in uniform.

I walked up to one such woman and asked her the question. She energetically explained that on this day 149 years ago, the 7 provinces agreed to join together to become Canada.

Fair warning to everyone: consider yourself warned that 2017 will be their Sesquicentennial, or 150th anniversary. I cannot imagine the party that will be on all the streets of Canada next July 1. Be prepared for some partying going on.

JULY 2

Today was completely a Vancouver Adventure Day. We walked the city's sidewalks all day, dazzled by shop windows, sometimes even stepping inside.

We took a tour of Vancouver on one of those open-roofed busses. The parks were beautiful and the city was nice and clean. At a park called Chinatown was a pond, surrounded by a Chinese garden filled with all kinds of oriental plants and trees. It was very busy; we were eager to get back on the bus.

Later, we walked through the Pacific Center, a downtown shopping mall. My biggest discovery and splurge was at Bath and Body Works' Semi Annual Sale. I purchased two travel sizes of body wash for a whopping $1.25 each. I love B&BW. One night, a long while ago, I decided to count every one of their products I had in my bathroom, and I tallied up 43. I had all different scents of body washes, lotions, lip balms, cuticle creams, hand sanitizers—you name it. I certainly can't do that anymore, here in the motorhome, so I buy small and few.

The highlight of the day was supper. We chose a modern-looking Chinese place. It had high plate glass windows on one entire side of the vaulted restaurant, so we had a great view of the activities on the street. Sorry I didn't write down the name, but the food was great.

JULY 3

It was our last day in Vancouver and we decided to take a Vancouver Whale Watch tour. We were picked up downtown, just a block from our hotel, and bussed to the little fishing village of Stevenson. That little town is also home to Disney's world of Storybook, the setting of the famous TV series *Once Upon A Time*. We bought our tickets, were issued yellow slicker suits, and walked to the Zodiac, a rigid inflatable boat. After a quick lesson about life preservers, we were off.

It was a great afternoon! Warm and sunny, the wind in my hair, the boat bobbing up and down on the sparkling water. I quickly removed the slicker and asked the guide how long we would be out today, as the advertisement had said a "3- to 5-hour tour." She replied that the length of time would be determined by how long it takes for the captain to find pods of whales on that day.

Then, only 25 minutes into the tour, she announced that the captains of their three boats had already discovered several pods, which was very unusual this close to shore. So, from that general area, we spent the next two hours trolling in the sunshine, oohing and aahing at the resurfacing of so many whales. The guide explained that there were at least nine pods in the area, some of them resident whales and others were transient whales. I certainly couldn't tell the difference, but with her Master's Degree in Marine Science, I'm sure she could. She kept us informed of all we were seeing.

We watched with awe as the Orcas breeched the waters again and again. Larry caught a magnificent photo of five of them surfacing the sea at the same time, in an orchestrated row. The picture is priceless. You've just got to look up this photo on our website.

The captain didn't stop with just the whales, he cruised us past eagles, sea lions, even seals, all within a few miles of each other. It was a delightful and amazing final day in Vancouver. We were in bed very early, as 3am would come quickly.

Genesis 1:28

28 God blessed them and said to them,
"Be fruitful and increase in number;
fill the earth and subdue it.
Rule over the fish in the sea and
the birds in the sky and
over every living creature that moves on the ground."

JULY 4

We were up at 3am and had the desk call a cab at 3:45.

We arrived quickly at the Amtrak station, only to discover that it was closed! We were to take the Amtrak's Cascade train back to Seattle. The tickets had said to arrive two hours before departure and we had done as instructed. It was still the middle of the night, dark, with unknown peril. We were the only ones waiting outside. Repeat after me: "I am a Child of God and have been marked with the sign of the cross forever." I know He will protect us and I am reminded once again: I will fear no evil!

> Psalm 23   A psalm of David.
>
> 1 The Lord is my shepherd, I lack nothing.
> 2He makes me lie down in green pastures,
> He leads me beside quiet waters,
> 3He refreshes my soul.
> He guides me along the right paths
> for His name's sake.
> 4 Even though I walk through the darkest valley,
> I will fear no evil, for you are with me;
> your rod and your staff, they comfort me.
> 5 You prepare a table before me
> in the presence of my enemies.
> You anoint my head with oil; my cup overflows.
> 6 Surely your goodness and love will follow me
> all the days of my life,
> and I will dwell in the house of the Lord forever.

    We could see two men in the dimly-lit park across the street. I was frightened. I did not want to become a statistic of urban crime. One of them felt it was his responsibility to come close, to explain when the station would open, that he too, was waiting for the train. There were homeless men lingering outside.

    Homelessness is one thing we've encountered on this adventure that we were not accustomed to. Every one of the large cities seemed to have homeless everywhere. Many were begging on street corners, camped in front of churches we visited, preying on the hearts of the religious, and in front of shops and restaurants. My heart goes out for them. We wanted to help. But, would we be giving support for an addiction? If so, should we just give them food? We pray for all of them. What would Jesus do?

> Matthew 25:35-37
>
> 35 For I was hungry
> and you gave me something to eat,
> I was thirsty and you gave me something to drink,
> I was a stranger and you invited me in,
> 36 I needed clothes and you clothed me,
> I was sick and you looked after me,
> I was in prison and you came to visit me.'
> 37 "Then the righteous will answer him,
> 'Lord, when did we see you hungry and feed you,
> or thirsty and give you something to drink?
> 38 When did we see you a stranger and invite you in,
> or needing clothes and clothe you?
> 39 When did we see you sick or in prison and go to visit you?'
> 40 "The King will reply, 'Truly I tell you, whatever you did for one of the least of these brothers and sisters of mine, you did for me.'

They finally opened the door at 4:30am—thank you, Jesus! I was exhausted from all the sun the day before and there was no place to sit outside. We were allowed to board at 5:30am and I was asleep before we left the station.

This train trip was certainly different from our scenic train ride in Alaska. I did get to see some beautiful scenery along the coast, but much of the route was through the cities' industrial sections, and not so beautiful. The entire trip took 3½ hours to Seattle, where our "limo" was waiting to take us back to Lake Pleasant, right on time.

What a once-in-a-lifetime trip these sixteen days had been! Even though we took many photos of this journey, not one of them does it justice. There is just no way to effectively capture those massive views of God's great creations; no way to smell the fresh crispness of the air.

We were delivered safely to the campground. We walked over to the storage area to start the car, which was parked in front of the motorhome, but it wouldn't start. Great! Thankfully, it was early enough in the day that we had plenty of time to deal with it. Larry and I muscled the car through the grass and weeds over beside the motorhome, and used the auxiliary batteries to jump start it.

We cranked up the rig without difficulty and drove it straight to Les Schwab to get the new tires for the rear. They had already replaced the one that blew, before we left for Alaska. All four tires cost us nearly $2,000, but they were over ten years old. The front two tires were replaced a few years ago, and were four years old. They're good for the time being.

When darkness arrived, we could hear fireworks around the campground, but we were plum worn out. We failed to report for America's Birthday Party this year, so perhaps we will celebrate wildly next year, when we plan to be in New England. But for now: sleep, peaceful sleep.

JULY 5

We slept like rocks. Lake Pleasant Campground, an urban campground is set back from the highway, around a lake. The grounds are packed with trees and bushes to absorb what little sound is left. And to their credit, there were beautiful hydrangeas in full glorious bloom throughout the park as well.

The sky was completely cloudy, in the low 60's, and spit rain on and off most of the day. It wasn't a great day to go sightseeing anyway.

Today must be a catch-up day, out of sheer necessity. There were suitcases full of dirty laundry, and our daughter had forwarded our mail. The box was full of bills to pay and other mail to review, so Larry would have plenty to keep him busy, while I got the laundry done.

Laundry isn't usually a problem. I have a splendid little Splendide washer/dryer in the motorhome. It has a single drum, so it doesn't take up much space. You put in a (small) load, choose your settings, and push start. It washes it, then dries it, without touching it again until it's done. It does a great job, as long as you can use it every day to keep up.

This huge backup of clothes was destined for the laundromat at the campground, which was very nice. It would be all done in an hour or so.

We ate a small supper and headed to bed early, listening to the rain.

With all the maintenance problems, I must remember…

Matthew 6:25-27   Do Not Worry

25 "Therefore I tell you, do not worry about your life,
what you will eat or drink;
or about your body, what you will wear.
Is not life more than food,
and the body more than clothes?
26 Look at the birds of the air;
they do not sow or reap or store away in barns,
and yet your heavenly Father feeds them.
Are you not much more valuable than they?
27 Can any one of you by worrying add a single hour
to your life?

> Matthew 6:32-34
> 32 For the pagans run after all these things, and your heavenly Father knows you need them.
> 33 But seek first his kingdom and his righteousness, and all these things will be given to you as well.
> 34 Therefore do not worry about tomorrow, for tomorrow will worry about itself.
> Each day has enough trouble of its own.

JULY 6

Now that our backlog was somewhat overcome, we got up early and purchased tickets online to take the Boeing Factory tour, which we had really been looking forward to.

But soon we discovered that the battery in the car had died again, and I had to bother the camper next door to beg him for a jump. He was kind and did it without complaint. We were so grateful we didn't have to wait for roadside assistance, that I again knocked on his door. This time was to give him a restaurant gift card and a ministry brochure for his kindness.

We returned to Les Schwab to spend another $125 for a new battery. Their service was excellent and the prices were competitive. The same fine young man who had repaired our blown tire assisted us once again. His momma should be very proud of him.

We were finally on the road to Everett, Washington, to our Boeing Factory Tour. Their point of assembly is hailed as the largest building in the world, by volume—200 million cubic feet. Here, they built first the 707, and then the

747, 767, 777, the Jumbo Jet class, and then the 787 Dreamliners.

They explained that Boeing 700 model numbers are for commercial aircraft. Just for your information, when they built those first commercial jets, they were going to call them 700. The marketing folks said it didn't have a ring to it, so they renamed it the 707 to make it sound better.

Just for your information, Boeing model numbers 300's and 400's are for military aircraft, 500's for turbine engines, and 600's for rockets and missiles. Our tour guide made the joke that now that they're making 787's, they're about to run out of numbers, so if we had any great ideas, send them in.

We were bussed from the Visitor Center to the various assembly buildings along the tour route. We had to walk a mile under the buildings in tunnels because they don't want you on the manufacturing floors. You finally take elevators to an upper floor, so you can view from above.

Everyone had been required to turn off their cell phones completely at the gate. We certainly understand why no photos were allowed. Boeing is a major defense contractor and the aerospace industry is very competitive.

From the walkways above, we could see hundreds of workers below, working on at least a couple dozen aircraft, all in various stages of completion. The employees looked like little ants going from task to task, from plane to plane. These huge jets are under roof in a line, being manufactured in different phases: some with or without engines, wings, tails, insides, all with primer, and some with finished paint jobs and logo markings. We saw some finished planes that were for Alaskan Airlines as well as an airline located in Dubai.

To put this in prospective, we've all seen video of production lines of automobile manufacturers. A car comes down the line, each worker does his or her task(s), and the car continues down the line to the next workers. Now take that process and put a gigantic Boeing 777 in its place. Now you can understand our amazement. We learned that it takes 80 days from start to finish to build a 777. But they have so many in various stages of progress, a completed plane rolls off the line every 3 days. But each of these planes are not the same. Keep in mind that each of them is being made to the specifications of the person or company that ordered each one.

No one was just standing around, everybody was busy and on a mission, unlike out on the streets, where one poor guy is digging a hole and five others are standing around, "supervising" him.

What an amazing "Made in America" factory tour!

Isaiah 40:31

31 but those who hope in the Lord
will renew their strength.
They will soar on wings like eagles;
they will run and not grow weary,
they will walk and not be faint.

Late that afternoon, we rushed to the south end of town to visit the Visitor Center at Microsoft. We arrived in time to see it, but they had it closed for a VIP group. They allowed us to go through their company store that offered everything Microsoft. It was sad to realize that the prices were higher than you would see in retail stores. I assumed it would be exactly the opposite.

Supper, then sleep after a great day of walking, driving and touring.

JULY 7

Today was a long travel day in the motorhome to Port Townsend. I-5 took us out of Seattle, down to Tacoma—at the bottom of Puget Sound. We drove across the Tacoma Narrows Suspension Bridge, over Puget Sound to Kitsap Peninsula, up to Port Townsend and then to Fort Worden.

The original Tacoma Narrows Bridge was destroyed in 1940. It collapsed into Puget Sound only four months after completion due to aeroelastic flutter. Thank goodness that bridges are built nowadays not to do that! The wind started the bridge swaying like a pendulum. As the wind worsened, the bridge began to roll, as well. It finally broke into pieces and fell into the water below.

The twin bridges that were built to replace the original bridge are the fifth longest in the US. All I could think of while driving across the twin span was, "Why couldn't they have built these spans to match?"

Heading up Route 16, we finally left the urban environment that we'd been in for weeks, into the rural pine forests of northwest Washington. We drove north to Route 3 over to US 101 west. Then we took Route 20 into Port Townsend, and finally Fort Worden State Park, which Larry rated a 6.

The village of Port Townsend is on the northeast tip of the Olympic Peninsula. It has all kinds of quaint shops and Victorian houses, most of which were built in the 19th century, when the village was in its heyday. The early residents called their city the "City of Dreams" because they thought it would become the largest port on the west coast. But it just never happened. Seattle instead became one of the busiest ports on the west coast. But it's still a picture-perfect little town.

To the east of the town is Fort Worden State Park, which served as an army post, originally built to protect Puget Sound from 1902 to 1953. "Admiralty Inlet was considered so strategic to the defense of Puget Sound at the turn of the century that three forts were built at the entrance with huge guns creating a 'Triangle of Fire' that could theoretically thwart any invasion attempt by sea."[20] The three posts would prevent any hostile fleet from reaching such targets as the Puget Sound Naval Shipyard and the cities of Seattle, Tacoma, and Everett. It was named after John Worden, commander of the USS Monitor during the Civil War. At the far northern point of the State Park, near the campground, is the Point Wilson lighthouse. Port Townsend—full of beautiful historic homes and quaint shops—lies across Puget Sound from Seattle and Everett, and the San Juan Islands lie to the north. The Sound and passageway to the Pacific becomes the border of Canada and the US.

We ate at a small seafood restaurant at the harbor in town, called Fins. The locals we had asked told us that Fins had the best seafood in town, and we were not disappointed. And we do love seafood!

---

[20] www.historylink.org/File/7524

Driving through Fort Worden, we were delighted to happen upon another special event. We were serenaded with fiddlers from all over the country who had come for the Centrum Festival of American Fiddle Tunes. They were scattered everywhere on the grounds, playing and practicing all over the state park. The sounds were mesmerizing. Each one was playing his/her own song.

> 1 Chronicles 23:5
>
> 5 Four thousand are to be gatekeepers and
> four thousand are to praise the Lord
> with the musical instruments
> I have provided for that purpose."

While walking the beach, Larry came across a huge dead Dungeness red crab. It was about three times the size of the east coast's blue crabs. We'd heard of these crabs at seafood places and restaurants along the Pacific coast, but hadn't seen one. I can't wait to try one all steamed and served with drawn butter.

Diana had texted earlier, asking that we get some "sea glass" for her. At that time, we had no idea what it was. When we were out walking on the beach, we saw a woman with her kids bending over, carefully searching for something small. We asked what she was looking for and she explained "sea glass". We learned that it is colorful bits and pieces of actual glass. It originated decades ago, when glass and other trash was dumped just offshore. Over the years, the surf breaks the glass, then tumbles them repeatedly, until they become small, smoothed pieces of glass. They are indeed beautiful. Some pieces—perhaps because of their color—can stick out like a sore thumb, but others are so small that they're hard to see, unless you specifically search for them.

It was quite the effort to collect perhaps two tablespoons of them, each smaller than a pea.

It was the perfect adventure, looking for the tiniest of things.

JULY 8

Today we celebrate 100 days of our Journey! Wow!

Less than five months ago, I was recovering from neck surgery, with two long screws that are now a permanent part of my anatomy. A blink later, I'm here in the Pacific northwest and half of our 2016 adventure is complete. When you stop and really think about your life plans with which He blesses you, it becomes an overwhelming experience.

Who would have thought!

> Psalm 145:1
>
> 1 I will exalt you, my God the King;
> I will praise your name for ever and ever.

As we toured the Fort Worden museum today, we had quite the history lesson. The museum had been created from one of the old wooden barracks. Its official name is the Puget Sound Coast Artillery Museum and it's full of artifacts from maritime relics and achievements.

Throughout the park, there were hidden gun emplacements and lawns that once were parade grounds. There were grand Victorian Homes, officers' homes, and the basic wooden barracks of working soldiers, all on countless rows of tree-lined roads.

It might sound boring to just hear of it, but it was a great way for history to come alive. There we were in the sunshine, the sun sparking off the ocean, and the wonderful music of the fiddlers wafting in the air.

Plus, no homework assignments and no tests. You just can't beat that type of an education!

JULY 9

We drove the motorhome west on US 101 to Olympic National Park. At the Visitor Center, we watched the educational movie and received another park stamp. This park has a lot of rain and about a million acres to protect.

"The park protects a vast wilderness, thousands of years of human history, and several distinctly different ecosystems, including glacier-capped mountains, old-growth temperate rain forests, and over 70 miles of wild coastline."[21]

While there, we saw a group of young hikers getting ready to climb the mountain. They had their gear spread all over the parking lot. The leaders were making sure each hiker had everything they needed for the trails.

We didn't stay long, as we had so far yet to go.

We drove northwest, then south two hours to the west side of the Olympic Peninsula on US 101. The road led us through a huge forest and past an enormous lake. It was quiet and looked like glass. The traffic was slow-going, which us allowed us plenty of time to enjoy the view, as the road followed the lake for about an hour.

---

[21] nps.gov/olym/index.htm

We were at the highest northwest point of the lower forty-eight. There was a fine mist in the air—not quite rain, but I suppose it was the usual for this area. We had reservations for Kalaloch Campground, still part of the Olympic National Park to the southwest. Larry rated it a 3. Although there were no utilities, the view was fantastic!

Kalaloch Campground is located on a high bluff about 45 feet above and adjacent to the Pacific Ocean. Even though it was mid-summer, the water in the Pacific northwest is not for the swimmer, because it's downright cold!

The campground is large and sits in a peaceful, quiet, and heavily wooded area of the rainforest. Needless to say, it was raining when we arrived.

We pulled out our military-grade rain gear for the first time and suited up. We got the walkies out, took the car off the dolly, and unhitched the dolly from the motorhome. With the walkies, I coached Larry as he backed in the rig.

Rain or shine, this campground is one of the most-visited areas of Olympic National Park. Although most of the campsites are not directly on the beach, several of them do overlook the ocean. We were lucky enough to secure one of these after our first night there. Larry got up early and scouted people leaving the park that morning. That specific park didn't assign slots and you could move around as you wanted, first come, first serve. The campground was full, and God blessed us with the awesome gift of a front-row seat.

Our spot was a small, barely off-the-road site. We parked the motorhome and got out to look. It was boxed in with vegetation on both sides and straight ahead was a limitless view of the Pacific Ocean. It was at low tide and I'd bet the surf was a quarter-mile out. Wow.

Kalaloch means "a good place to land" in the Quinault language, and there is no shortage of natural areas to explore.

"The Pacific shoreline just below provides ample habitat for marine life: tide pools reveal crabs and sea urchins at low tide; sea otters float on the surface of submerged kelp beds; shorebirds nest on beaches; and whales and dolphins occasionally emerge offshore. Beyond the national park's 73 miles of coastline lie three national wildlife refuges and one marine sanctuary."[22]

Hidden in either fog or rain clouds (or both), a view of Mt. Olympus was not to be had during our stay.

Leviticus 26:4
4 I will send you rain in its season, and the ground will yield its crops and the trees their fruit.

JULY 10

We stayed in this same place for several days, right on the overlook. The tide came and went, just as it does back in Myrtle Beach. But as I said yesterday, this tide really goes OUT!

Larry found a trail that led down to the beach. It was nearly hidden in the brush, and it took careful navigation to get down the many steep and uneven steps of dirt and railroad ties that led to the sand.

---

[22]recreation.gov/camping/kalaloch/r/campgroundDetails

Once there, we were in a treasure trove! There were shells of course, but many of them were large and unbroken. We rarely see that in Myrtle Beach. There were loads of crab shells, driftwood, and even whole sand dollars.

At night, the sky was adorned in all its celestial beauty: moon, stars, planets, and the majesty of the milky way. Each night a campfire kept us warm, as we sat outside to enjoy the sounds of the creatures who lived around us and the pounding of the surf nearby. You just can't achieve this kind of quiet in urban settings.

As we drove out of the park one afternoon, we couldn't help but stop and admire a very unusual rig camped right here in the same park. The small camper was a retro Pleasure Craft decked out in white and turquoise. It was a perfect match to the white and turquoise vintage Ford Country Squire wagon that towed it. It had all been restored and shined like new. To complete the picture (we did take pictures), they had stuck two pink flamingos and a Tiki torch in their yard. What a cute blast from the past!

Philippians 4:7

7 And the peace of God,
which transcends all understanding,
will guard your hearts and your minds in Christ Jesus.

JULY 11

Larry took a hike down to the beach this morning alone. All this cold and damp weather is taking a toll on me. I stayed behind and rested in the warm motorhome.

As he'd walked down those treacherous steps again today, past the driftwood and down the sand, he came to a weird-looking tree. He took some photos of it and did a little research.

The Kalaloch Tree Cave is a tree along the beach that, due to erosion, has developed a large cave under its roots. The tree hasn't fallen, but for many years has looked as though it would at any given moment. Larry said he didn't get close and took his pictures from afar, because it did look ready to collapse.

The sound of the surf seemed very loud today. The waves were crashing far out, at low tide. There was enough room to play a collegiate game of football down there. It was an unusual day of blue skies and sunshine, and the seabirds were enjoying the beach as much as Larry was.

I did join him later that afternoon. There were families scattered on the beach, and this one particular family built a huge sand castle. He said they had been working on it all day, and it was one of the most impressive amateur castles we had ever seen. Then we picked up unbroken sand dollars from all over the beach.

By evening, it was a bit chilly. We enjoyed another campfire, complete with marshmallows and hot chocolate. Priceless.

Genesis 1:10

10 God called the dry ground "land,"
and the gathered waters he called "seas."
And God saw that it was good.

JULY 12

The day was spent traveling Route 101 back to Tacoma. We spent the night at Olympia KOA in Olympia, Washington, which Larry rated a 2. We were on our way to Mt. Rainier.

The KOA was a sad little campground that really needed a lot of love and remodeling. Even the three-foot utility pole at our site was rotten and fell over as Larry plugged in our electrical cord. We'd only needed a place to pull in and sleep, so we made do. We should have saved the night's fee and just parked at a Walmart somewhere.

I have personally stayed in a lot of KOA's over my lifetime. In their heyday, the KOA name was assurance of the best there was. I don't know what has happened over the years, but we are more disappointed than not when we stay in one now. I know there are exceptions to this generalization. We're just careful when we reserve a KOA.

JULY 13

We left by way of Route 706 out of Tacoma to Mt. Rainier National Park.

Mt. Rainier is an active volcano at 14,410 feet. It's not as high as Denali, but it's still pretty doggone big. The National Park service claims it to be "the most glaciated peak in the lower forty-eight."

The closer we came to the National Park, the more abundant were the wildflowers and evergreens. Spring is just arriving at these higher elevations, despite it being the middle of the summer.

We arrived at the Cougar Campground in Mt. Rainier National Park, Washington, that Larry rated a 3. There were no utilities, but the rig will provide all that we need, as it always had, with water, holding tanks, generator, batteries and, for Larry's sake, satellite TV.

Wildflowers were everywhere, in all colors of purple, pink, red, blue, white, and green. They were in all sorts of shapes and sizes. They covered hillsides and meadows, and bordered the roads.

The entrance to the park is called Longmire. We stopped at the Visitor Center there, treated ourselves to a quick lunch, then explored the area.

Our walk took us across an old logging road bridge. It had been made of timbers and had a pleasing smell to it. We saw that the bridge was rated at 10,000 pounds. We could never have driven our rig over it, because it weighs many times that.

The bridge took us across a dry glacier bed that was full of rocks but no water. It didn't look like a dry river bed, it actually looked like a river of rocks had come through. I'm sure it will be rushing with snowmelt in the spring, whenever that is.

Song of Songs 2:12

12 Flowers appear on the earth;
the season of singing has come,
the cooing of doves is heard in our land.

JULY 14

We drove up the mountainside to a section of the park named Paradise. Once we arrived, we agreed that it was aptly named. It's at a higher elevation in the park with views in all directions. The parking lot was full and there were cars parked all up and down the winding road. We were blessed to find one last handicap site close to the Inn. Thank you, Jesus. I don't think either one of us could have made it up that big hill.

We went to the Visitor Center, watched the park movie, and received another stamp in my Passport. We walked the long, paved trail and were not disappointed with the view it rewarded us. It was perhaps a mile round-trip. We were blessed with panoramic views, wildflowers, streams, and waterfalls. It was beautiful, and worth every step of effort. Folks were walking, hiking the trails, and biking everywhere.

We got back in the car and drove about an hour to the northeast side of the mountain. It's the highest road in the park and dead ends at Sunrise, the highest point that can be reached by vehicle at 6,400 feet. The entrance to this side of the park was backed up with cars and we had to wait about an hour while one poor ranger collected fees. It was summer vacation time. All we had to do was flash our Access Pass to get in.

The temperature dropped as we drove to the top, but the view was tremendous! You could clearly see a cave carved into a turquoise blue glacier. Hikers were trekking up there to get a closer look, but my telephoto lens works just fine, thank you very much. We'll go anywhere, as long as we can get there by car. Haha.

JULY 15

We packed up the rig and headed back down from Mt. Rainier to Route 12 to Randall, Washington. Route 131 took us to Northwoods, then Highway NF30/Meadow Creek Road, Wynn River Road, and Middle Creek Road took us to our destination.

We were traveling in line with the volcanos of Mt. Rainier, Mt. St. Helens, and Mt. Hood. We went on to the deep forest of Gifford Pinchot National Forest.

We should have never been on this road; it was for small cars only. This was the day we realized that we needed something to provide routes designed for RV's or big rigs, and not just Google Maps.

This road is closed in winter. There were switchbacks, bumps, low limbs, and holes everywhere. There was nowhere to turn around, but at least the great views made it worth the error.

Much later we would discover cracks in our air conditioning covers up top and figured they must have happened this day. Duct tape does work wonders when the alternative is spending over $200 for new covers. Who actually sees them, anyway?

A note to everyone: don't take the road on the eastside of Mt. St. Helens—be sure to take I-5 on the west side!

We found a roadside viewing area and took photos of Mt. St. Helens with some beautiful purple wildflowers, and the blue sky. Along with the greenery of the forest, it's a picture postcard for sure. It's one of our best.

> **Luke 12:27**
>
> 27 "Consider how the wild flowers grow.
> They do not labor or spin.
> Yet I tell you, not even Solomon in all his splendor
> was dressed like one of these.

When we finally arrived at Paradise Creek Campground at Mt. St. Helens, Washington, we were in a deep forest of tall trees that were so thick, the sun couldn't shine through them. What little light broke through was dim. The park, which Larry rated a 2, was along a mountain stream. There were no utilities here and absolutely no means of communication, including no Wi-Fi. It was the very first time I'd seen rangers keep track of campsites by hand. They did have hand-held radios, but they told us that even that was poor.

We were to stay here for two nights, but the devil took advantage of this wilderness to strike once again: he blew the drain plug in the hot water tank. With the plug blown, the pressurized system couldn't direct water anywhere in the rig, as it all leaked out of the heater drain.

Larry rigged a makeshift plug so that we could shower in the morning. He's really turned out to be the quicker fixer-upper! Just call him MacGyver.

JULY 16

Today, we drove the rig down the Wynn River Highway to Carson, Washington, on the Columbia River, then headed west on Route 14 into Stevenson. There, on Second Avenue, is Columbia Hardware, a small but well-stocked hardware store that had our drain plug. God went before us and provided a great big space along the highway where Larry could park the rig easily.

We could see the Cascade Locks they use for barge navigation, then we crossed the Bridge of the Gods. The bridge passes over the Columbia River at the Washington/Oregon state line. It was so beautiful. Another perfect picture postcard! There were high cliffs on both sides of the river, complete with green trees, cascading waterfalls, and fern gorges. Beautiful.

Now into Oregon via the Vietnam Veterans Memorial Highway west, aka I-84. This parallels US 30 where there are lots of falls and gorges. There are 26 falls in this area over vertical basalt walls along the Columbia River Gorge. This area is graced with the greatest concentration of waterfalls in North America, particularly along the Oregon side of the western Gorge. Horsetail, Bridal Veil, Triple, and the most popular Multnomah Falls.

Located on Crown Point, east of Portland is a viewing area called the Vista House. "Vista House was built in 1917 on one of the most beautiful scenic points on the Historic Columbia River Highway. It was constructed to provide travelers a place to rest and refresh themselves as they made their way down the magnificent Columbia River."[23]

Columbia River Gorge National Scenic Area is really a rain forest. This greenery of trees, ferns, and waterfalls from the cliffs flowing down from Mount Hood is God's beauty tenfold! They say from one vantage point off of east Larch Mountain Road, you can see Mt. St. Helens, Mt. Rainier, and Mt. Hood all lined up, forming the Cascades Volcanos. This is also part of the Pacific Ocean Ring of Fire.

---

[23] http://vistahouse.com/

We tried to see it and take some photos, but it was covered in dense fog all day. We never really got to see Mt. Hood in all its glory.

JULY 17

We drove to Ainsworth State Park Campground. It's east of Portland, in Troutdale, Oregon, and Larry rated it a 3. He chose to stay here because it made a great central base camp from which we will visit the Portland and gorge areas.

We took the car to explore the area. Being a Sunday, and the middle of summer, you couldn't get anywhere near Multnomah Falls. There were people parked in every conceivable spot. Forget seeing anything up close today; we will have to return later in the week.

We drove into Portland instead and stocked up on groceries.

We had gone so many nights without cable or satellite that Larry decided we should stock up on DVD's while at Walmart. We bought about ten, with many of them with multiple movies—that should hold us for a while. Then we went to the movies. Ironic, huh?

When we returned to the motorhome, we watched one of our new movies, as well. After resting up today, perhaps we will get to hike Multnomah Falls tomorrow.

JULY 18

We woke up to another cloudy day and moved the rig to a different site at the campground. The site we were on was only available for one night. We did give out a lot of kid packets here, as there were kids everywhere. We know God had to be smiling at that.

We set aside a block of time to make up packets, about twenty-five at a time. We turn off the TV and concentrate on the love and hope we want to be in these packets. We pray for the kids who will receive them. We gather items that we've ordered from CEF and OCC and other suppliers, then print coloring sheets, introductory letters, and envelopes for the grownups.

Back to worldly works, QuickBooks seemed to rear its ugly head again today, but this time it was truly operator error. When the CSR installed some new software last week, they had created a new shortcut from my Desktop, which I didn't see. I tried to open the program and clicked the same old shortcut. Oops. Yes, you can all laugh at that. Duh.

Diana texted back and forth with us most of the day. I guess she really missed us while we were off the grid in the heart of the forest.

Larry drove us 14 miles to see Mt. Hood, so we could try to see all the mountains in the Cascades in a row but, we couldn't see a thing but the low-lying clouds. This will require another trip if we have the time.

We tried again at Multnomah Falls and by the grace of God, found a place to park. There were still lots of people there, exploring every level of the Falls. It is a magnificent creation, and the amazing sound the water makes can be heard all around. To stand there and watch its power was mesmerizing. Awesome. Breathtaking.

The cliffs where the falls begin are 611 feet above, there are actually two different falls at the top. They fall as one 542 feet to the next platform, where they create the lower falls for the last 69 feet.

We walked up a lot of steps to the lower platform, which was close to the falls. We chose not to take the steep trail up to the upper bridge. We are just getting too old. My brain thinks I'm 26, but my body screams "yeah, you wish!"

There is a large area to be explored, from near the top of the falls to the water pool runoff blocks away. We hiked down from an overpass, through the brush, to stand close to the water. We spent some time down there. There weren't as many people and it was cool and quiet. The sounds of the trickling water combined with the falls in the distance made the area so peaceful.

We climbed back up to the roadway and decided it was time for supper. We ate at Falls Lodge, right at the foot of the Falls. The restaurant was made of glass panels and our table had an unobscured view of the Falls. Although it was cool, someone had propped the doors to the patio open, so we could hear them, too. I don't remember what we ordered, but their hot coffee sure was good.

Psalm 42:7

7 Deep calls to deep in the roar of your waterfalls; all your waves and breakers have swept over me.

Back at the motorhome, we checked in with Mom and then watched another George Clooney flick, *Three Kings*. All is well with the world.

JULY 19

We took I-85 west the short distance to Portland Fairview Campground in Portland, Oregon, which Larry rated a 5.

Another cloudy day, not much suited for outdoor adventure, we took off across the Columbia River to take the tour at Pendleton Wool Mills, in Washougal, Washington.

I don't buy much in wool, I'm strictly a wash-and-wear type of girl. This tour was an amazing discovery, beginning with how wool comes from sheep (we already knew that), fleece is spun into threads, dyed to various colors, woven into cloth, and finished to sell.

It was mind boggling to watch and hear all the massive machinery working, spinning then weaving threads of brilliant colors. There were large "forms" that had hand-spun threads to mount on the looms, ready to go whenever needed.

This mill was established six generations ago, in 1863. We were personally taken through the buildings to see each of these steps firsthand. Pendleton is very, very particular about the quality of the fabrics they weave and the slightest imperfections render them seconds.

It was good to see happy people, proudly working on an American-made product. The finished products were like none other and it showed in the smiles and greetings we received.

After the tour, we did a post office run. While we were putting gas in the car, Diana posted a picture on Facebook that showed the World's Largest Continual Chocolate Waterfall that was right here in Portland at a place called The Candy Basket. We Googled it and we were only one block away!

The 20-foot-tall Chocolate Cascade was right inside the front door. I learned it had been gushing goodness continually since 1992. It was indeed impressive, but not so much the tiny store. But it was worth the stop.

Back at the motorhome, we were finally able to enjoy an 80-degree sunny afternoon. It was about time. It was the middle of the summer, after all.

For weeks after the tour, it seemed that we saw Pendleton Wool products in all sorts of places that carried high-end blankets and throws, purses and backpacks. And we had seen them made.

It was another great day of discovery.

Deuteronomy 18:4

4 You are to give them the first fruits of your grain,
new wine and olive oil,
and the first wool from the shearing of your sheep

JULY 20

Today was just a non-remarkable errand day. It was also a very frustrating day, because the stupid steps are not working again. Out comes the 3-step ladder to help us get into the motorhome once again. We cannot figure out the rhyme or reason for when they come and go. Believe it or not, there will be a day that we conquer these steps! Larry's shins are showing the signs of these steps coming and going as they please—Black and Blue!

We grilled pork chops for supper and watched a movie.

Mostly, a quiet day of rest.

JULY 21

The sun is still shining today and the temperature is in the low 80's. Finally, a full day of both sun and warm.

After a quick trip to Costco, we came back and enjoyed the pool.

Before this next comment, let me explain first that I didn't have a pool in my life growing up. My parents took me to Florida every year, and those were the only times I ever got in a pool. Larry had had an above-ground pool at his house for years. When we started dating, I would get in the pool with him and his sisters. Quickly, they turned into these crazy wild beasts! How could I find a safe corner in a very round pool?

Well, on this particular day at the campground, Other People's Kids (OPK's) had filled up the pool before we arrived. And they were all crazy wild beasts. They were screaming and yelling and running, they repeatedly canon-balled into the pool. I was a nervous wreck. Their supervising elders were all around. Am I the only adult here who fears concussions and broken bones?

In my defense, let me also say that I'm an only child. My daughter is forty years old. My only grandbaby is a Black Lab Mix, named Zoe. I just don't take chaos well anymore, especially when the potential for bodily harm is in the equation.

We discovered mid-swim that the hot tub had been opened just the day before, and no kids were allowed. Off we went to the outdoor spa, away from the pool area and had a lovely afternoon.

We had supper plans for tonight in Portland. We actually had a date, of sorts! And I would finally get to meet a person I had heard so much about. Larry first met Fabiola (Fabi) on a mission trip to Guatemala, where she served as his interpreter. Fabi is originally from Venezuela and migrated to Guatemala via Medical Missions Ministry during her university years. She moved to Portland, Oregon, to live with her aunt while studying Christian youth programs. It was a delightful supper, learning all about this young lady of whom my husband has spoken so kindly, so often. She is an amazing young woman, clearly on mission for God.

Back in the motorhome, we were happy to see another familiar face, this time on the television. Kristen Van Dyke was doing the weather report for a local Portland TV station. She had her start back in Myrtle Beach, after her graduation from the College of Charleston. She had come a long way.

JULY 22

We rose early to drive today, but it was raining. We delayed departure for a few hours, hoping it would stop, but it didn't. We finally packed up in the rain and pulled out. Those rain coats we bought back home sure have come in handy here in the Pacific northwest. It rains a lot here!

We drove south on I-5, the main north and south expressway for the west coast. Traffic was horrible, by the way. Then we took US 20 to South Beach State Park, Newport, Oregon, which Larry rated a 3. It was nice enough for a state park, but we will have to hike about a half-mile to the beach, which we did. I sure wish we would have biked it.

The drive was about three hours, and we did drive out of the rain eventually. It's sunny here, but much cooler—in the low 60's.

As much as I wanted to explore the coast, there was something much more imperative at the moment: Larry's prescription refill. Larry always gets his prescriptions through his Humana Medicare Part D mail order. We order ninety days at a time online, it comes in the mail, all is well, no big deal. There was much disagreement about just whose fault this was, as I set up his daily drugs but he reorders them, but he ran out of one prescription. Being the female half I am usually right, but we are human, and we are married, and we do disagree. The problem was that four of the drug stores in town didn't even carry the drug. I finally found one pharmacist who did have 80 tablets, only a fraction of the 270 on the refill. We'll take them! That gives us nearly a month to work out the rest of the details for more.

A crisis averted, we went to a very popular local place called Mo's for great seafood. It's located in the fishing harbor part of the town. At the last moment over supper, Larry decided we should go take photos of the sunset. We raced to the Yaquina Head lighthouse, and arrived just in time. We were blessed with seeing a whale, dozens of sea lions, hundreds of birds, and one spectacular sunset.

This lighthouse at sunset was one of our best pictures. It was such a beautiful, spectacular, amazing view. Yes, all three of these words and it still doesn't do it justice.

> **Luke 4:40-42**
>
> 40 At sunset, the people brought to Jesus all who had various kinds of sickness, and laying his hands on each one, he healed them. 41 Moreover, demons came out of many people, shouting, "You are the Son of God!" But he rebuked them and would not allow them to speak, because they knew he was the Messiah.

JULY 23

We got up early, for today was another travel day. As we do every time we prepare to move again, we open all the window shades. I secured all the interior doors—there are five. I put away all things that usually sit on counters. Larry disconnects all utilities from the outside, I turn off the heat pumps, and make sure the fridge is on gas. I shut down the inverter, pull up a couple of throw rugs, move the mini fridge and computer printer, then pull in all three of the room extensions. Larry starts the engine. The last thing we do is hit the button to bring up the levelers…

And they won't retract.

Just like back in Denver, we were stuck again! It had to be an electrical problem. Plus, the steps were not working again. What aggravation! I went up to the ranger station to inform them. It was the middle of summer and the place was booked full. We knew we had to move, as our reservations had only been for last night; people would be arriving in a couple of hours to claim their spot.

Larry placed a call to Good Sam Roadside Assistance to dispatch a repairman to our location, while I was busy praying. Larry was trying the switch repeatedly. Finally, they retracted. God does answer prayers, if it is in His will. I concluded there was nothing left for us to do here, and we were free to leave. Thank you again, Lord.

We traveled south down US 101, and were amazed at the beautiful scenery of the rocky shores of Oregon. We turned inland on Route 38 to Route 138, then headed back to I-5 south. The mountains took us through deep forest. We witnessed a vast change in the landscape today, and it was all beautiful.

We spent a lot of hours on the road today to bring us closer to Crater Lake National Park. You can sure tell the kids are out of school for the summer. Everything is busy: restaurants, parks, beaches, campgrounds, roads, and highways. America sure loves its vacation time.

God went before us to find a place for the night. We stayed in a little campground called Tri-City RV park in Myrtle Creek, Oregon, that Larry rated a 4. We tried to get into Seven Feathers Casino Campground, rated 10/10/10 by Good Sam, but it was full for tonight.

We do use Good Sam's rating system to find campgrounds. We find it accurate and it's considered the gold standard of campground rating systems. The three-number rating they award to each campground can be found in their Campground Directory or online. Good Sam explains:

"How do these numbers work? The three-number rating is a snapshot of the campground's amenities, cleanliness, and environment. Each of the three ratings is based on a scale from 1 to 10, with 10 being the best.

"For each of the listed subcategories, a campground may receive 1 point, a half-point, or no points. A small percentage of campgrounds attain the coveted 10/10*/10 ratings, meaning top marks in every category. Those will be highlighted in a special section of the print directory.

"A park must receive a 5/7/5 rating and meet specific minimum requirements within each category to qualify for membership in the Good Sam Park Network. If a listing in the directory has no ratings or UI is indicated, our teams didn't inspect this campground.

Facilities:

"Evaluates the level of development of RV sites, hookups, recreation, swimming, security, laundry services, interior roads, registration area and Internet access.

Restrooms and Showers:

"Rates the cleanliness and physical characteristics of toilets, walls, showers, sinks/counters/mirrors, and floor. If a park achieves a full point in each of the above, it receives a star (*) that indicates exceptionally clean restrooms. Also rated are restrooms' interior construction, odor, supplies, number of facilities, interior appearance, exterior appearance, and location as it relates to park spaces.

Visual Appearance:

"Appraises the park's setting and site layout, function and identification of signage, overall exterior building maintenance, noise, trash disposal, litter and debris around the grounds and sites, and appearance of grounds, sites, and entrance area.

"Each campground's rating is determined by a consultant team made up of highly trained RVers who travel hundreds of miles each year to cover the private RV parks in their region. In all, 38 teams crisscross North America, making visits to the campgrounds in their territories and taking a complete tour of each facility to compile their report.

"When the Good Sam RV Travel Guide and Campground Directory is published, consumers can depend on a ratings system honed from millions of miles traveled and countless hours of campground inspection. Over the decades, directory editors and field inspectors have factored in insights of thousands of RVers to find out what consumers value in comfort, convenience, and enjoyment. As a result, the numbers encapsulate everything that a consumer should know about a campground. With a single glance at these three numbers, RVers will know how developed a park is and whether or not it will meet the camping experience they are looking for."[24]

We were settled there by late afternoon and took it easy through the evening. Both of us went to bed early, because we have another long day of driving ahead of us tomorrow.

JULY 24

Today was another travel day to cover the rest of the trip to Crater Lake National Park, Oregon, to stay in Mazama Campground, that Larry rated a 2. This low rating should not discourage you from camping there. A low rating is typical of National Parks. They're usually not easy to get to because

---

[24] https://www.goodsamnetwork.com/rating/

they're located is such remote areas. They usually have no utilities and the campgrounds (including bathrooms and showers), were built back in the 1940's or 1950's. It just is what it is. If you camp with a tent and the showers are important to you, then you might reconsider. But for those of us who bring it all with us, they are quite sufficient.

The roads were minor, rural roads: Douglas County Hwy 1, Tiller Trail Hwy, Route 227 and lastly Route 62. We went east, then north, then west, then south, then east again. There were plenty of switchbacks, valleys, and hills to climb. Larry became quite skilled on these tight and twisty roads. While he was driving, I was looking down and out the window by my seat where I became quite aware of how close we were to driving off into some deep ravine! I refused to drive!

Our experience with the campground did not start out well. They assigned us to a campsite, we go to it, and there's a tent set up on it. Each of the sites indicated whether it was for RVs only or tents only. This one was not for tents. None of the spaces had utilities. It was a huge site as campsites go, so we set up on it, as we'd been told.

It was a hot afternoon, well into the 80's, where the season daytime highs are usually around 70. And no air conditioning. Yes, I'm a wuss when it comes to heat.

Later the tent people came back and the man insisted that we move. Back and forth we go, and we say, can't we just share the site? Their tent was a good 25 feet from the motorhome and there was plenty of parking space for both cars. He said it would make his girlfriend nervous, and she would not share the site!

So, even though he was the one on the wrong site, and he was leaving in the morning, the ranger came and asked us to move. It wasn't fair, but it was still the whole matter of tearing down and setting up again. Well, at least one good thing came out of the whole fiasco: we could get better satellite, despite the trees.

We drove to an overlook at sunset to see the stars. We even saw a shooting star! Once you escape the lights of urban areas, the stars will reveal themselves in all their glory. You just have to look up. If you haven't ever seen the Milky Way in the absolute dark, well, you must!

Crater Lake is absolutely beautiful, day and night.

Psalm 147:4

He determines the number of the stars
and calls them each by name

JULY 25

In the car, we left the campsite and drove the entire Rim Drive around Crater Lake. It was a bright, sort of glowing color. Larry started calling it "Crater Blue", because it's like no other blue he'd ever seen. Because of its water clarity, it is an amazing deep blue color, and different than glacier blue. It is beautiful from every angle. Every view from the drive was just as beautiful as the last.

We stopped at most of the scenic views and took lots of photos. We learned the park was founded in 1902 and its depth of 1,943 makes it the deepest lake in the US, and the ninth deepest in the world. The lake is actually a collapsed volcano and measures five miles east to west and six miles north to south. It's so perfectly clear that it's like looking at a circle of glass.

This is a very unique lake, for many reasons. There is no inflow to the lake, other than rain and snowmelt. There is no outflow from the lake either, other than evaporation. Its water may be the most pristine on earth.

Scientists say that a violent eruption triggered the collapse of the volcano, Mount Mazama, and formed Crater Lake. There are two islands in the lake, Wizard Island, and the Phantom Ship, which really does look like a pirate ship. We took pictures to prove it – check it out on the website.

As we've mentioned before, American Indians were here long before it was a national park. Members of the Klamath tribe could have actually witnessed its forming 7,700 years ago, and they have long considered Crater Lake as a spiritual site.

In Sand Creek Canyon, on the south side of the volcano, there are some weird formations called the Pinnacles. They're unusual volcanic pumice spires extending high into the air, remnants left on the steep sides of the canyon from volcanic activity and lava flow.

While driving back to the campground, we discovered a wildflower meadow. We parked the car to walk through. It was absolutely amazing! There wasn't a marked trail as such, only a narrow foot path created by those who had come before. There was a tiny creek that crisscrossed through the meadow, and sometimes you would have to walk across stones in the creek. There were colorful wildflowers as tall as I am, and others barely higher than the ground, of every color imaginable. It was definitely not handicap accessible, but only short rises and falls for us older folk.

Annie's Creek Restaurant was right there in the national park lodge, so we enjoyed supper there. While we were eating, we watched a mother come in with three small kids to eat. It appeared that they had been out on the trail a few days, as they had gear and were themselves, unkempt. Larry voiced that it really took some guts to be out in the wilderness on the trails with kids, alone, considering the bears, mountain lions and snakes.

Back at the motorhome, we had some time to watch satellite TV (FOX News, of course), then headed out with the camera to watch the sunset. We parked at a gravel pullout and had it all to ourselves. The sun was a glowing orange as it slipped behind the mountains, surrounded by clouds of pink and purple. Awesome. It was a perfect evening to enjoy God showing off in all His splendor.

JULY 26

The levelers and the steps were continuing to be trouble. We decided to escape them by driving south on Route 62 to Medford, Oregon, and take a factory tour of Harry & David. Being candy makers once ourselves, we've always had admiration for their retail stores and the quality of goodies they put in their gift baskets.

We wanted to take the rig into Medford in the hopes that someone could fix the problems, but everyone we called joked about seeing us after Labor Day. No thanks.

We finally found a place back up in Myrtle Creek that said he could take us the very next day. That fact, in and of itself, should have thrown up a red flag. So instead of going to Harry & David, we packed up the rig and headed back to where we had just come from.

If you remember, the last time we were up in this area, the Seven Feathers RV Resort and Casino was full. They had room for us this time. We were eager to stay at a place that was rated so highly.

The RV Resort is on the opposite side of I-5 from the Casino. Once we checked in, we were escorted to our site. This was the first time we'd been thoroughly questioned about how old our motorhome was. "What make and model is it?" "What year is it?" They actually had to approve of our staying there. Any motorhome more than ten years old or looks bad cannot enter here. It's a nice resort and they want everything to look nice, I can understand that. Ours rig is ten years old now, a 2006. If we came back next year, would they turn me away?

The streets are beautiful blacktop, all the curbs and sites are poured concrete. It was beautifully landscaped with trees and flowers, and amenities galore. This campground was planned by someone who knew what would attract the RVers. An absolutely perfect 10! There was always a Casino van looping through the campground. If you needed a ride anywhere locally, all you had to do was stand at the front of your site and it would pick you up on the next round.

After we unhitched the car, we immediately went for a swim in their indoor heated pool. Our appointment to get the levelers and steps fixed was for the next day, and now our main electric cable was giving us trouble. The male end of the electrical cable plug had broken so we needed a new one.

The rest of the day was spent on cleaning, maintenance, and repairs. After spending the past couple of weeks with the windows in the motorhome open to Mother Nature, it was time to clean it from top to bottom. Larry tried fixing stuff on the outside to avoid repair costs, but to no avail. I took the car into itty bitty Canyonville (one mile away) and got everything on my list at the Dollar General.

After we cleaned up, we took the van over to the Casino where we enjoyed the $7.50 buffet. You can usually get low-cost food at casinos. When you're retired on a fixed income, every dollar counts. The Casino has this huge eagle statue in front of it with hanging purple, pink, and red flower baskets everywhere. They really know how to landscape and market their casino. They not only have a beautiful campground, but a state-of-the-art truck stop with upscale amenities, a well-maintained rest area for weary drivers, and restaurants. They want you to get off the interstate and enjoy this beautiful oasis. And gamble some, for sure.

JULY 27

We arrived at the repair place Myrtle Creek RV Repair. After the owner saw what we needed and looked at our problems said he could not take us in "until two days from now." It would give us a few days to enjoy the campground and the area. So, we made an appointment for the day after tomorrow, shook hands and left.

We headed back down I-5 about sixty miles to Medford, Oregon again, this time to finally tour Harry & David. It was another awesome afternoon of discovery. We have been up and down this section of I-5 so many times now. It's pretty, and the view through Grants Pass is nice, but enough is enough.

We learned that Harry & David has been in business since 1934. The campus is sprawled out over 55 acres. We were loaded into a small bus to begin the tour, which lasted about an hour.

When I personally think of Harry & David (having been in the popcorn business myself), I think of their chocolate-drizzled popcorn—Moose Munch—then, their chocolate delights. But I forget that a lot of their business is in fruit. They have an orchard division named Bear Creek Orchards that continues to maintain over 2,500 acres of pears and peaches in the area.

Their busiest mail-order season is, of course, Christmas, and second is Mother's Day. But they were still busy the day we went, hand-packing lots of pears and other things into boxes for shipping. The smell was amazing! They have numerous big buildings for offices, manufacturing, and warehousing. A tanker was unloading a shipment of coconut oil for their popcorn. A whole tanker truck! We used coconut oil back when we had our popcorn shop, Pop 'N Stuff, and we thought going through a 40-pound can was a lot.

We finished at the gift shop and found the deal of the day. As peaches were currently in season, they must have had quite the overrun. We purchased a bag of peaches for $1.00. They were delicious. For taking the tour, they gave us each a little gift box with cookies and chocolates.

We found a Panda Express for lunch, then I got a much-needed haircut next door. We enjoyed the latest *Star Trek* movie at the cinema, grabbed groceries at Walmart, and drove the 1½ hours back to Seven Feathers.

The casino had been issuing tickets for a car giveaway that happens in three more days. That car was awesome! It was a deep purple/plum Dodge Charger. We decided to go every day, if just to get the tickets. We claimed our tickets and headed back to the campground. We grilled burgers outside and watched satellite for a bit.

We covered a lot of miles today, and it was all good.

JULY 28

We drove the motorhome to the repair guy's garage to see what he could fix today. Fingers crossed.

Taking our time, I drove us to wine country. We drove Route 238 to Jackson, Oregon, just west of Medford, to a small historic little town in the heart of wine and fruit country. The entire area is just beautiful. The roads wind through the slightly hilly country. Most of the hills are covered in beautifully manicured rows of grapevines. The vineyards and immaculate, groomed and planted in perfectly straight rows. I have no idea how they do that. We also saw orchards of peaches and pears.

There are homes throughout these areas as well. Some of them are small and simple, others are sprawling mansions. We chose one vineyard as it opened for the day.

It was Dancin' Vineyards. It was in the rolling hills and you could see the grape vines for what seemed like miles. There were high fences and large entrance gates—now this is what I imagined the Napa Valley looked like. We enjoyed a wine tasting, then decided to have lunch there. We sat outside at an umbrella table and enjoyed the beautiful colors of the flowers and the scents of the herbs planted all around us. There was even a pond full of water lilies and fish. We ordered wine that was served with unusual crackers and equally unusual cheeses. The day was warm and sunny. Perfect.

After stopping at a few other wineries, Larry drove us back to check with the repairman in the late afternoon. He said he had diagnosed what was wrong, but there were no parts to be gotten during our planned time here. Wouldn't he have known that to begin with, I wondered? Geesh.

The day was perfect until we were backing up the motorhome. I do believe my husband suffers from this newly-named condition of "Hangry." It's when you get all angry because you haven't eaten in a while. Hungry plus angry equals hangry. I held my tongue and prayed for my frustrated husband instead. Hours later, he actually apologized.

Of course, he's forgiven. We are all forgiven.

Matthew 20
The Parable of the Workers in the Vineyard

1 "For the kingdom of heaven is like a landowner who went out early in the morning to hire workers for his vineyard. 2 He agreed to pay them a denarius for the day and sent them into his vineyard.

3 "About nine in the morning he went out and saw others standing in the marketplace doing nothing. 4 He told them, 'You also go and work in my vineyard, and I will pay you whatever is right.' 5 So they went.

"He went out again about noon and about three in the afternoon and did the same thing. 6 About five in the afternoon he went out and found still others standing around. He asked them, 'Why have you been standing here all day long doing nothing?'

7 "'Because no one has hired us,' they answered.
"He said, 'You also go and work in my vineyard.'

8 "When evening came, the owner of the vineyard said to his foreman, 'Call the workers and pay them their wages, beginning with the last ones hired and going on to the first.'

9 "The workers who were hired about five in the afternoon came and each received a denarius. 10 So when those came who were hired first, they expected to receive more. But each one of them also received a denarius. 11 When they received it, they began to grumble against the landowner. 12 'These who were hired last worked only one hour,' they said, 'and you have made them equal to us who have borne the burden of the work and the heat of the day.'

13 "But he answered one of them, 'I am not being unfair to you, friend. Didn't you agree to work for a denarius? 14 Take your pay and go. I want to give the one who was hired last the same as I gave you. 15 Don't I have the right to do what I want with my own money? Or are you envious because I am generous?'

16 "So the last will be first, and the first will be last."

JULY 29

Today was supposed to be a free day. We had nothing planned—a world of opportunity out there to see. There was the casino across the street, the indoor pool…but then, the air conditioners quit working! The main electrical cord plug had bit the dust and caused the air conditioners to fail. Oh, no! It's 102 degrees outside!

Long story cut short: this afternoon, we made lots of telephone calls and rushed trips to town and another really rushed trip to a town an hour away, to an RV parts place before they closed and nearly running out of gas before we got there.

We purchased a replacement for the male end of the plug. We took it back to the rig and set to work. We were sitting outside in the brutal heat. Head to head, we both worked diligently to rewire the plug. We finally finished and plugged in the rig. In this heat, it would take some time to know if the air conditioner problem was fixed. If not, it was going to be a miserable night.

Lunch was a distant memory, so we decided that we deserved Mexican for supper, so we drove down into little Canyonville and had a delightful meal at El Paraiso. Once we arrived, I decided that I deserved an icy cold Margarita, too.

We finally took a dip in the pool to cool off, and by the time we returned to the rig, it was nice and cool.

God Answers Prayer! It will be a very good, cool night.

JULY 30

It was certainly a calmer day, now that the air conditioners were working well. We figured we would just stay inside, safe from the heat today and get some work done. Larry spent all day online, making future campground reservations. I spent all day posting July's transactions and reconciling the checkbooks.

We grilled supper, then headed over to the Casino. Hourly ticket drawings will be held up until the 11pm drawing, when the car would be given away.

We discovered an evening of BINGO going on upstairs. Now, I've occasionally played BINGO in church halls for decades. But I had never played it with an iPad. Well, it wasn't actually an iPad, but it was some type of hand-held touch pad. We paid our fee at the registration table and the lady hands us this thing. Excuse me, what do we do with this? She started it up and gave us a 30-second tutorial. Then we were left to our own devices. It was the coolest thing ever!

The pad played fifteen cards a game. It knew from its controlling computer what game we were playing, and what would constitute a BINGO. Each time they called a number, it instantly appeared marked on the card, the pad reprioritized the cards, by putting them in order by the total numbers covered. The first card was always the busiest card. When we were blessed with getting down to one number, that number would blink on the card. We quickly came to the conclusion that the pad did absolutely everything necessary except stand up and yell, "BINGO!"

They did play some paper cards during intermission, and we were forced to spend a whole dollar to purchase a hot pink dabber to play. We didn't win any of those games, either.

We went back to the floor and I won $7 on the slots. Not bad. Let me make it clear that we are not gamblers. We go in to play with a set budget in mind, something small like $10 or $20. When that's gone, we're done. Larry hates to play because he says he always loses. I just play for fun, entertainment, the excitement, the possibility of winning.

By 11pm, everyone was crowded near the entrance, where they would draw the winning ticket for the car. It was smoky inside, so we decided to wait outside in the cold. They had some of those nice gas warmers set up, so it wasn't too bad. Larry was fading. He was really pushing himself, because it was way past his bedtime.

It was finally time for the drawing, and you had to be present to win, so we went back inside. There had to be 100,000 tickets in that thing, maybe more! They rolled and rolled the large cage, then read the number on the ticket. Nope, it wasn't us, but a woman just a few feet away screamed. Then she cried. She was blabbering some story when a Casino worker interrupted and asked loudly, "Are you the same lady whose car broke down on the way here today?"

I was delighted to know that the winner wasn't some high roller that didn't need another new car. This woman was truly in need and God provided for her in a most amazing way.

God is good, all the time. All the time, God is good.

JULY 31

It was another early morning to drive to Harris Beach State Park in Brookings, Oregon, which Larry rated a 5. South, down I-5 again, southwest on US 199 and then north again on good old US 101, along the Oregon coast. We needed to fuel up the rig. Larry got out and began to pump when this attendant ran up and offered to do it. Larry declined his offer, but the attendant explained that it was against the law in Oregon for him to pump his own fuel. This was the first state we'd encountered that didn't allow self-serve. We didn't complain, but we thought it was worth mentioning.

We officially drove into California, then drove back into Oregon. California proved to be our 19th state in a little more than 120 days. We have done some traveling!

We don't like to backtrack, but it seems we've been doing a lot of that this past week. Today, we drove past a campground in Redwoods National Park, where we have reservations in just a few days. The giant redwoods are a sight to behold. We'll get back to them later.

The State Park is simple, and nice enough. We quickly drove to town in the car and went grocery shopping. We ate Chinese back in the motorhome, then headed down to the overlook to take photos of the sunset, which was beautiful. The pics we took this particular evening also wound up as some of our absolute best photos. The sun was a brilliant, bright, glowing orange ball of fire. It was a wonderful way to end the day.

It had been a clear day, but was chilly now. Where in the world was summer?

AUGUST 1

We had a knock on the door. A fellow camper explained that he had taken some of our packets for his kids and wanted to thank us for making them available, then praised our Motorhome Ministry. He offered a small donation to cover their cost. We had a great conversation about God in today's world. This is what this mission is all about. Doing what God wants each of us to do: spread the word of the Lord.

I was grateful for this man's encouragement because the devil was on our backs again. The levelers were now as unpredictable as the steps. Larry had been calling everywhere, trying to get someone to fix them.

The last guy had said it would take up to two weeks to get the parts. So, today Larry was calling ahead to areas we would be visiting two weeks from now, asking them to order the parts and put us in their schedule. "No, we won't order the parts until we diagnose that they are necessary." But we will pay in advance for them, if you order them. "No, we don't do that." Larry was so upset, and rightly so. How were we ever going to get these things fixed, without sitting in the same place for 2-3 weeks?

I decided to drive into the little downtown of Brookings. I stopped at a yarn/quilt shop I'd seen, *By My Hand*. It was actually two storefronts with a large opening in the middle—one side for fiber crafts and the other side for quilting and sewing crafts. Laurie was the lady who ran it, and she had some unique and terrific stuff in there. She was so nice, and we chatted a while. I can't dare buy anything in here, as I already have enough craft supplies to last through three broken legs!

I like ACE Hardware stores, so I dawdled in there next. They're usually in small towns and sometimes you can find the neatest stuff. I found a silicone collapsible funnel in there for $1. It's a great space saver.

When I returned to the motorhome, Larry was outside, still upset by the levelers. He'd been trying to diagnose the problem for weeks; what in the world could I do to help? I don't know anything about this stuff.

I quietly went inside and Googled it. That's a common response to things nowadays, just Google it. Even though Larry said he'd already done that, a fresh set of eyes wouldn't hurt. I put in all sorts of key words about the motorhome, the brand of levelers, whatever I knew.

I began to read. I knew it wasn't in the hydraulics, he had checked that long ago. Perhaps the circuitry? After reading just a few minutes, I approached him cautiously (you wives understand this) and said, "Um, why don't "we" take off the driver panel and check the connections for a loose wire? You've tried everything else. It wouldn't hurt to try this." He was game to try anything, at this point.

We unscrewed the cover plate and had barely raised it up when the problem became obvious. An electrical connection into the controller was loose. It must have gotten that way by all the bumpy roads we'd traveled. One minute later, the repair was complete. Dang. That was way too easy (and by the way, it's never malfunctioned since). They work GREAT!

Then Larry said something totally unexpected: "Well, while you're on a roll, you can figure out how to fix the steps, too!" Ooh, now the pressure was on. Back to Google.

He was under the motorhome, under the steps when I returned just about 5 minutes later. He had the electrical meter out checking connections and electrical currents, for the hundredth time. "Um, I have read several repair forums and I believe I know how to fix the steps," I said, "Do you have a hammer?"

He came out from under the rig, looked me straight in the eye and said, "Yeah. Why? What do I need a hammer for?" I knew what he was really thinking: you are such an idiot. A hammer. Right.

"Well," I explained, "It says sometimes motors have a bad spot in them, and if you tap it several times with a hammer, it will work."

So, he crawled out and got the hammer. He slammed that motor harder and more times than necessary, more out of pent-up frustration than anything. He secretly wished his actions would prove I was an idiot.

Time for the big test. I started the engine of the rig and closed the door. The steps withdrew, as they should. Aha! I opened the door and they extended. Is it true? Closed the door. Opened the door. Again. Again. And again.

Praise Jesus in Heaven! Thank you, Lord! They work!

From that point, the repair would be easy. We now knew for sure that the motor was faulty. Larry ordered the motor and had it sent to our PO Box in Myrtle Beach. It did take several weeks, but it was no matter now. We kept the hammer handy, so that every time the steps didn't work,

Larry slammed it again. It worked every single time—and every single time now, we laughed.

AUGUST 2

We moved the motorhome today to a harbor-front campground, Beachfront RV, Port Brookings, Oregon, which Larry rated a 3. It was just a few miles from the State Park. The sites are simple, but this one is waterfront, on the beach in the harbor area.

With full utilities now, I spent all day catching up the laundry and enjoying the view.

It was a very short walk to the beach. It wasn't a pretty beach like you would see back in South Carolina. The sand is much darker and there are lots of rocks—small pebbles to huge boulders—everywhere. The water was muddy, but I wasn't planning to get in anyway.

The sun was shining and the breeze felt good.

We grilled shrimp for supper, enjoying the view of the waterfront.

AUGUST 3

It was another beautiful, sunny day in Oregon. I went back to the yarn shop again today, just for something to do.

I spotted a completed knit cap that really got my attention. I have knitted literally hundreds of caps for charity over the years. I won't go into detail here, because most of you aren't interested in knitting patterns, but I did put it in the back of the book, for those of you who are. When I got back to the motorhome, I began a new bright red ribbed cap, with white as a secondary, interwoven color—my high school colors. It turned out great, and it was only one of many that I mailed to my home church, to be included in Operation Christmas Child Shoeboxes.

Larry wandered the harbor and walked the neighboring jetty. He took photos of the pelicans and the crab boats, as they were coming in for the day. He followed one back into port. The skipper had caught a good number of red Dungeness crabs. Then he'd set up shop at the dock. He was selling the crabs for $10 each, alive or quick boiled. Larry paid for one already cooked, and the skipper gave him further instructions on how to reheat it later.

Larry returned to the motorhome, toting his crab in a bucket, announcing that he had caught supper while he'd been out. We laughed. Later, with drawn butter, it was delicious.

AUGUST 4

I didn't make any notes regarding this very un-notable day. I know that it was finally warm and sunny enough (both on the same day) that I sat outside in a camp chair for over an hour. I also managed to get myself a sunburn.

But I had no regrets. The weather up here in the northwest has been so cloudy and rainy and cool, I was delighted to be outside long enough to earn a sunburn.

Tomorrow is a travel day, so I made sure that absolutely everything was washed and up to date, and that the freezer and fridge were full.

AUGUST 5

We departed early and headed down US 101 to head through the redwoods of California in the motorhome. We would spend the night at Jedidiah Smith Redwoods State Park, in Crescent City, California, which Larry rated a 3.

The Redwoods National Park and State Park is about 65 square miles. It was only a short distance down the coast from Brookings. It's usually foggy in the mornings and it takes most of the afternoon to burn off. Today was no exception. We were blessed to have a day without rain, but it sure remains humid.

The trees are so BIG and high. The redwoods' real name is *Sequoia Sempervirens*. If you've never seen them in person, you just can't imagine the height and sheer mass of the trees. They can reach heights of 425 feet and be 26 feet in diameter. They once grew in a much larger area, but are now confined to a narrow strip in the Pacific Northwest. Some of the trees have been here before the birth of Christ— over 2,000 years old and still alive! A lot of redwoods succumbed to loggers in the 1800's, so we're grateful they are now protected by the National Park Service.

The campground was a navigational nightmare! The canopy was low and the road was narrow and winding. Larry slowly maneuvered through the maze of trees. After we took off the car, backing into the tight site took careful communication on the walkies to keep from hitting any trees. This campground was set up decades ago, and just wasn't made for today's larger motorhomes. But we took it slow and careful and we made it. No bumps, bruises, crashes, or scratches, on me or the motorhome. Once we set up, we were off in the car to explore.

We drove the car first to the Visitor Center to see the park's movie and get my Passport stamped. Once again, we learned of the Native Americans who were first to settle here. The special bond they have with nature is apparent in all the National Parks, who do an amazing job of educating the public regarding restoration and conservation.

We drove on to Stout Grove, about a mile away, which was a massive grove of some of the highest redwoods in the park. We parked the car and walked the half-mile loop through the redwoods and ground ferns. The trees are magnificent and so high! The sunlight was struggling to shine through the canopy. There were fallen trees that have been left untouched and rotting.

We took lots of photos here, too. Some of the fallen trees had fallen with their roots intact, and ten times as wide as we are tall—like sixty feet wide! It was a beautiful, quiet, and magical walk through the ancient redwood giants.

We left the Grove and headed down a winding dirt logging road through the Redwoods in their full glory. There was a mist there, almost unearthly, that seemed to shimmer in the broken sunlight. After just a few miles, we arrived in Crescent City, California.

We visited The Crescent City information center and the beachfront Thomas H. Kuchel Visitor Center on the way south on US 101 to Napa Valley. The coast is stunning. The blue Pacific Ocean, waves, surf, and sun, along with patchy fog create stunning views from cliffs alongside of the highway. We drove back to the motorhome and enjoyed a small supper. What an amazing day it had been!

AUGUST 6

We spent a lot of hours on the road today, in the motorhome. We passed beautiful sunflower fields and vineyards throughout Sonoma County. We have tried to limit driving to three or four hours a day, but we really wanted to get to our destination in Napa Valley, California.

Since entering California, the first thing we noticed was the condition of the roads. They are the worst! They all seem to be badly in need of repair. They have the highest gas taxes in the nation, but the worst roads. Go figure!

The motorhome rounded another bend and there stood a fifty-foot Paul Bunyan and Babe blue ox! It was clearly a tourist trap and it worked. They got us to stop!

We soon realized this wasn't a typical tourist trap. Its name is "The Trees of Mystery" in Klamath, California, and it's located 36 miles south of the Oregon border on US 101. It's on private land and was founded in 1931; it's surrounded by Redwood National and State Parks.

For over 65 years they have been entertaining and educating visitors from around the world about this natural preserve and Indian museum.

There were trails through the redwoods and even a Skytrail gondola lift, that took us 1,570 feet up, so we were above the redwood forest canopy. You could see the forest as well as the ocean from up there. We walked past the Brotherhood Tree, a massive redwood tree at 297 feet high and 19 feet in diameter. It was definitely worth the stop!

After spending hours driving through the beautiful California forests, we arrived at the Sky Wilderness Park, a county-owned park in Napa Valley, which Larry rated a 2.

We arrived late in the day, set up quickly and headed out for supper at the Panda Express in Napa.

Outside the restaurant, sitting almost in front of the door, was a Mexican woman holding up a cardboard, hand printed sign that read, "My husband was deported and I have no money to feed my 2 kids." My heart was heavy, as was Larry's. Once inside, we asked the restaurant staff about her and were told that she's out there several days a week. Larry was led to give her a little something. He did speak to her in some of the little Spanish he knows, "Jesús te ama," translated means Jesus loves you. Larry gave her some money, which he felt God was telling him to do.

I have always felt firm about illegal immigrants: if you come illegally, then you broke the law. It shouldn't be a surprise if we make you go back. It's not as though you can't come at all, and there is a way to do it right. Do it right.

We rarely give cash, because we never know how it will be used. Napa Valley seems so affluent, but there is also poverty.

We are indeed seeing lots of things we'd never seen before, and I believe God wants us to share these things with you in this book, to get you thinking about these matter, too. Hopefully, we are becoming better souls because of these journeys, and perhaps you can be, too.

---

1 Samuel 2:7

⁷ The LORD sends poverty and wealth;
he humbles and he exalts.

AUGUST 7

We took off in the car to explore Napa Valley! We did drink a glass of wine here and there. Oh my, a Christian who drinks, and a Baptist no less! But, there is no place in the Bible that Jesus forbids drinking spirits, but there are plenty of places that God warns us to stay sober. What few occasions we do drink, we drink only one.

> 1 Peter 5:8
> Be alert and of sober mind.
> Your enemy the devil prowls around
> like a roaring lion
> looking for someone to devour.

We both love only the sweeter wines, so they can keep all that dry stuff. But, to visit where most of the wines are made was a travel day to cherish.

The valley is between mountains on all sides. The lush greenery in the landscape is full of grapes in the fertile soil of central California. It is nearing the harvest season when we arrived, and a few have already begun. There are about 400 wineries with tasting rooms in the Napa Valley, and over 600 if you include Sonoma county. We couldn't visit them all!

So, we went to a few that we thought would be the most interesting to visit. These wineries are showcases for their wine and label. They are beautifully landscaped with chateaus like mansions all over the hills. Some structures display beautiful architecture most reminiscent of old Europe and some were modern contemporary designs. The valley is made up of several smaller towns.

"Visit the towns of Napa Valley and find out what makes each one distinct.

<u>Calistoga:</u> Famous for their hot springs and mud baths, Calistoga is the place to unwind and relax.

<u>St. Helena:</u> A picturesque town with scores of shops, wineries, restaurants, and swanky hotels.

<u>Oakville & Rutherford:</u> Visit these two towns for some of the best Cabernet and Chardonnay wines in Napa Valley.

<u>Yountville:</u> Yountville is a food and wine lover's dream that also boasts a lively culture and arts scene.

<u>Napa:</u> Find a vibrant night life and unexpected blend of urban activities in the town of Napa."[25]

A list of some of the notable wineries in the area that we toured:

<u>Artesa Winery:</u> From the main road, all you can see is the top of the back of the building, which is built down within the hill. But the winery itself is an artistic sanctuary with a multi-level fountain overlooking the hills and valley.

<u>Beringer Vineyards:</u> We toured this winery and their barrel cellars, and learned their history.

<u>Castello di Amorosa:</u> a medieval castle in the midst of chateaus, complete with a moat, a drawbridge and a herd of goats. There were beautiful flowers amid the landscaping.

<u>Chateau Montelena:</u> an old French-looking building made of stone and covered in ivy. It was our first tour.

<u>Inglenook:</u> Francis and Eleanor Coppola purchased the property in 1975. You've all heard of Francis Ford Coppola the director, aka Nicholas Cage's uncle. It had

---

[25] napavalley.com

beautiful stained glass and a wooden staircase entrance, overlooking a huge fountain. Down among the barrel cellars, there were beautiful tasting rooms for any size of gathering, with large, hand-painted murals. There was a beautiful lattice overhead filled with grapevines, burgeoning with grapes. I took photos of a bird who had nested among the vines. There was also a very interesting film history museum upstairs.

Robert Mondavi Winery: After the tour, we ordered a glass of wine and a cheese tray for lunch. We ate outside at an umbrella table, overlooking acres of grapes.

PEJU Province: The winery and tasting rooms were surrounded by acres of grapevines. There were large yellow flowers blooming outside on tall stalks. They resembled sunflowers but had a bloom like a massive zinnia, over a foot across. The staff explained they are Teddy Bear Sunflowers.

Mumm Napa: there were mountains of colorful wildflowers everywhere!

Domaine Carneros: This was a beautiful structure with outdoor seating at tables with umbrellas. From the back, we could see them forklifting cases of freshly-picked grapes (they allowed us to take some). Grapes for wine-making are really tiny—about the size of a pea—somewhat bitter, and not at all like the sweet table grapes you eat. We could look in the large doors to see the clean and tidy warehouse and the stainless-steel processing equipment inside.

Round Pond Estate: they had a beautiful palm tree-lined driveway.

I took photos of a cute little winery down in town that was built in an old Texaco-looking gas station. The old garage area had been converted into a wine-tasting bar, with a large sign above the bar, "Lubrication."

Just a note: we began to notice there were rose bushes planted at the ends of the grapevine rows in many of the vineyards. We assumed that it would have something to do with pollination, but we were wrong. We learned both roses and grapevines are susceptible to some of the same diseases. Roses help to show early signs of mildew, which is a fungal disease, so that the grapevines can be treated early. Wow, who knew?

Wine tasting can get really expensive over the course of a day, most of them we saw were $50ish - each. The tours are pricey, in the $100's too, depending upon what's included. There were a lot of young millennials from the upper crust of San Francisco and Silicon Valley area. Some were dressed to the hilt, as if going to a formal dinner party, the ladies wearing fashionable hats to match their dresses and shoes. The men were decked out too, with their facial hair, expensive shirts, and loose ties. They were having a great time.

If you are visiting here, you should take the time and money to take at least one tour and tasting. After visiting the valley, it's no wonder that the USA is becoming the largest wine producer in the world, second to none.

> Amos 9:13
>
> ¹³ "The days are coming," declares the LORD,
> "when the reaper will be overtaken by the plowman
> and the planter by the one treading grapes.
> New wine will drip from the mountains
> and flow from all the hills.

AUGUST 8

Today we visited the famous Jelly Belly factory in Fairfield, California. Jelly Belly Candy Company, formerly known as Herman Goelitz Candy Company and Goelitz Confectionery Company, manufactures Jelly Belly jelly beans and other candy. We sold literally hundreds of tons of these little beans over the eighteen years we owned Pop 'N Stuff. I once considered myself quite the Bean Connoisseur! Those little beans really do have a special place in our hearts, and I have been looking forward to this tour for years.

To finally see them making a batch from raw materials to finished product was really a WOW experience. They make dozens of flavors and colors of beans, and the ingredients for each batch are measured by hand. Although machines do a lot of the production work, they are carefully tended to by employees who want only the best finished products. Toward the end of the production cycle, there was one woman whose sole job it was to pick out the Belly Flops, the beans that are not up to quality standards in size, shape, or color.

Throughout the tour, we could view close up the dozens of portraits of famous folks—made completely with Jelly Belly beans! Princess Diana, Ronald Reagan, Elvis Presley, the Mona Lisa, Ma & Pa Kettle, Wonder Woman,

Harry Potter, Yoda, and lots more. See them at jellybelly.com.

The store is fantastic with everything Jelly Belly. I can't believe we bought five bags of Belly Flops and enjoyed them for weeks. We even enjoyed a special wine pairing at the end of the tour. For a nominal fee, they paired samples of five wines to some of their confections and chocolates.

While running some other errands in Fairfield, we decided to try Jack in the Box for the first time. We were cheerfully greeted by the young lady who asked for my order. I was the only person in line, so I explained that it was my very first time at a Jack in the Box. I took a few moments and decided to order their Classic Buttery Jack with cheese, fries, and a drink. Simple. I made sure she understood that I did not want mustard on my sandwich. The food was slow to come, and I used the time to get our drink cup filled. But I couldn't, because there was no Diet Coke. I told the cashier, but she apologized that there was no one available to change the syrup box. We settled on Diet Root Beer instead. Finally at the table with our food, I discovered mustard on the sandwich. I returned to the counter and requested another sandwich, this one without mustard, please. The same cashier cheerfully complied. I returned to the table again, and Larry complained about the fries, as they'd obviously been fried in old grease, and tasted nasty. I went up to the counter again and politely complained about the condition of the fries. The cashier replied she was aware the oil needed to be changed, but they hadn't had time to change it. She offered me onion rings in exchange. "Weren't they fried in the same oil?" I asked. "Oh, no," she said. Okay, onion rings. They were just as bad.

I went back to her again and politely asked to see the manager on duty. I'd worked in retail most of my adult life, and I know what a request for the MOD means. The person in charge is to drop everything and take care of the problem at hand. The cashier left the counter, but came back alone. "The manager said she can't talk to you right now. She can't refund your money, but you can have anything you want to replace the fries." Unbelievable! As soon as we got back to the motorhome, I wrote a scathing email to the company. I was patient and polite at every turn, as was the young cashier. I received a prompt reply AND a personal phone call from corporate management.

As I went through the story all over again on the phone, my main complaint was not just the food, but the unseen manager who chose not come forward. As I had said in the email, I repeated to the man on the phone that I had no intention of trying Jack in the Box again, to be treated like this. He apologized again and said he would be sending me some coupons in the mail, asking that we give them another try. Weeks later, in a box of mail from Diana, there were indeed coupons, each for a complete meal. We decided to try again, since there was no cost to us.

I regret that I don't recall where we used those coupons, but the cashier took one look at the coupon and said, "You had either a great experience or a really bad one to receive one of these." I smiled and said, "Really bad." This time, the service was great, the food was exactly as ordered, hot and delicious. Lesson learned: give someone a second chance. This time, it was well worth it.

We ran some errands while in Fairfield, then hit another couple of wineries this beautifully warm and sunny Jelly Belly day.

What a day!

AUGUST 9

We drove the motorhome the short 55-minute trip from Napa Valley to San Francisco, by way of Route 29 to Route 37 west. We stayed at Marin RV Park, Greenbrae, California, that Larry rated a 3. It was basic but sufficient, more like a parking lot with hookups on the edge of the bay.

This first day, we walked from the campground several blocks to the ferry terminal. We were a bit confused at first about how to purchase tickets and where to go to ride, but with the help of strangers, we figured it out. We left the Larkspur Ferry Terminal and rode across the cold and choppy bay water to the main San Francisco ferry terminal along the wharf. The ferry was nearly full, busy with late-morning commuters. The weather surprised us, because after all, it was August. We had worn only light jackets and the wind cut right through us. The wind over the cold water becomes a natural air conditioner.

Coming out of the terminal, we chugged right past San Quentin. It was an eerie feeling passing that cold structure, knowing that Charles Manson was in there somewhere, along with others on death row.

Scott Peterson was there, too. He was convicted of killing his wife Laci, who was 8 months pregnant with their first child, Conner, and dumping her body in San Francisco Bay on Christmas Eve, 2002. He has maintained his innocence, but the jury found otherwise.

> Numbers 35:16
>
> [16] If anyone strikes someone a fatal blow
> with an iron object,
> that person is a murderer;
> the murderer is to be put to death.

We could finally see the famous Golden Gate Bridge in the distance. When it was completed in 1936, the structure was painted with primer. When citizens were asked what color they wanted it painted, the majority said they liked it just the way it was. It has been painted and repainted with primer color ever since. It stood tall in its usual foggy grandeur. Out in the distance in the bay, we could see the notorious, now vacant, Alcatraz Prison. The National Park Service offers tours of Alcatraz, but tickets are required and so much in demand, that you have to get them months in advance. We finally docked at the main ferry terminal, which is quite nice, lined inside with dozens of shops and restaurants.

There were crowds of people that morning, although we'd missed the earlier rush hour. In Larry's opinion, you wouldn't need a car to live here. They have excellent mass transit systems: ferry, bus, and rail trolley cars.

We passed many homeless as we walked through the wharf area. They were invisible to those on their daily commute. We prayed for them. We took a very crowded, 1940's rail trolley car to Fisherman's Wharf.

The wharf area is composed of Pier 35 to Pier 41, wooden piers that stretch out into the bay. There are shops, restaurants, museums, and even a merry-go-round. There were large displays of fresh fruit and candies.

The bells they ring on the rail trolley cars sound just like the old Rice A Roni commercials: The San Francisco Treat! The city's cable cars are the only National Historical Monument that can move.

There were people everywhere, elbow to elbow in some places. It was a sunny but cool day. The smells were mixed. The bay was fishy smelling and yet you could smell cotton candy and funnel cakes. Sea lions were abundant, and they are really stinky.

We decided we would spend tomorrow taking a sightseeing bus tour of the city.

We rode the ferry back during rush hour (what were we thinking?) and walked back to the campground before dark. It had been a busy but great day.

AUGUST 10

Yesterday, we had walked from the campground to the ferry terminal. Today, we rode our bikes. Well, Larry rode his, but I had a terrible time with mine. Most of the journey was through this really narrow, high-sided concrete walkway, with busy highway traffic just over the left side and water just over the right. I understood the purpose of the sides, I just couldn't steer the bike within that small margin of error. I walked it partway, collided with the concrete a couple times, and actually fell once. Poor Larry kept stopping to check on me, with a look of pity on his face. After crashing my knee and knuckles into the concrete and drawing blood, I was pretty upset by the time we reached the pier. Why can't I get this bicycle-riding thing down as I did when I was a child?

When I'd calmed down, Larry joked later he was afraid the headlines in the San Francisco Chronicle the next day would read, "Old Lady falls off Bicycle onto Expressway and becomes Road Kill." Funny.

We finally arrived, chained the bikes and took the ferry, same as yesterday, then bought tickets for the Hop On Hop Off bus tour.

The bus took us as far as the Visitor Center at the foot of the famous San Francisco-Oakland Bay Bridge. It was a tight, congested, and busy place, with people parking, eating, and getting ready to walk the Bridge trail. Everyone had to get off the bus and wait to Hop On another one that would take us across the bridge to Sausalito. The small town is across the bridge, on the "quiet" side of the bay.

The trip over the bridge is definitely etched into my memory. It was 60 degrees today, but it was windy. Between the cold water in the bay, overcast, foggy, and windy, the resulting wind chill must have been in the low 40's. Riding on the top deck of the tour bus in my light jacket pulled up over my head, I thought I would freeze, get blown off the bus, or both. In hindsight, it was hilariously laughable.

Traffic was coming and going with commuters and tourists. As we crossed, you could hear the bridge sing: hmm.

We got off in Sausalito to walk around. It was full of little shops, pubs, and restaurants. And it was busy. For lunch, we settled in at a hole-in-the-wall café called, Venice Gourmet with only four tables, outside on the waterfront. We watched everyone enjoying the day while enjoying clam chowder, cheese, and a panini.

We enjoyed so much and saw so much more by letting others drive us around. We never once used our own car there.

We got on and off the bus several times in the two days we rode it. Today we got off the bus and walked the hilly streets through Chinatown. The first Chinese arrived in San Francisco in 1848, and it was like stepping into another country. The signs of the shops that lined the streets were all in Chinese, and filled with products from China. Large red Chinese lanterns were strung back and forth, above the streets. I wanted to see what treasures were held inside each store!

We ate lunch at a beautiful Chinese restaurant, called The Far East on Grant Avenue. a very ornate establishment with fancy Chinese art and statues. The waiters and hosts were all dressed in traditional Chinese clothes. We enjoyed a traditional fortune cookie after a filling meal of Sweet and Sour Chicken. Larry left a Motorhome Ministry brochure and seed packet in the hopes that God's word would be read in this place, too.

After lunch, we set out to find where those fortune cookies had been made. Thank God again for Google; Frank took us right up Grant Avenue, turned us west on Jackson, and then down Ross Alley.

The storefront was so small, we nearly missed it. But the wonderful aroma and the line out the front door assured us we were in the right place.

The Golden Gate Fortune Cookie Factory has been supplying fortune cookies around the world since 1962. We stood close to watch three Chinese women working at three odd-looking machines.

The batter is poured into molds automatically, then travel on a conveyer belt system through an oven. The cookies come out baked, small, round, flat, hot, and soft. The operators carefully place the small paper fortune on each cookie. Then each cookie is folded over a steel rod and the machine crimps it into a fortune cookie. They work very quickly, before the cookies cool and harden.

We watched in amazement at how quickly they're made. Every several seconds, the women have made three more. There was a man there, offering samples in hopes of making a sale. It worked. We bought several packages to enjoy. We then noticed a sign that said if you took a picture, you must pay fifty cents. We paid the fee and snapped the photo.

FYI: did you know that fortune cookies were originally invented by someone from Japan that lived in San Francisco? Who knew?

The bus also took us through the famous Haight-Ashbury district, where the hippie culture was born. The "Summer of Love" of 1967 actually began in the winter before. Those times were filled with sex, drugs, and rock 'n roll. My opinion is that it's pretty much like that still today, 50 years later.

The hippie movement was born as a revolt to the government and the Vietnam war—a revolt against the American establishment. Sounds familiar, doesn't it? The bus passed psychedelic-looking shops and bars, set between large Victorian houses in all sorts of colors. I remember one shop had the giant shapely legs of a woman with fishnet stockings hanging out of a second-story window. I suppose they considered that "art."

"While the Haight-Ashbury eventually became known as the center for hippies, acid, and acid rock music, it was also the center of many artistic efforts, including painting, poetry, performance art, comics, posters, and literature of all kinds. The Haight-Ashbury's music scene thrived and continues to shine like a beacon of the psychedelic age, as everyone now knows the music of the Grateful Dead, Jefferson Airplane, Big Brother and the Holding Company, along with Janis Joplin, Quicksilver, the Steve Miller Band, and friends from Berkeley including Creedence Clearwater Revival and Country Joe and the Fish, and many other lesser-known but amazingly talented bands."[26] They lived here because the rent was cheap. Not so today. Jimmy Hendrix even has a mural on the side of a building dedicated to him.

One thing we noticed was the great number of homeless in the area. I researched this further to discover that "Data Shows San Francisco Has Second Highest Homeless Population in United States"[27], second to New York City. In the downtown financial district, through the city parks were groves of tarps, tents, and cardboard boxes for the homeless. It was all very sad to see.

We both witnessed a guy unzipping his pants to pee in front of everyone on the bus. He wasn't even embarrassed, just brazen. This will not be the first nor the last time we'd see this. Where have our morals and common decency gone?

---

[26] rockument.com/blog/haight-ashbury-in-the-sixties/

[27] abc7news.com/news/data-shows-sf-has-2nd-highest-homeless-population-in-us/1407123/

The bus passed by Lombard Street, the crookedest street in the US, beautifully laden with colorful flowers. We also saw Filbert Street between Hyde and Leavenworth Streets, the steepest in the city—at 31.5 degrees!

The driver pointed out that congresswoman Nancy Pelosi lived on top of one of the hills near the bridge. We also saw OJ Simpson's High school, which was named after him, then after his trial, was renamed Galileo High School. We passed the house used in the TV series *Full House*, and was just down the street from the house where the late Robin Williams played *Mrs. Doubtfire*.

We went right past St. Paul's Catholic Church. It is a large, grand structure, a parish church of the Roman Catholic Archdiocese of San Francisco, that you would recognize as the church used for *Sister Act*, starring Whoopi Goldberg. And did you ever see the movie *Bullet* with Steve McQueen driving up and down the hills? The guide told us it was filmed all along the bus route. And many of you remember *Streets of San Francisco*, starring Karl Malden and the very young Michael Douglas. (I loved that show!) The list could go on and on, but these are all examples of moments that have touched our lives that can be traced to this area.

We got off the bus at the Ghirardelli Chocolate Factory. The factory is no longer there, but their retail store and ice cream parlor have plenty of magnificent offerings. They even gave me 2 free samples, just for walking in! It was a sunny, blue sky day. The cold water of the bay kept the entire area cool. There were plenty of folks down there swimming, most with wet suits on. I personally think anybody that swims in that cold water *without* a wet suit is just nuts.

We walked to the San Francisco Maritime National Historical Park and National Monument, located on the edge of San Francisco Bay, in the Fisherman's Wharf neighborhood. It was a small place, and I got another stamp for my Passport.

For supper, we strolled to Cioppino's and enjoyed their famous seafood stew. "Cioppino is a tomato-based seafood stew that was invented by the San Francisco Italian fisherman of North Beach in the 1800s, using whatever seafood was left over from the day's catch. Often it was crab, shrimp, clams, and fish, which were then combined with onions, garlic, and tomatoes. Then everything was cooked with herbs in olive oil and wine. Originally it was made on the boats while out at sea and in the Italians' homes, but as the Italian restaurants started sprouting up around the wharf, Cioppino moved into the restaurant and became a very popular dish."[28] It was delicious! Although I've never made it, you can find the recipe in the back of the book.

AUGUST 11

Today was our last day in San Francisco and we wanted to be sure we hadn't missed anything. We rode our bikes to the ferry again. Well, I tried to ride and took the ferry again to cross the bay. At least today was sunnier and seemed a bit warmer than it had been.

We walked up to the Hop on Hop Off stop and rode it all the way. We had a different tour guide, of course, who told the stories just a little bit differently than the guy had done the day before.

---

[28]avitaltours.com/san-francisco/history-of-san-francisco-cioppino

We remembered places that we had whizzed by way too quickly yesterday and tried to get photos today. We noticed more Victorian purple houses than we had noticed before, and just the sun shining made things look different. I thought of Diana because she loves anything purple. Our tour guide even sang *I left My Heart in San Francisco* at the end of the tour today. Tony Bennett would have been proud.

It had been a wonderful trip here in city on the Bay; one we will never forget.

Genesis 11:4

⁴ Then they said, "Come, let us build ourselves a city, with a tower that reaches to the heavens, so that we may make a name for ourselves; otherwise we will be scattered over the face of the whole earth."

AUGUST 12

Today was a travel day to San Jose, California.

Do you know the way to San Jose? It was quite the popular song back in the 60's. We took I-580 in rush hour to the I-880 through Oakland. Then, US 101 took us to the next campground, Coyote Valley RV Resort. As usual, we put up our Motorhome Ministry banner and our free kid packets. We had chosen to stay here because its location would serve as a central base camp to travel to Silicon Valley, and other area attractions.

The Facebook office was a 37-minute trip north on US 101 to Palo Alto, California. We took a picture of the sign and drove the campus. There are so many buildings and employees on bikes going from place to place. But, no Visitor Center; we were disappointed.

We left and drove only 13 minutes to arrive at Google. It was a lot like Facebook—plenty of buildings and people riding colorful bikes to get between buildings. Google also had no Visitor Center, only a store full of high priced Google-branded "stuff": T-shirts, caps, cups and mugs—a tourist shop for sure! We took photos of the campus and the Google sign.

We have been using Google for most of the trip, and I have a great respect for it. I mean, Frack has made his share of mistakes, but look at the amazing things it *can* do. Their maps and directions have been a Godsend in a strange area where we don't know the roads. It's even more helpful with parking this big rig, especially with a tow dolly. With a dolly, you can't just back up and turn around, and a simple stop at a McDonalds could turn into a catastrophe! I can pull up an area on Google Maps so close, that I can see their entrance and exit, the number of parking spaces and decide if there's a place to park or turn this beast around.

To the south, we visited NASA at the Ames Research Center, about 8 minutes from Google. We didn't even know NASA was there; we just saw a sign on the freeway and decided to stop by. It certainly makes sense to have a research center in the heart of Silicon Valley. Their Visitor Center was a small but interesting place to learn about their programs—past, present, and future. There was information about the Mars Lander and the information it will provide for future space travels. I took a picture of myself as seen by a thermal monitor. Funky. We even got to see a moon rock!

When we finished at NASA, Apple's main campus and retail store in Cupertino was only 11 minutes away. We parked and tried to enter their retail store, but it was packed elbow to elbow with twenty-somethings. They were grabbing up iPhones, iPads, all of those new watches they have now, and every accompanying accessory they could put their hands on. The amount of money exchanging hands during our short visit was mind boggling. How do they afford to eat?

We had one last stop we wanted to make in this busy, congested, but pretty area. We drove another 14 minutes to arrive at eBay main headquarters. It was a glass building that I figured would be much bigger. And it was another place with no Visitor Center.

I'd like to make a suggestion to anyone with power who's reading this book: all you guys in Silicon Valley need Visitor Centers. We were just two of how many people in the area who would have enjoyed seeing the personal side of your companies. A place to walk through, filled with amazing pictures of amazing moments, facts and figures about your origin, development, and ongoing success. Maybe a look at the computer or server you started out on. Facts about the history of your company. Sure, we could look it up online and read it, but that's no fun to us. And your on-site stores shouldn't be more expensive than your goods in the open market. It's something to think about.

Among high-tech leaders, only Microsoft and Amazon are not here, but in Seattle. We wanted to visit Amazon, but forgot that it was in Seattle. It seems the leaders of the pack stay very, very close to one another.

We took the drive back to the motorhome and enjoyed supper. Then we watched *The Heist* on DVD. It was a complicated, let's-go-rob-a-casino movie, but I did enjoy it.

There should be a meteor shower tonight, and I went to bed wondering if it would be worth getting up in the middle of the night to watch. Probably too much light here, anyway. Nah, way too tired to get back up.

AUGUST 13

It was a much quieter, slower day in San Jose.

We caught up on *Scandal* on Netflix, I did some laundry, then we watched some more. We enjoyed the pool and the hot tub. It felt so good to lay there in the warm sun until I dried.

We enjoyed White Castles for lunch, then made a quick trip to Walmart for some groceries.

While eating supper, we heard a knock on the door. The campground manager introduced himself and apologized for the interruption.

He relayed that the campground owner had called him. Apparently, our Motorhome Ministry banner had offended someone, who had called the owner to complain. We could tell the manager was very upset to have to carry out these orders.

Well, this wasn't the first time. We immediately came out to remove the "offensive" stuff, all the while the poor guy kept on apologizing. We told him how some folks feel we're soliciting, but we're not. We don't ask for donations. We don't charge anything for the materials. But, we will comply.

Larry refrained from rating this campground, for obvious reasons. The manager made it clear that he didn't agree with the owner, and it was sad that the owner mandated this on behalf of only one complainer. But we reassured the poor guy that we clearly understood his predicament. God, bless you, sir.

We will "dust" our feet off, and move on to the next city tomorrow, anyway. God is in control.

AUGUST 14

We left early, because we had a long day ahead. We have been looking forward to Yosemite!

We drove long across the central part of California. The extreme drought was obvious. Farmers throughout the area were clearly Trump supporters, with large signs and billboards everywhere we looked. This sure is the exact opposite from what the large cities out here proclaimed.

The farmers are crying out for water to be diverted to these rich growing fields instead of up to San Francisco. I would come to learn just how much of our produce comes from this part of California. Further research of this subject amazed me. California is the largest producer of almonds in the world, and the second largest producer of pistachios. I had no idea that California grows the following percentages of total US production: "95% of apricots, 100% of artichokes, 90% of avocados, 90% of broccoli, 75% of cantaloupe, 80% of carrots, 95% of celery, 99% of dates, 100% of dried figs, 98% of kiwi, 92% of lemons, 90% of lettuce, 95% of nectarines, 99% of olive oil, 97% of plums, 99% of pomegranates, 80% of strawberries, and 99% of walnuts. And, they're the largest producer of both garlic and tomatoes."[29] Wow.

We traveled Route 152 east to Route 140 east right into Yosemite Campground. But, not without frustration. Again.

On our way through the Sierra Nevada Mountain, the oil and water warning lights on the dashboard suddenly lit up. This had never happened before! Larry pulled over to the side of the road, a major feat, considering the deep ravine within feet of my door.

The motorhome was overheated. We let it cool a bit, then added coolant and some oil. We drove on, and everything seemed okay.

The road was narrow and winding, a challenge for this big rig and tow. There were tunnels and drop offs to the stream. It's a good thing Larry's a pro at this now, but he drove slow and cautious.

The traffic coming in with us was bumper to bumper. It was busy, but it was summer. Everything was filled.

At one point of the road, we had to cross a VERY narrow temporary bridge across the stream. I looked out my side of the rig to see a large landslide that had buried the entire road. There were actually two of these temporary bridges on this newly laid detour.

But then, the engine lights came on again. With no place to pull over, Larry continued to fret each mile we

---

[29] keepcaliforniafarming.org/which-foods-come-from-california/

drove. The next time he could pull over, he checked the oil stick: we were three quarts low! He always carried one quart, but he had already put that one in earlier. Where in this world could we buy oil for a diesel truck engine?

We finally pull into the registration area. And guess what? Wait for it…the steps didn't extend. The devil was having his way with Larry today!

Larry rated the North Pines Campground at 5, simply because they didn't have any utility hookups. It was very much like Yellowstone, but the beauty here in the valley made it great.

We pulled into our campsite to learn that it was 103 degrees here today. And no air conditioning! But the sun set quickly and it began to cool. Somewhere in the night it was 50 degrees and we slept soundly.

Despite all, God is good. We are here. We are safe. We are blessed.

AUGUST 15

The reservations we had here had been made one year in advance. In August of last year, we both had gotten up early, opened both computers and stood ready for the 7am release of campsites. We looked and sounded like two crazy people trading at the opening of the stock exchange. The system requires you to request a specific site to reserve, so Larry had prepared two lists of sites that would be large enough for our rig, and each of us started at the top. No, that one's taken. Nope, that one, too. No, to the second one. YES!! I captured the third campsite on my list. We were going to Yosemite!

"Yosemite National Park includes nearly 1,200 square miles of mountainous scenery, including high cliffs, deep valleys, tall waterfalls, ancient giant sequoias, and a large wilderness. Millions of people visit Yosemite each year to experience its beauty and its many opportunities for enjoyment.

"Not just a great valley, but a shrine to human foresight, the strength of granite, the power of glaciers, the persistence of life, and the tranquility of the High Sierra. First protected in 1864, Yosemite National Park is best known for its waterfalls, but within its nearly 1,200 square miles, you can find deep valleys, grand meadows, ancient giant sequoias, a vast wilderness area, and much more."[30] Over four million people visit this park each year, and in 2016, we will be counted as two of them.

When God made this valley, He made it to be a part of Heaven on earth. There are sheer cliffs standing 7,000 feet up on all sides. There are usually waterfalls, but due to the draught and the time of year, most were dried up.

First matter of business was to get the steps fixed. Larry spent some time under the rig, trying to figure out what was wrong, after they had worked so well. He finally resorted to the hammer, bang, they worked! We were finally ready to start a day of adventure.

But the first stop had to be to get the oil we needed for the rig. Larry had gotten so upset yesterday at the sheer mass of cars wandering about, that I drove today. I praised God that this was a national park that had automobile services available, as many do not. We quickly purchased a gallon jug of exactly the right type of oil. It would not have

---

[30]nps.gov/yose/index.htm

been good thing to drive it out of here, back out to civilization without the necessary oil. Now, everything would be just fine.

> ## Psalm 121
>
> ¹ I lift up my eyes to the mountains,
> where does my help come from?
> ² My help comes from the LORD,
> the Maker of heaven and earth.
> ³ He will not let your foot slip,
> he who watches over you will not slumber;
> ⁴ indeed, he who watches over Israel
> will neither slumber nor sleep.
> ⁵ The LORD watches over you,
> the LORD is your shade at your right hand;
> ⁶ the sun will not harm you by day,
> nor the moon by night.
> ⁷ The LORD will keep you from all harm,
> he will watch over your life;
> ⁸ the LORD will watch over your coming and going,
> both now and forevermore.

With business out of the way, our hike to the Visitor Center was nice. It was 90+ degrees in the sun, but the shade of the huge trees made it bearable. We enjoyed the air conditioning, the official park movie, and another stamp.

We ate little for supper, the heat taking our appetites away. There were only three brief periods of the day when campers were allowed to run their noisy generators: breakfast, lunch, and supper. We ran it from 5-7pm, but it sure didn't help much. We went to bed early. It was hot, but a scooch less hot than yesterday.

Another God-blessed day.

AUGUST 16

We drank up the sights of the valley while driving up to the highest reaches of the park by car. There were outback rocky terrains through thick forests of giant sequoias, babbling streams and grassy meadows.

We stopped at the other Visitor Center at Yosemite Village. Again, we enjoyed their air conditioning, their movie and learned even more about the park. They had different stamps, so I stamped my Passport some more.

It was still so hot during the day, so we picked up our lawn chairs and walked the short distance to a stream—actually, the Merced River—that ran slowly through the campground. We set up our chairs as close to the water as we could without sinking, then stuck our bare feet into the cold water. It was wonderful!

There were several little groups of people enjoying the river that afternoon. One was close to the banks and playing in flotation devices. Another group, to our right upstream, was playing around a felled tree.

Then we smelled something awful. The smell I have now learned is marijuana. Our noses took us in the direction of its origin, a small group of thirty-something men and women. They were sitting in chairs, chest-deep in the middle of the river, with floating coolers of beer at arms' reach. They were passing joints around, talking and laughing loudly.

Larry and I couldn't believe it. Alcohol is frowned upon in National Parks and they were making no effort to conceal even that. But weed?

Other than for medical purposes, marijuana was still illegal in California. And in a Federal Park? Geesh. People never cease to amaze me, and some folks are just plain dumb. The smell would have knocked down a ranger passing anywhere nearby. Yogi Bear and Boo Boo wouldn't have cared much for it, either. It smelled more like Pepe Le Pew.

The heat and poor sleep was really getting to me, so I went back to the motorhome to lay down. Larry took his bike and rode around for a while. He said it did his heart good to witness families and their kids playing and jumping from a granite boulder into the cool stream. The kids were having a ball. They were climbing then jumping, over and over again. He just sat and watched them for an hour or more. It was like a natural water park right in the midst of Yosemite.

With no one else around, he rode peacefully along one of the back roads to Mirror Lake. It was supposed to be a beautiful lake with mirrored cliffs reflecting from above. After an exhausting ride up the steep grades, he was disappointed to find only a dried-up lake. California's drought has really taken its toll on this beautiful park.

We turned on the air conditioners during the generator hours of 5-7pm. But again, it wasn't much help.

We did enjoy a beautiful sight that evening, though. First one deer, then another appeared out of the trees right across the street from us. Then they crossed the road and ate quietly from a bush right outside our windows. Nature is so beautiful. Then another early bedtime.

AUGUST 17

If I hadn't already known that the heat was making me sick, I'd swear I had the flu. Achy all over, I stayed in bed later than usual, until I couldn't stand the heat any longer.

We ate a small lunch, packed a cooler of water and crackers, then got into our blissfully air-conditioned car. We headed first to Tuolumne Meadows, about 15 miles away. It's a vast, flat meadow with granite cliffs serving as a perimeter in the distance. There was plenty of wildlife grazing. On the way, we passed a beautiful alpine lake that was crystal clear and shimmered with blue. We stopped and admired the breathtaking beauty. Later, we pulled over to watch several mountain climbers, both men and women, inch their way up a sheer cliff, pulling themselves up with a safety rope. The highest of the mountains were still snowcapped, despite that it was late summer. Tuolumne Meadows had a small Visitor Center for me to get yet another stamp. There was a large tent setup as a restaurant, so we enjoyed a sandwich before driving back to the campground.

Next, we headed to the high elevation of Glacier Point. It took us another 15 miles to get there, but in the opposite direction. The Google map showed it as only a mile away as the crow flies, with a gain of 7,000 feet in elevation. But, of course, we didn't have the means to fly there, so we had to take the long road.

The view was amazing! We could actually see the campground from here, although it appeared as small as a thimble.

While we attempted to enjoy the view, there was a 20-something "kid" horsing around by climbing the overlook, which made us quite nervous. One slip and he would have gone completely over the cliff. Larry finally said something like, "I really don't want to see you die today, would you please get down?" He replied, "I got new hiking boots on." Yeah, right, that will save you! Again, why do people make such bad choices? There are signs all around, warning of the dangers of climbing on the rocks, that had probably been there since the day that the first guy fell off.

The view from there was breathtaking. You could see the "Half Dome", a huge granite dome mountain with a sheer cliff on one side, several waterfalls, and wilderness all around. There were the different greens of the forest, the grey-pink granite and the blues of the waters and sky. And visitors were coming and going all over the place. There was a store that was the "only show in town" and it was packed.

The journey today took us through many different areas that had been marked by fire. We learned about how forests replenish themselves after a fire. Some of these fires had been recent, and some of the areas had signs, telling you that this natural replenishment is from 2005 or 1996. I know that fires are in a forest's circle of life, but the charred carcasses of the trees were still painful to see.

We had planned to drive to Mariposa Grove to witness the giant sequoias, but the road was closed for a restoration project. It won't be open again until the summer of 2017. We weren't too disappointed because we had seen that area during a whirlwind trip down the west coast back in 1987.

During our visits to national parks, we continued to be amazed by the melting pot of cultures who come here. Many days, we were among more Asians than Americans, and often the only ones in a group that spoke English.

Yosemite seemed busier than Yellowstone, but I think that's because Yosemite celebrates the same number of annual guests, but confined in a very small valley.

One thing was for sure, people really noticed our banner. Kids were everywhere, walking and biking by. They seemed to approve. We gave out lots of packets!

All praise and glory to God! We were working for Him, spreading His word, and seeing the country to boot!

Hallelujah!

Psalm 42

[1] As the deer pants for streams of water,
so my soul pants for you, my God.
[2] My soul thirsts for God, for the living God.
When can I go and meet with God?

AUGUST 18

Man, oh man, I'm actually running a fever today, without much respite in sight. We had driven everywhere there was to drive to keep in the cool of the car, and the generator hours just don't cool things off much.

I don't mean to be whiney, it's just the way it was.

Our reservations have us leaving on Saturday morning, in two days. Since we've already seen everything, I wonder if he would consider leaving tomorrow?

AUGUST 19

Considering there were no utilities onsite, we would have to pack up and move the rig today just to dump the tanks and refill with fresh water. I quietly asked Larry if we could just leave? The traffic would probably be worse if we waited until Saturday, don't you think?

He was all in favor of missing a little traffic, so we packed up for the trip. It would be five hours until we reached Lake Tahoe.

We took Route 120 west, Route 4 east, Route 49 north, Route 88 east, Route 89 north and finally to US 50 east. Google Maps was busy chattering the whole way. Many times, we passed beautiful waterways, glistening in the sunlight. I took photos of a tiny little town we passed through that had a banner stretched across the main street which read, "Welcome to Groveland." Quaint. The heartbeat of America.

I traveled today missing my mom. She had died on this very day back in 1971, just before I started my senior year of high school. Forty-five years ago, Wow. She died after a painful three-year battle with cancer.

We realized that if we'd driven for days on this US 50 east, it would take us back to the town of Milford, Ohio where we both grew up. Sobering, reflective. This road leads to home.

We drove through plenty of dry central California. The roads were typically bumpy, as were some of the back routes taking us north in the foothills Sierra Nevada Mountains.

By the time we were driving our last leg into Tahoe, it was obvious that half of the population of San Francisco was driving in for the weekend. Gambling was popular on the Nevada side of the lake. Big casinos were right at the border (and I mean RIGHT at the border), welcoming folks for this last big weekend before many go back to school.

We sure couldn't go the posted speed limits on those winding roads! We had been told that California law requires a driver to pull over, if you have more than five vehicles behind you. We pulled over several times, when the roads allowed.

As we broke through the mountains, the first glimpse of Lake Tahoe was just spectacular. It's a freshwater lake at an elevation of 6,225 feet, and straddles the border between California and Nevada, west of Carson City, Nevada. It's the largest alpine lake in North America, being 21 miles long. It's also the sixth largest lake in America, behind the great lakes, and the second deepest. Only Crater Lake is deeper.

Although there are plenty of ski resorts around here for winter fun, the lake during the summer offers up all sorts of wet activities. There were boats, water skiers, and jet skis all over the lake.

It had been a great day of travel…until we arrived at the campground. We pulled in to register at the Lake Tahoe Valley Campground, South Tahoe. Larry rated this a 3, but mainly due to the confusion at check in. I noticed when we pulled in that it was a heavily wooded campground. I emphasized to the clerk, "Are you sure this site will hold a 36-foot motorhome?" Oh yes, yes.

We went to #281, as instructed. There was a tree on each side of the opening to the site, right at the road. Hmmm, I don't know about this.

We took the car off the tow dolly, the dolly off the rig. We each grabbed a radio and went to work.

I will censor the next forty long minutes by saying that we attracted a great deal of attention. If Larry can't back it in, it must be my fault for giving poor directions. This syndrome Larry suffers from goes all the way back to 1978, when we bought our first boat. Ask my neighbors. They confess to hiding behind their hedges across the street to watch the entertainment. They said sometimes they even brought popcorn. True story.

The guy parked in the site on the other side of the narrow road came out to nervously watch us getting closer and closer to his truck. He offered to move it and I nearly kissed his feet! That gave us another five feet to work.

I offered many times to go up to the registration and request another site, but no. Larry was The Man, and he could park anything (if I would just do my job!) I told him flatly that the only way this rig would fit on this site was to be air-dropped there or if the motorhome would bend in the middle. It must be a "man" thing.

Finally, with the opinions of two other guys (note: guys) in the audience assuring him that we should have never been given that campsite, I went back to get another site. #290 was just another fifty feet up the same road, in a clearing. Took us all of two minutes to back it in.

The campground was okay, on the outskirts of town. The sites were just dirt and pine needles, and the utilities hadn't been upgraded in a long while. But everything worked. We wanted to get into the state parks in the area, but they had already filled. They were closer to the lake and offered wonderful views.

But here we were, safe and sound. And unlike the state parks, we had full utilities!

Thank God for air conditioning!

AUGUST 20

We had to move this morning to the site we had reserved earlier (remember that we left Yosemite a day early). This one was a pull through, praise the Lord. Piece of cake.

A major cleanup was desperately needed. We'd had the windows open for the past five days and a fine blanket of dust covered everything. We'd tracked in pine needles and grass, and laundry was backed up everywhere.

We stripped the beds, gathered towels and washed down everything. It will take days to get the laundry done. Now, with the motorhome cool and clean and the laundry started, we took off in the car to explore.

It took 71 miles and several hours to drive completely around Lake Tahoe. It's beautiful, but there were people everywhere. All during the drive, we were looking for someplace to park to stand still and look at the lake. There were hundreds of lots and spaces, but believe me when I say every single one was filled.

Finally, at the overlook at Emerald Cove, we found a place to park. The view was awesome. The turquoise clear water was so beautiful with the picturesque blue sky. We could see a paddle-wheeler taking tourists for an afternoon cruise.

Finding only one more parking space all afternoon, we just kept on driving. We finally decided on a nice little Italian restaurant named Primo's for supper, which we thoroughly enjoyed.

Back to a clean, cool motorhome and more laundry. Then a shower, movie, and bed.

Another blessed day.

> Matthew 13:47
>
> Once again, the kingdom of heaven
> is like a net that was let down into the lake
> and caught all kinds of fish.

AUGUST 21

Today would be a quiet day, considering we'd covered the entire perimeter of Lake Tahoe yesterday.

We went to the cinema to see *Ben Hur*. It was an excellent movie, filled with wrongdoing, innocence, and redemption. It had not been billed as a Christian movie, but we were delighted that it included the compassion of Jesus during that time. It also illustrated how the characters of the movie were affected by Jesus's crucifixion. It was great.

We love movies and storytelling but Hollywood seems to think that every movie has to include sex and cursing to attract audiences. Well, I can tell you that stuff doesn't attract *this* target audience. Larry and I have had a passing joke over the years. We'd see a preview at the movies and Larry would say, "Who in the world would pay good money to see that?" I reply, "Honey, we are not the target audience."

I truly wish the Motion Picture Association of America film rating system would break down the R-ratings to explain why it's an R. Is it full of sex? Is it full of cursing? Give them an R-F862, for the number of times the F-bomb is used. Is it full of violence? I've seen movies full of documentary violence that didn't have a single cuss word in it. Just a thought.

Even as Christians, occasionally we take a chance on an R-rated movie. If it's a decent story line, I may tolerate some mild cussing. But there have been a few times that we got up and walked out. And nothing offends me worse than using the Lord's name in vain…repeatedly. We do our best to research before we go, but sometimes you just can't find that kind of stuff in a review.

The cinema was in an outdoor shopping complex filled with lots of brand and unknown stores. Full of popcorn and soda, we walked the area out of curiosity, then decided on a small, simple meal at the local KFC.

AUGUST 22

On the Road Again (sing it), this time for Reno, Nevada.

We left the mountains of Lake Tahoe and came out onto the flat, dry desert of Nevada. On the way, it was clear to see the transition: the hills were naked, rounded mounds. No trees, no grasses, no bushes. Nothing. This would be our first of many days spent in the desert. That was sure different than the rainforests of the Pacific Northwest! We drove through Carson City to Reno via US 50, east to I-580 then into Sparks, Nevada. We encountered a couple of tunnels on the way, which always make Larry a bit nervous, but we sailed through each one without a hitch. We finally arrived at Sparks Marina RV Park in Sparks, which Larry rated a 9.

The campground is paved with tidy, concrete pads. It was well-landscaped with all sorts of amenities. We took advantage of the pool and hot tub for sure. The water felt so good, out there in the desert sun.

There was a young family at the pool and they asked about our Motorhome Ministry. We spoke at great length, because they were curious. It was our hope that we made an impression upon them regarding the importance of raising their two small children in the Word. It is our hope and prayer.

In this world, we will never know how our planted seeds will flourish. But I yearn for the day in the next world, that we will.

Isaiah 55:10

[10] As the rain and the snow come down from heaven,
and do not return to it without watering the earth
and making it bud and flourish,
so, that it yields seed for the sower
and bread for the eater,

We took the afternoon to visit Reno. It was a Monday afternoon, the summer season was over and there's wasn't much activity, either on the streets or inside the casinos. After we parked the car, we passed several beggars on the way to the first casino. To avoid further encounters, we stayed inside, walking from one establishment to the next.

When it was time for lunch, we dined cheap. I enjoyed the prime rib with soup and fries for $5.99. Larry figured we could always take home leftovers, so he ordered himself a steak with soup and fries for $4.99. What a great deal, and it was very good! And we did take home leftovers!

The casinos were as flashy as Vegas on the inside, but the outside streets paled in comparison. I don't know it was due to the lack of recent rain or just a general state of affairs, but the streets looked dirty and unkempt. Personally, it creeped me out. So, when we walked outside again, I had seen enough. The sky promised storms at any moment, so we headed quickly to the car.

We passed a new shopping mall on the way back to the campground and we decided to explore. We entered a huge store named Scheels, which we had never heard of. They have all things hunting, fishing, fitness, and more. They even had a full-sized Ferris Wheel in the center of the store!

"Special attractions include eight life-like bronze sculptures; two 16,000 gallon aquariums full of brilliantly colored fish; a 35 foot-tall, 800 square foot Wildlife Mountain; a 65-foot, 16-car operating Ferris Wheel; a Home Décor and Gift Lodge; a nostalgic shooting gallery, Roller Ball, a Buck Hunter simulator, and a 5-sport simulator with sports including basketball, soccer, baseball and football, where customers can test their skills. The Walk of Presidents and many more amenities makes this shopping adventure unlike anything the Reno-Sparks retail customer has ever experienced."[31]

---

[31] scheels.com/shop/scheels-catalog/scheels-store-rs

We went up to the second floor and discovered a bunch of animatronic presidents who came to life with the touch of a button. Wow!

It's ironic, now that I have no more problems or pain in my neck, I have been suffering terribly with lower back pain. I've had it for a while, and even went to the emergency room for x-rays back home a few years ago. The doctor told me that I have arthritis in my lower back and hips; that the bones are all raggedly on the edges. She asked what I had done for a living. "Well, for about twenty years I owned popcorn and candy stores. I worked standing 18 hours a day on concrete floors, lifting 50-pound bags of popcorn and sugar." Yep, she said. That would do it. Now it's worse than ever.

While we were at Scheels, Larry encouraged me to see if they had any kind of brace that would help. I was delighted that they did, and it really wasn't all that expensive. I wear it when I think we're going to be walking a great distance, although it does leave me a little short-winded. Perhaps losing about twenty pounds would help with that latter problem.

We arrived at the campground for another swim, which was great, then enjoyed what was left of the day.

---

1 Chronicles 4:10

[10] Jabez cried out to the God of Israel,
"Oh, that you would bless me and
enlarge my territory!
Let your hand be with me, and keep me from harm
so that I will be free from pain."
And God granted his request.

AUGUST 23

Although nothing had been planned, today turned out to be one crazy day.

I'm up and ready to hit the pool, when Larry told me to sit my butt down and call Intuit, again. How many months in a row does this make? What should have been a 5-minute task of running and emailing client statements, the program wouldn't email. Larry was ballistic. One hour and fifty-three minutes later, it worked. Now the whole day seemed a loss.

Larry went off on another cleaning spree—the carpet, this time.

We had planned pool, post office, drive downtown for $10 steak and lobster. What actually happened was Intuit, laundry, I went to post office, Larry scrubbed the carpet like a wild man and I had to finish it. Supper was at the motorhome, although the stuffed salmon we'd gotten from Costco was delicious. An evening of watching FOX News, then bed. Whew!

AUGUST 24

Today was a driving day to take us to Salt Lake City, Utah. We couldn't make it all the way today, so we stopped at a little place called Double Dice RV Park in Elko, Nevada, which Larry rated a 5.

It was a pleasant day, right up until the steps wouldn't work again. But have no fear! We grabbed the hammer and BANG! Now, they work. This was getting to be fun.

We didn't want to take the car off the dolly just for one night, so we ate frozen P.F.Chang's and watched a Will Smith movie, *I am Legend,* which totally creeped me out. But, then again, it doesn't take much to creep me out. I am a wuss when it comes to horror-type movies. No thanks.

Our electric service was acting crazy and we blamed it on the campground. It kept setting off the wash machine, and the red lights would flash. Oh, if we'd only listened to its warning. A surge protected strip blew as well. What's up with this?

AUGUST 25

Today was another driving day, and another change of scenery. The closer we got to Salt Lake, the more level the landscape became. We drove right through the Bonneville Salt Flats, a densely-packed salt pan in Tooele County in Northwestern Utah. The landscape was now, for miles in every direction, nothing but white salt. This area is a remnant of the ancient and long-gone Lake Bonneville and is the largest of many salt flats located west of the Great Salt Lake. I could never have imagined anything like this. We both saw mirages in this area, appearing like large lakes of water ahead of us. But when we got there, there was just more salt. Cool.

We didn't have reservations here, so I called ahead to the Great Salt Lake State Park, which was located right ON the Great Salt Lake. There are only five sites and we were blessed to get one. Larry rated it a 5.

Later that evening, we walked out to the end of the little campground and took amazing pictures of the sunset over the water. A bus with Asian tourists came to the parking lot to see the sunset, too. When we walked back to the rig, one old couple from the tour, who didn't speak a word of English approached us and gestured as if they wanted to go inside our motorhome. We motioned for them to enter. I guess they don't have motorhomes in China, or wherever they were actually from. They stayed only a minute, then nodded repeatedly to thank us.

We went to the Visitor Center and got another stamp for my Passport. We learned that the Great Salt Lake is the largest salt water lake in the Western Hemisphere, and the eighth-largest terminal lake in the world. It's comparable to the Dead Sea in the Middle East. In vast contrast to so many bodies of water, there were no boats, no swimmers, or any other activity that we could see. We learned that miniature brine shrimp and brine flies are the only creatures that can tolerate the high salt, and they feed on the algae. If you attempt to swim in it, you just float quickly to the top; it's nearly impossible to go beneath the surface.

As we traveled the city over several days, it was always clear when we were getting back close to the campground. Right across the street is the Garfield Smelter Stack, 177 feet wide at the bottom and 1,215 feet high. It serves to disperse exhaust gasses from the Kennecott Utah Copper smelter at Garfield, Utah. It can be seen from just about anywhere in Salt Lake City.

Zechariah 14:8

[8] On that day living water
will flow out from Jerusalem,
half of it east to the Dead Sea and
half of it west to the Mediterranean Sea,
in summer and in winter.

AUGUST 26

We drove out to Antelope Island today, north of the main city. It's a 42 square-mile island just outside Salt Lake City, surrounded by the Great Salt Lake. There is also another state park campground there, but it had no utilities. I'm so grateful we could get into the campground we did. Life is so much easier with electric, water, and sewer hookups.

We were delighted to see a lot of bison and deer. But we noticed a lot of fire burned areas. We learned later that nearly 28,000 acres had burned very recently. But it was still a beautiful road trail with plenty of bison grazing in the fields of the island. We saw lots of those singular males, too.

We grilled pork chops for supper and enjoyed another beautiful sunset. It was another movie night in the wonderful air conditioning. It was yet another blessed day.

AUGUST 27

We celebrate as God has allowed our journey to reach 150 days today. Thank you so much!

We moved the rig to Salt Lake City KOA, which Larry rated a 7. We had a tough time getting the wifi set up, but everything else was great.

The KOA is located just a few miles from the Mormon Tabernacle campus. We spent the afternoon and evening exploring Temple Square. They had missionaries from all around the world, leading tours in every building. Their young students are required to work for the church for a year at the main campus here in Salt Lake. They were all very nice and I enjoyed learning about something else in the world of which I knew very little.

We went in for the tour, knowing next to nothing about the Mormon belief. Larry told them what we do as missionaries, then asked questions as to their beliefs. Larry and I believe "that the Bible, composed of the Old and New Testaments, is the Word of God, a divine, supernatural revelation. We believe the plenary, verbal inspiration of the original writings of the Scriptures, and that thus given, they were wholly without error of any kind."[32] After Larry explained this belief to our guide, he asked her, "Doesn't the Book of Mormon add to the Bible? The young Asian girl who was our guide explained about the lost gold plates, which were left out of the Bible. That was our first red flag: God wouldn't have left out a book of the Bible, even if it had been "lost" at the time. It is complete and without error.

The story goes that, "Joseph Smith, Jr., the founder of the Church of Jesus Christ of Latter-day Saints (LDS, or Mormons), claimed that after both God the Father and Jesus Christ visited him in 1820, an angel named Moroni, an ancient Nephite warrior, visited him in the fall of 1823. Smith was told by Moroni how he had buried gold plates fourteen centuries earlier not far from the Smith farm near Palmyra, New York. The angel said that they contained a record of ancient inhabitants and the 'source from whence they sprang.'"[33] "Smith claimed he was prohibited from retrieving the gold record for another four years. The story of the gold plates is an absolutely essential part of the Mormon narrative, for in the eyes of many Latter-day Saints, the coming forth of this record, and its subsequent translation into the Book of Mormon, legitimizes their belief that Smith was indeed a prophet sent by God to restore the true

---

[32] langstonbaptist.com/what-we-believe/

[33] The Book of Mormon, The Testimony of the Prophet Joseph Smith

Christian faith lost long ago due to a 'great apostasy.' The story of the gold plates cannot be underestimated, for without them there can be no Book of Mormon. Though many members of the LDS Church are very familiar with this story, the details surrounding how Smith obtained the plates, how he "translated" the plates, and how a few chosen men saw the plates, have compelled some within the LDS Church to challenge the main components of the account in order to make it sound more credible"[34]. The book of Mormon is a translation of these plates by founder Joseph Smith., who claims that he returned the plates to the angel Moroni.

I had no idea that the Mormon Tabernacle was such a massive campus. It was meticulously landscaped and beautifully maintained. We ate supper at their Lion House, which served great home-cooked food. It was a small restaurant on the temple campus "which was built in 1856 and was the family home of Brigham Young, the second president of The Church of Jesus Christ of Latter-day Saints and the first governor of the state of Utah.[35] We were picked up at the campground by a shuttle system of Mormon volunteers to go to and from the temple area each time. An elderly couple served as our drivers each day. We gave them a brochure from our ministry for them to read as well as they gave us information on their religion. It was a beautiful, fascinating day.

---

[34] equip.org/article/problems-with-the-gold-plates-of-the-book-of-mormon-2/

[35] templesquare.com/lion-house/

> Revelation 22:18-19
>
> **¹⁸** I warn everyone who hears the words of the prophecy of this scroll: If anyone adds anything to them, God will add to that person the plagues described in this scroll. **¹⁹** And if anyone takes words away from this scroll of prophecy, God will take away from that person any share in the tree of life and in the Holy City, which are described in this scroll.

AUGUST 28

We got up early and headed downtown to Temple Square to attend Music and the Spoken Word. Nearly all of you reading this has most certainly heard of the Mormon Tabernacle Choir. Being a choir enthusiast, I couldn't wait to hear them sing!

I learned that Music and the Spoken Word has been broadcast live for more than eighty years now. "Without interruption, it gives voice to peace, hope, inspiration, and the goodness of God. No other broadcast can claim such a heritage."[36]

During the summer months, guest attendance is so great that they hold the service in their Conference Center across the street from the Tabernacle on Temple Square. The place is gigantic. The acoustics were perfect, and the music of the orchestra and choir were absolutely angelic. It was like watching a Hollywood production: the lights and sound, the announcer, the music, the cameras all worked in faultless precision.

---

[36] mormontabernaclechoir.org

We walked the grounds after the hour was done, but I was feeling poorly again. I can't blame it on the heat—maybe it's something in the water, I don't know. We did take an elevator to the roof with a chaperone, a volunteer to help explain to us what it is to be a Mormon. On top of the Conference Center hall is a complete landscaped roof, like a park complete with monuments, statues, streams, waterfalls, and trees., all planted on the roof. It was a few acres in size. It was easy to forget you were on a roof, except that the view it afforded was amazing.

We went back to the motorhome and I slept the entire afternoon, while Larry poured through the Book of Mormon we'd been given the day before. When he finished, he proclaimed that it had been an interesting read, indeed. We remain secure in the Baptist faith.

Larry: *Everyone is entitled to their own beliefs as guaranteed by our constitution and the free will given to us by God. Most people are raised and taught their parents' beliefs, just as Mormons are raised and taught their parents' beliefs. Lugene and I both came into the Temple campus with an open mind.*

But what bothers me are several important beliefs they have that go against mainstream Christianity. They don't believe in the Trinity. This is a big one, as the Trinity is, without doubt, Biblical. They don't believe you have been saved by the Grace of the Resurrection, but ultimately, by your own works. The Book of Mormon describes degrees or levels in heaven, but no literal hell. Another belief is that their modern-day saints will each rule their own part of a universe as a god. It's obvious the Mormons worship the same God that we do, and they are very devoted in those beliefs. Their buildings and churches are so perfectly structured and maintained. But their Book of Mormon has some serious contradictions to the holy word of the Bible itself.

I prayed I would feel better tomorrow. There's so much left to see and learn!

AUGUST 29

Today was a short travel day to make our way to the southern part of Utah and all the National Parks they have. Did you know that there are more National Parks in the state of Utah than any other? We will visit all five of them in the next several weeks.

We were amazed to see lots of reds in the trees. I guess the elevation would be responsible for an early fall here in the mountains.

Our first stop is Mountain Valley RV Resort in Heber, Utah, heading out of Salt Lake on I-80 west to US 40 south, which Larry rated a 10. It was the highest-rated Good Sam Park in the state of Utah, for good reason. It was everything the reviews said it would be.

The pads were cement with bright green grass around them with flowers and trees on every site. We had other reservations in place, so we could only stay one night here. This would be a place I would love to stay long-term.

The day was sunny, warm, but not hot. The humidity was desert low. And the pool and hot tub were just perfect. There was one cigarette butt I saw on the parking lot, but, other than that it was perfect.

Considering it was a one night stay, we didn't bother to take off the car. We enjoyed watching the infamous *Forrest Gump*. It had been so long since we'd seen it, it seemed like the first time. What a wonderful movie. I love the quote "Life is like box of chocolates, you never know what you're gonna get". Until you've taken your first bite, this is so true!

After an early supper, we headed back for another dip in the pool. The mountain scenery at sunset is something everyone should experience. The sun dances with its shadows on the mountain slopes as it sets.

Early to bed for an early morning. Thank you for another wonderfully blessed day, Lord.

AUGUST 30

It was a day of travel to the Arches National Park in Moab, Utah. We had reservations at the Moab Valley RV Resort there in Moab, which Larry rated a 9. From Heber, UT we traveled southwest to Provo by way of US 189, past Deer Crossing Reservoir, a beautiful lake. As we continued, we came to Bridal Veil Falls, a roaring natural waterfall in scenic Provo Canyon. You can actually hear the falls from the highway! Then, southeast on US 6, to I-70 east and then US 191 southeast into Moab.

Our drive blessed us with the sights of so many different types of rock formations. All the dirt here is red, the cliffs are red, the frumpy mounds are red, and the dirt by the side of the road is red. It reminded Larry of a childhood game, *Red Rover, Red Rover...*

The National Park Service site promises, "Visit Arches and discover a landscape of contrasting colors, landforms, and textures unlike any other in the world. The park has over 2,000 natural stone arches, in addition to hundreds of soaring pinnacles, massive fins, and giant balanced rocks. This red rock wonderland will amaze you with its formations, refresh you with its trails, and inspire you with its sunsets."[37] We drove to the Visitor Center to begin our visit with the park movie and secured a stamp in my Passport.

Our explorations in the park did not disappoint. Again, we'd never seen or even imagined beauty such as this. Pictures and movies don't do it justice. You have to see the whole picture and enjoy the magnitude of the experience. The park service names the rock formations to what the rocks and arches look like: Three Sisters, Balance rock, Courthouse Towers, Leafless Tree, and The Windows. Wind, rain, erosion, and time have made this wonderland in the red rocks.

It was really hot, though. My photos for today include a screen-shot of my Wunderground app, showing it was 102 degrees on this day. The relative humidity was so low, it had a heat index of only 98 degrees. This was a welcome change! We have finally caught up with summer. It seems we have been a season behind all year.

We took the car into bustling little Moab and thoroughly enjoyed some Thai food, for a change. The restaurant was called Singha Thai Cuisine. We had a new dish, but I can't think of its name for the life of me. It was a relatively small restaurant but, it was an excellent choice.

---

[37] nps.gov

Back in the coolness of the motorhome (have I said enough, thank you God for air conditioning?), we watched a movie and hit the hay.

It had been a long, good day.

AUGUST 31

We got in the car with plenty of water and drove up through the National Park.

The hiking guide had 15 different hikes, rated from easy to difficult. Some of them are so difficult that you're required to have a ranger accompany you. We took one of the easy trails up to the Windows Arch. Any photos we saw or took cannot do it justice. The Windows Arch is several stories tall, the window being carved by wind, water, and time. It was amazing. God is such an artist.

It was hot, so I requested an air-conditioned nap back at the motorhome. Even Larry slept. But while we were sleeping, the devil had paid us a visit and the front air conditioning unit was on the fritz. Oh, no.

We spent a couple of hours Googling and calling local repair people. It finally started cooling again, although we really couldn't put our finger on exactly what had happened or how we'd "fixed" it. All of these different electrical problems that just didn't seem to be related to one another. There was no way to troubleshoot.

We had a knock at the door and found one of the park employees. Usually a knock means bad news. But, the woman at the door brought us some boxes that had been delivered. She saw the banner and read the packaged address on the labels on the boxes. She said she was a Christian and asked polite questions about the Ministry. She took a kid packet to give to her niece.

We received some of our ministry materials as well as a box from a RV parts depot. It was finally the part to fix the steps! Yay! Or at least it should have been. Don't you know it? They sent a controller for the steps and not the motor. Larry called them up promptly and explained their error. They apologized and will reship tomorrow. But, it will have to be sent to a campground down on our reservation list, several days from now.

The satellite had been acting stupid, too. In the heat (and while checking the air conditioners), Larry had taken off the satellite dome and I ran the scans. After a while, it became clear: the dish could only find satellites when the dome was off. He called the manufacturer. It was still under warranty, so they agreed to send another one to our next campground. Yay! Thank God for warranties.

We took a drive on a less-traveled road, Route 128 that curved alongside the Colorado River. After several miles, we parked the car and got out to wander, and eventually wound up right down on the riverbank. While we were there, a group of rafters arrived and used that exact area to come up out of the water. The tour guide was a guy, and the rafters were all girls in bikinis. They were all running quickly to the outhouses. Must have been a long excursion! We were there in late afternoon, and the sun disappears quickly behind the tall peaks. As it sets, it casts shadows on the steep mountain sides.

The pool was once again wonderful; the day overall, blessed.

JUST ONE MORE THING...

My great hope is that you've enjoyed my ramblings about our travels this past year. What an adventure it has been! And Motorhome Ministry has planted seeds of the Gospel in every single place we have visited. But it doesn't stop here. HIS ROAD TRIP TWO is well in the works and should be available by summer, 2017.

It will include all the details about our experiences at the Albuquerque International Balloon Fiesta, the Grand Canyon, Las Vegas, and over a month of amazing adventures in the great metropolis of Los Angeles. We went on Wheel of Fortune, saw a movie star in Malibu, and did you know there are ancient tar pits just blocks away from Rodeo Drive?

Then, there are more amazing National Parks and Presidential Libraries, we stayed all over the great state of Texas, and celebrated Mardi Gras in New Orleans. We still have plenty of technical difficulties, which are always comical in hindsight. Of course, Frick, Frack, and Frank continue their habitual bickering along the way.

But my greatest hope is that, despite my humanness, you have been able to see Christ in me; well, Christ in us. And my prayer is that you would desire Him for yourself. Some folks have the misconception that Christians think they're better and above other people. We are most definitely not. We're sinners, just like you, but forgiven.

We have confessed our sins, asked that God would forgive us, and have become new creatures in Christ.

It's really very simple.

You can become a new creature, too:

> Romans 10:9-10
> ⁹ If you declare with your mouth, "Jesus is Lord,"
> and believe in your heart that God
> raised him from the dead,
> YOU WILL BE SAVED.
> ¹⁰ For it is with your heart that you believe
> and are justified,
> and it is with your mouth that you profess
> your faith and are saved.

> John 3:5-7
> ⁵ Jesus answered, "Very truly I tell you,
> no one can enter the kingdom of God
> unless they are born of water and the Spirit.
> ⁶ Flesh gives birth to flesh, but the Spirit
> gives birth to spirit
> . ⁷ You should not be surprised at my saying,
> 'YOU MUST BE BORN AGAIN

Billy Graham Ministries' website explains that, "Jesus Christ says that we must be born again. How do we become born again? By repenting of sin. That means we are willing to change our way of living. We say to God, "I'm a sinner, and I'm sorry." It's simple and childlike. Then by faith we receive Jesus Christ as our Lord and Master and Savior. We are willing to follow Him in a new life of obedience, in which the Holy Spirit helps us as we read the Bible and pray and witness."[38]

I personally believe that, "Those who leave everything in God's hand will eventually see God's hand in everything." I see God's hand in everything, every day. I

---

[38] billygraham.org

hope you can understand why, after reading my words of faith.

> **2 Peter 3:9**
> ⁹ The Lord is not slow in keeping his promise,
> as some understand slowness.
> Instead he is patient with you,
> not wanting anyone to perish,
> but everyone to come to repentance.

> **Psalm 121:7-8**
> The Lord will keep you from all harm,
> He will watch over your life
> The Lord will watch over your coming and going
> Both now and forevermore.

Stay tuned. By the will of God, the adventure will continue...

MY FAVORITE RECIPES

RECIPE FOR FROGMORE STEW

<u>For a batch to feed 3-4 hungry folks, you will need the following:</u>

1 gallon of water

Juice of one lemon

Salt to taste (I use 1 ½ TBSP)

3 TBSP Old Bay Seasoning (shrimp boil)

Few thin slices of onion

1 pound small red potatoes, quartered with skins on

1 pound Kielbasa sausage, sliced into bite-size pieces

6 mini ears of frozen corn on the cob

1 pound frozen shrimp with tails on

> In a large stock pot over medium-high heat, bring to a boil: water, lemon, salt, Old Bay Seasoning… (or your favorite)

Then add potatoes & onions, & continue to boil for 5 minutes.

Then add Kielbasa & continue to boil for 5 minutes.

Then add corn & continue to boil for 5 minutes.

Then add shrimp & continue to boil for 5 minutes.

Feel free to add other items like squash or baby carrots if desired.

When done cooking, drain well and dump on the table.

To have a unique and authentic experience, spread brown paper on the table, dump the Frogmore Stew on the paper** and eat with your fingers! No plates or utensils allowed.

> **To avoid any damage to your table, be sure to take appropriate precautions to protect your table-top from heat and moisture. Enjoy!

HISTORY OF FROGMORE STEW

Beaufort historian, Gerhard Spieler, believes that the recipe was the invention of local shrimpers who used whatever food items they had on hand to make a stew.

Richard Gay, of Gay Seafood Company, also claimed to have invented Frogmore Stew. On National Guard duty in Beaufort in the 1960s, he was preparing a cookout of leftovers for his fellow guardsmen and he brought the recipe home to the community of Frogmore with him, putting out copies of the recipe at his seafood market and selling all the necessary ingredients.

RECIPE FOR "ERIN'S CHICKEN STUFF"

Preheat oven to 350 degrees

SHOPPING LIST:

1 pound of cooked chicken, shredded
(you can use fresh chicken or canned, drained)
1 block of cream cheese, softened
1 cup of mayonnaise
1 cup of shredded cheddar cheese (I use mild)
1 bag of Tostito's Scoops

Mix together the chicken, cream cheese, and mayonnaise.

Mix all ingredients well and put in a 9 X 9 bakeware, suitable for serving

Bake for 30 minutes

While still hot, cover in shredded cheese.

Each person can spoon and fill his Scoops.

Enjoy!

RECIPE FOR AWESOME POTATO SOUP

Get out the Crock Pot.

SHOPPING LIST:

    32oz bag of frozen hash browns (I bought Ore-Ida shredded)
    32oz can/box of chicken broth
    10oz can of condensed cream of chicken soup
    8oz package of cream cheese
    1 ½ cups shredded sharp cheddar cheese
    ¾ cup crumbled bacon
    ½ tsp fresh rosemary, minced

In the Crock Pot, mix together all ingredients <u>except</u> the rosemary.

Cook on High for 3 hours

When serving, add rosemary and another sprinkle of cheese, for garnish.

Once, when I didn't have 3 hours to slow-cook it, I cut this recipe in half, and cooked it on the stove.

This recipe was found on a public feed in Facebook. I regret I cannot give credit for where it originated, because it's great.

FYI: Did you know they make liners for Crock Pots? You line the pot before adding your ingredients. When you're all done, there's no cleanup, no soaking or scrubbing—you just throw away the liner!

IT'S NOT IN THE BOOK, BUT EVERYBODY NEEDS THE RECIPE FOR MY "DADDY'S CHILI"

My Daddy, Harlan, was so proud of his recipe for chili. It was the only thing he ever cooked, and it was always a special production. My way only takes an hour or so, but he always put in lots of water so he would have to cook it down all day long! He wouldn't tell me his "secret ingredient" for years—it was something I don't like; I guess he figured I wouldn't eat it if I knew! It's very mild, but it's easy to spice up. Enjoy!

Get out a stew pot.
SHOPPING LIST and some prep work:

> 3 pounds lean ground beef
> 2 stalks of celery, finely chopped
> 1 medium onion, copped
> 2 cans of condensed tomato soup
> 2 15oz cans of tomato sauce
> 2 15oz cans red kidney beans, drained and rinsed well
> 1 TBSP chili powder (or more, to taste)
> 1 good squirt of yellow mustard
> Shredded cheddar cheese
> Oyster crackers
> Salt & pepper to taste

Brown the ground beef, celery, & onions. Drain excess grease.
Add all other ingredients PLUS 3-4 cups of water.

Cook at least an hour at a slow simmer, keep stirring the bottom often, to keep from scorching.

I often take spaghetti and break it up into short pieces and throw it right in with the chili to cook, to extend the batch.
Serve with oyster crackers and shredded cheddar cheese.

AND WHEN DADDY MADE CHILI, MOM MADE COTTAGE CHEESE SALAD

I arrived for some special occasion at Mom & Dad's. I remember Mom greeting me at the door with a spoon, saying, "Taste this." Before I would, I asked what it was, and she repeated herself. After several rounds of this comedy, I relented and tasted it. It was light and sweet and had fruit in it. Yum! That's when she laughed and told me that it had cottage cheese in it, and she knew I hated cottage cheese.

Get out a large bowl.

SHOPPING LIST and some prep work:

> 12-16 ounces of small curd cottage cheese, any percentage milkfat
> One regular box of Jell-O (NOT sugar free) any flavor--I've tried strawberry, orange, lime, raspberry, cherry...
> Small can of crushed pineapple, drained
> Small can of mandarin oranges, drained and halved
> Small jar of maraschino cherries, drained and halved
> Small container of Cool Whip, thawed
> Optional: crushed pecans

Empty cottage cheese into the large bowl. Add box of Jell-O. Mix well.

Be sure that you've drained the fruits well before you add. Mix well. Add the entire container of Cool Whip. Mix well.

Add nuts, if desired (I personally do not). Cover and chill before serving. It's a big hit at church pot lucks!

AUNT GINNIE'S BIG BATCH BBQ

My mother-in-law used to have great big family gatherings at her house, and we would all show up. There was food everywhere! I learned many years later that it was her sister, Ginnie that provided the BBQ I enjoyed so much at those pot lucks. This is great served on buns with coleslaw and a slice of cheese, tucked right into the sandwich. De-light-ful!

Get out a large skillet and a large stew pot (or your Crock Pot)

SHOPPING LIST and some prep work:

      4 pounds hamburger
      4 small onions, chopped
      1 green bell pepper, seeded and chopped
      4 pieces celery, thinly sliced
      1 cup of BBQ sauce, (she used Open Pit Hickory)
      3 cups of catsup
      1 cup sweet pickle relish
      Salt & pepper to taste

Brown hamburger, onions, bell pepper, celery. Salt & pepper to taste. Drain well.

In the old days, you would put the hamburger mixture in a stew pot. Nowadays, just put it in a modern-day Crock Pot.

Add BBQ sauce, catsup, and pickle relish.

Simmer for 3 hours. High for Crock Pot.

LOIS' PICNIC SPAGHETTI

And no family gathering is ever complete without my mother-in-law's Picnic Spaghetti. We all loved it so much, she always had to fix a double batch. It's the best! You can serve it hot, but I like it COLD.

SHOPPING LIST:
>1 small can of Hunts tomato sauce
>8 pieces of regular bacon
>8oz package of Muellers thin spaghetti
>1 medium green bell pepper
>1 TBSP granulated sugar
>½ TBSP salt
>1 small white onion

FIRST, prepare a pot of water and bring to a boil.

- Chop onion and bell pepper into small (1/2" x 1/2" pieces)
- Fry bacon in medium-sized skillet until crisp. Remove from heat. Remove bacon to cool, but <u>KEEP GREASE</u> in skillet
- Reheat the grease in skillet until hot again, then cook pepper & onions, only enough to soften, not long.
- When onions clear, add tomato sauce to the skillet.
- Bring mixture to a boil, stirring well.
- After bacon cools, put in plastic bag and crumble.
- Add the salt, sugar, and crumbled bacon.
- Mix well, then turn down burner and simmer for 10 minutes, stirring occasionally.

WHILE THIS SIMMERS, your water should be ready to cook the spaghetti. When done, drain it well and put in a large dish or pan. Pour the skillet sauce onto spaghetti. Mix thoroughly. Enjoy!!

DEB'S ZUCCHINI CASSEROLE

My best buddy, Deb has a reputation for growing monster zucchini. I mean, she's raised 'em to nearly the size of baseball bats. She has a zillion way to serve zucchini, and they all come with a side of homemade zucchini bread. Here's one of the recipes I personally enjoy, because it's easy, and a great way to hide zucchini from my husband.

SHOPPING LIST and some prep work:
      2 zucchini, cubed (hereafter referred to as "zuc")
      1 large sweet onion, chopped
      ½ clove of garlic
      1 can condensed cream of chicken soup
      1 box Turkey or Chicken Stove Top dressing
      1 8oz bag of shredded cheddar cheese
      1 small can chicken do NOT drain liquid

Preheat your oven to 350*
Prepare the Stove Top dressing per the directions on the box. Set aside.

Sauté the zuc, onion, and garlic in a medium hot skillet; cook until onions are clear. Add the condensed soup and the chicken. Mix well.

Take a 2-quart casserole dish, and spray with vegetable spray.

Layer ½ of the stuffing on the bottom.
Layer ½ of the zuc mix
Layer ½ of the cheese
Layer the rest of the stuffing
Layer the rest of the zuc mix
Layer the rest of the cheese on top
Bake at 350* for 20-30 minutes. Yum.

CIOPPINO

I've never made this, but I thought you might like the recipe:

SHOPPING LIST and some prep work:

    3 tbsp. olive oil
    1 large fennel bulb, thinly sliced
    1 onion, chopped
    3 large shallots, chopped
    2 tsp salt
    4 large garlic cloves, finely chopped
    ¾ tsp dried crushed red pepper flakes, add more to taste
    ¼ cup tomato paste
    1 (28-ounce) can diced tomatoes in juice
    1 ½ cups dry white wine
    5 cups fish stock
    1 bay leaf
    1 pound manila clams, scrubbed
    1 pound mussels, scrubbed, debearded
    1 pound uncooked large shrimp, peeled and deveined
    1 ½ pounds assorted firm-fleshed fish fillets such as
        halibut or salmon, cut into 2-inch chunks

Heat the oil in a very large pot over medium heat.

Add the fennel, onion, shallots, and salt and sauté until the onion is translucent, about 10 minutes.

Add the garlic and ¾ teaspoon of red pepper flakes, and sauté 2 minutes. Stir in the tomato paste.

Add tomatoes with their juices, wine, fish stock and bay leaf.

Cover and bring to a simmer. Reduce the heat to medium-low.

Cover and simmer until the flavors blend, about 30 minutes.

Add the clams and mussels to the cooking liquid.

Cover and cook until the clams and mussels begin to open, about 5 minutes.

Add the shrimp and fish.

Simmer gently until the fish and shrimp are just cooked through, and the clams are completely open, stirring gently, about 5 minutes longer (discard any clams and mussels that do not open).

Season the soup, to taste, with more salt and red pepper flakes.

Ladle the soup into bowls and serve.

Recipe courtesy of Giada De Laurentiis

http://www.foodnetwork.com/recipes/giada-de-laurentiis/cioppino-recipe.html

EASY KNITTING PATTERN FOR A WINTER CAP

SHOPPING LIST
- #8 needles
- #10.5 needles
- ruler
- stitch markers
- worsted weight yarn, about 2 ounces
- yarn needle

To begin, cast on 70 stitches on #8 needles

Purl all stitches on the first row

Ribbing Rows:
*K1, P1 repeat to end of row
Repeat row until piece measures 2 inches

Change to #10.5 needles

Body of the hat:
Row 1: Knit all stitches
Row 2: Purl all stitches
Repeat Rows 1-2 until piece measures 7.5 inches. End with a Purl row.

Decrease Rows:
*K2 together, **K8**, place marker on right needle*, repeat to end of row.
Purl next row-slide markers for left to right needle as you go.

The markers make it possible to avoid counting each stitch! K2 together at the beginning of each "knit" row, then

K2 together right after you slide each marker! Keep using them until the last row.

*K2 together, **K7**, slide marker onto right needle*, repeat to end

Purl next row.

*K2 together, **K6**, slide marker onto right needle*, repeat to end

Purl next row.

*K2 together, **K5**, slide marker onto right needle*, repeat to end

Purl next row.

*K2 together, **K4**, slide marker onto right needle*, repeat to end

Purl next row.

*K2 together, **K3**, slide marker onto right needle*, repeat to end

Purl next row.

*K2 together, **K2**, slide marker onto right needle*, repeat to end

Purl next row.

*K2 together, **K1**, remove all the markers as you go

Bind off.
Turn hat inside out and sew seam together to complete.

BACK OF THE BOOK STUFF

Some folks wonder how we can possibly live full-time in about 350 square feet? We downsized from a 2,300 square-foot home with a huge kitchen, 3 bathrooms and a 2-car garage for storage, so YES, there were some adjustments to be made! We had yard sales for three weekends running, sold all our furniture, and brokered our antiques. I gave dozens of books to a senior living facility and some to our county library. Some precious memories could not be parted with, and could not accompany us, so they did go into storage for a time. During the yard sales, a woman introduced herself as a worker from a local Habitat for Humanity store. Not only would they pick up furniture, she said the local store would pick up anything and everything we had left over, as long as it was all in boxes, and easy to load. When we had packed, sold, donated, and brokered everything that we could, I gave her a call. It was a tremendous service to me.

Now on the road, there are times, I must admit, that I just have to get out for a while. I usually feign a need for something and take the car and Frack out on a drive to Walmart, Dollar General, or whatever's available in the area. I feel so much better when I get back.

And even though Larry nibbles in little bits all day, he has finally come to understand that I like to eat out, especially to sample unique area cuisine. If I've been inside for days—because of writing, weather, or whatever—much he's better now at suggesting that we go out to shop, eat, or go to a movie.

But get used to the idea that there are going to be times that both of you want to be in exactly the same place at the exactly the same time…usually the bathroom! Just be considerate of who's whining the loudest.

Some folks wonder if we could give them some pointers? Larry would say that planning is of the utmost importance, especially if you travel when school is out of session. At those times, you can't just roll in somewhere and expect there to be vacancy. Plan your route well, because at 8 miles to the gallon, you sure don't want to backtrack! Larry's really great at drilling in and planning, and had all of our National Park reservations in advance of our departure, most of our State Parks, and a great deal of our private parks, as well. He put in a lot of time, while I was recovering, searching the routes, computing travel times, comparing rates and ratings of campgrounds. He had searched areas to see what attractions were there. The out-of-season weather has been our biggest surprise, but you can't control Mother Nature!

Some folks wonder if there are any apps out there, to help them on the way? Larry's phone is chuck full of helpful apps!

ALLSTAYS is an app that every person with an RV should have. You can search campgrounds and read personal reviews, find Walmarts who allow boondoggling with reviews, truck stops, rest stops, propane, dump stations, height clearances along a route, rig maintenance and repair. Their reviews have helped us avoid poor choices on the road.

ULTIMATE CG app shows where there is free camping allowed on public lands. This is how we had the opportunity to stay at White Sands.

CHIMANI is an app that gives you great information on all National Parks, national monuments, historic sites, memorials, recreational areas and more.

TRIPOSO is an app that gives you everything you need to know about the places and cities you plan to visit.

GAS BUDDY is an app for finding the cheapest fuel on your route. Members are constantly updating prices, and a recent reported drop of even a few cents on diesel can save you lots of cash on 100 gallons. TIP: if you can, always fill up away from the interstate. We have seen interstate truck plazas charge up to forty cents more than a small-town guy just off the interstate. Gas Buddy will help you find those deals. But also Google it, to be sure their lot has room for your big rig.

MY MEDICAL is an app for keeping your medical records with you, wherever you go, whether you're traveling away from home, or not.

WUNDERGROUND is an app from Weather Underground that will show you live weather from every weather station out there. When you open it, it automatically homes in on exactly where you are and what weather forecast, live radar and any weather alerts that are active at that time. Priceless!

GOOGLE MAPS (aka Frack) is an app that everybody should have for everyday use. Frack is pretty great on the long haul, but sometimes needs some human interpretation. It also has no idea that you're a high-profile vehicle with another vehicle in tow, so it may take you somewhere you really shouldn't be.

SYGIC TRUCKERS GPS (aka Frank) is what we've just begun to use. You begin by telling the program how long you are, what height you are, and what load you are, so it keeps you away from places you shouldn't be. One important talent loudly warns you of exceeding speed limits, and upcoming rest areas and railroad crossings.

RVingVIP is a maintenance app, a desktop program to keep track of all the maintenance issues of your RV.

DISHALIGN and **DishForMyRv** are invaluable tools to assist you in manually setting your dish antenna to satellite feeds.

TOLL CALCULATOR GPS helps you determine which route costs less when traveling on toll roads with a large motorhome and a "toad" (tow vehicle). This could save you hundreds of dollars, if you plan to be in areas with multiple toll roads.

TOLLSMART is another toll calculator app.

Find a good **LEVEL TOOL**. Every single time we pull into a new campground, we need to level. There are lots of apps out there that can assist you with this.

BANK AND INVESTMENTS apps are very important. One thing we learned years ago, the hard way. When you leave on a trip, your debit card company wants to know ahead of time. We had lived in South Carolina for so long that, one year when we went home to Cincinnati and used our debit card, the bank declined it. They continued to decline it until I called in and asked what was going on? Their security assumed that my card has been stolen, because it was being used in an area that I never frequented—it went against my spending pattern. They made a note of where I was and for how long, and the problem was solved. Now I'm sure to notify them before I go anywhere out-of-state, to avoid surprises.

Some folks wonder what to do with their mail? If you're a member of Good Sam, they offer forwarding services. They assign you an address that you give out, they collect your mail until you ask them to forward it to you. We personally, have a PO Box back home. Diana picks up everything, opens anything unusual and screen shots us copies, if it's something urgent.

Some folks wonder about using their computers on the road? This is our biggest challenge and our largest expense. We initially chose Verizon for our cellular service because they had the best coverage across America. The Verizon Jet Pack is mobile and works wherever our Verizon cell service works. AND, they have recently changed to Unlimited. This rocked our world completely! Most private and some state campgrounds advertise FREE Wi-Fi, but it's usually just a token offering, and rarely works well, except in the middle of the night. So, don't depend on what campgrounds are offering, make solid, dependable plans of your own.

Some folks wonder if there are any National Park programs they should join? If you are 65 or older, or permanently disabled, you should definitely apply for a lifetime Access Pass and pay the one-time $10 fee. Every National Park has an impact fee they charge for entering the Park. The Access Pass will have your name and photo on it, and it's good for you and anyone in your vehicle. Larry has one, so I don't need one because I'm always with him. Some federal campgrounds even offer a 50% discount on campground fees. It's saved us hundreds of dollars this past year.

Some folks wonder if there are clubs or memberships they should consider joining? We use several camping clubs. Just for your information, the average we've spent per night on the road is around $40 for full hookups, where high-end resorts could cost you $70-$100 per night. Special events like Mardi Gras, in New Orleans, one campground (we did not stay here) was charging nearly $300 per night. National Parks and State parks average around $30. Casinos, sometimes offer a great night of camping, cheap like, $20 or less—one let us stay for free—in the hopes they get you in their casino. Of course, you can't beat Boondoggling, it's FREE! Here are some of our personal thoughts about each:

GOOD SAM CLUB is a great value for the annual fee. It saves us 10% each time we use it and most private campgrounds do accept it. Their website has the BEST reviews of campgrounds, and Larry based most of our reservations on those reviews. They offer supplemental programs that you can sign up for, as well: Roadside Assistance, Motorhome Insurance, Travel Assist Medical, Extended Warranty, Motorhome Financing, Coast to Coast, Discounts at Camping World, Flying J, Pilot, and others, RV Forum, Mail Forwarding Services, and much, much more.

PASSPORT AMERICA is another good value for some half-priced stays. The drawback is that there are a lot of rules regarding its use and there are many campgrounds that don't accept it.

COAST TO COAST. We have saved money with this membership, but it's costly to join up front. Usually the campgrounds are older and off the beaten path, but for $10 a night, sometimes it's worth the trip. Before buying, I'd suggest you search the internet for discounters and other agents, and be sure there would be participating campgrounds in the area you'll be visiting. Some of them can be really nice and cheap, but we have stayed in others that have been mediocre, at best. Your nightly fee may be $10, but then it's $5 more for 50 amp electric, $5 more for Wi-Fi, $3 more for cable (you cannot opt-out—true story). They $5 you to death, until what you pay is closer to their normal rates.

KOA VALUE KARD. Many KOA campgrounds are aging, but there are still some really nice ones out there, just check out the reviews. We pay an annual fee and receive 10% at KOA across America. Just be sure to read the reviews written on them, before pulling in. They don't accept any other discounts, not even Good Sam.

RESORT PARKS INTERNATIONAL / RPI. We do have this, but haven't used it at all this past year, because we have the Coast to Coast membership. They are similar and we have it because we have Coast to Coast.

ENCORE is a benefit of Coast to Coast, and we have used it for a 10% discount.

THOUSAND TRAILS. We don't use this since we have Coast to Coast. Some of the participating parks are old and outdated as well as being out of the way. I think it's their way of attempting to attract folks that would not come otherwise.

ENJOY AMERICA. We have used this to save 50%, but like Passport America, there are some rules you must follow. This came with our RPI membership, as well.

Some folks wonder if we could offer any tips to making reservations? Accept the fact that reservations are a MUST for popular destinations and/or popular times. Any time kids are out of school—even for a three-day holiday—people are out and about. Make reservations at least 60-90 days out. If you want to stay in places like Yellowstone, Yosemite or Cades Cove in the Great Smoky Mountain National Park, you must make them a YEAR in advance of your date. For example, we want to enjoy a White House tour in 2017. We learned that, post 9/11, you must request that reservation through your State Congressman or Senator three to four months in advance of your desired date. Research your destinations. Print out everything you reserved, your dates, an exact address for your GPS, and any confirmation numbers. Keep them in date order, organized and ready for your arrival. We keep ours on a clip board on the dash.

We use **Recreation.gov** and **ReserveAmerica.com**, a great deal for park reservations.

We are weather wussies. We have been through multiple hurricanes and three blizzards. We like warm weather, so if you're in search of 70-degree weather in the winter like us, I have news: so is everybody else! Places like Key West, Florida, the Gulf State Beaches, South Padre Island and Galveston, Texas fill up fast for the winter. You should probably make those reservations a YEAR in advance, too. In Texas, they called us Winter Texans. In Florida, they'll call you Snowbirds. We love being called names.

Some folks wonder if we could help them get organized? Organization is a must. I have only a tiny fraction of the space I had in my nice home. I brought one piece of Corning Ware and rarely use it. I have two skillets, three saucepans, again, which I rarely use, because I nuke or Crock Pot almost everything. I brought four plates, four bowls, and two large bowls. If we ever have company, we'll eat off paper, no problem.

BUY SMALL. When I went back to work several years ago and Larry started shopping, he would bring home huge packages of stuff from Sam's Club and Costco. Early on, we had thirty-six rolls of toilet paper stuck away in every cabinet, nook and cranny, under the dinette, and under the bed. "But it was cheap," he said. I have finally taught him that a nine-pack of Scott is just fine. My washer/dryer uses one tablespoon of detergent per load. I had purchased Mrs. Meyers in a bottle with 68 loads. He buys a gigantic Tide that will probably last me two years. There's just no need for that, with such precious limited space. Larry's sense of humor often tells me, "If you can't eat it and s**t it, then don't buy it." Not Funny. And then he buys 6 huge tubes of toothpaste, that we will take up precious space until he turns 70. Buy small. You can always buy more.

Some folks wonder if we have any tips for repairs and maintenance? I would recommend first using an RV forum at **www.rvforum.net** or **www.rv.net/forum** for information regarding your specific rig and maintenance. There's a strong chance that other folks have experienced the same problem you have, so you should be able to easily find solutions to your problem. Always carry a good set of basic tools and a drill set because, believe me, you WILL need them. Other basic spares would include: engine oil, coolant, silicone, sealant, distilled water, Gorilla Glue, duct tape, and water filters.

Basic needs you may know, but you may not:

Always use a <u>water regulator</u>. Many campgrounds will warn you that they have high water pressure, so I always use a regulator, regardless. And always carry a spare—they fail without any warning whatsoever.

You should carry at least 25 feet of <u>water hose</u>, and a spare. Since typical hoses take up room and kink, I bought one that shrinks up when not in use, and another coiled one. Also, keep on hand a couple of 3-foot sections of water hose. If the campsite spigots are too low to the ground, they really come in handy. They also make rinsing your holding tank a whole lot easier.

You will also need 30 feet of <u>electric cable</u> (I've never needed more than that). A good <u>surge protector</u> is needed as well, for your electrical connection, and <u>adapters</u> to connect to different amps offered.

To avoid any problems, you should have FOUR 10-15 foot sections of <u>sewer hoses</u>.

To access <u>cable</u> connections, a 25-foot coax should do.

Some folks wonder how to handle keeping up with our doctors? We sat down with our doctors before we left our home base. We explained our plans to travel and requested that they write our prescriptions in a way that would enable us to get them filled as needed, for the next 12 months. None of our doctors had any problems in doing just that. I can personally recommend CVS Pharmacy for this. They seem to be almost everywhere, and your refill information is right there in their computer. Walmart or Walgreens probably do this, too. As long as there were refills left, I have never had a problem in getting our prescriptions filled.

When we planned our trip, we planned to return to our home base in the spring, when the weather would be warm. We'll spend thirty days back home to take care of dentist and doctor appointments, where we will get those refills rewritten for another year.

Some folks wonder about all of those factory tours we took? Other than the scenery and wildlife at the National Parks, those tours were some of our best times! Each time we arrived in a new area, we Googled it. Most cities and city Chambers of Commerce have official sites to encourage travelers to visit there. All you need is the name, and you go to their official site for possible tours, times, and prices. Most have been absolutely FREE, and those that charged, the fees were minimal. We have already been to the following:

- Jelly Belly, Fairfield, CA
- Freightliner, Gaffney, SC
- Harry & David, Medford, OR
- Gibson Guitar, Memphis, TN
- Hallmark, Kansas City, MO
- Tabasco, Avery Island, LA
- Budweiser, St. Louis, MO
- Celestial Teas, Boulder, CO
- Boeing, Everett, WA
- SAS Shoes, San Antonio, TX
- Hammonds Candies, Denver, CO
- Pendleton Blankets, Washougal, WA
- Jim Bean, Clermont, KY
- Landstrom's Black Hills Gold, Rapid City, SD

I don't know if you'd call these factory tours, but we enjoyed:

- The US Mint in Denver, CO was amazing too.
- The Money Museum Federal Reserve Bank of St. Louis

In 2017, we plan to see at least the following:

- Cape Cod Potato Chips, Hyannis, MA
- Ben & Jerry's, Waterbury, VT
- Coke, Atlanta, GA
- Hershey, Hershey, PA
- The White House, Washington, DC

Don't miss the Presidential Libraries … Buy a membership if you are going to visit more than one in a year.

OUR ROUTE

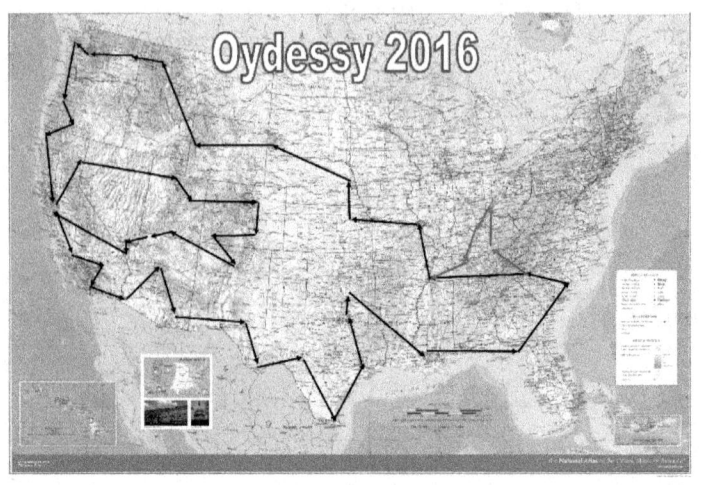

CAMPGROUND RECAP

Larry rated these campgrounds based on our personal experience there; we know your personal experiences may differ greatly. Some low ratings are simply due to the fact they offered no utilities, while other low ratings are due to the condition of the campground or problems we encountered while staying there.

April	Kentucky Horse Park, Lexington, KY, Rating 5
April	KOA Louisville South, Shepherdsville, KY, Rating 6
April	Diamond Caverns RV Resort, Park City KY, Rating 3
April	KOA Music City, Nashville, TN, Rating 9
April	Queen Casino RV Park, East St. Louis, IL, Rating 8
April	East Kansas City KOA, Oak Grove, MO, Rating 7
April	Deer Creek Valley RV Park, Topeka, KS, Rating 9
April	Cherry Creek State. Park, Denver, CO, Rating 8
May	Manor RV Park, Este Park, CO, Rating 4
May	Chimney Rock Pioneer CG, Bayard, NE, Rating 4
May	Chadron State Park, Chadron, NE, Rating 6
May	Custer State Park, SD (Blue Belle CG), Rating 5
May	Badlands National Park, Interior, SD, Rating 6
May	Rushmore Shadows Resort, Rapid City, SD, Rating 6
June	Deadwood KOA, Deadwood, SD, Rating 3
June	Hardin KOA, Hardin, MT, Rating 2
June	Absaroka Bay RV Park, Cody, WY, Rating 5
June	Canyon Village CG Yellowstone NP, Canyon Village, WY, Rating 3
June	Lincoln Road RV Park, Helena, MT, Rating 6
June	St. Mary CG, Glacier NP, St. Mary, MT, Rating 3
June	Icicle River RV Park, Leavenworth, WA, Rating 8
June	Lakeside RV Park, Everett, WA, Rating 6
June	Lake Pleasant RV Park., Bothell, WA, Rating 6
July	Ft Worden Beach CG SP, Pt. Townsend, WA, Rating 6
July	Olympic National Park., Kalaloch, WA, Rating 3
July	Olympia CG, Olympia, WA, Rating 2
July	Mt. Rainier NP, Cougar CG, WA, Rating 3
July	Mt. St. Helens, Paradise Creek, WA, Rating 2
July	Ainsworth SP CG, Troutdale, OR, Rating 3
July	Portland Fairview CG, Portland, WA, Rating 5
July	South Beach SP, Newport, OR, Rating 3
July	Crater Lake NP, Mazama CG, OR, Rating 2

July	Seven Feather RV, Canyonville, OR, Rating 10
July	Tri-City RV Park, Myrtle Creek, OR, Rating 4
August	Harris Beach SP, Brookings, OR, Rating 5
August	Beachfront RV, Port Brookings Harbor, OR, Rating 3
August	Jedidiah Smith Redwoods, Crescent City, CA, Rating 3
August	Skyline Wilderness Park, Napa Valley, CA, Rating 2
August	Marin Park, Greenbrae, CA (Bay Area), Rating 3
August	Yosemite National, North Pines Campground, .Rating 5
August	Lake Tahoe Valley Camp. South Tahoe, Ca, Rating 3
August	Sparks Marina RV Park, Sparks, NV (Reno), Rating 9
August	Great Salt Lake State Park, Magna, UT, Rating 5
August	Salt Lake City KOA, Salt Lake City, UT, Rating 7
August	Mountain Valley RV Resort, Heber, UT, Rating 10

We have chosen to leave the following parks unrated, due to negative treatment we personally received during our stay, regarding our Motorhome Ministry.

April	Myrtle Beach State Park, Myrtle Beach, SC,
June	Briarcliffe RV Park , Myrtle Beach, SC
August	Coyote Valley RV Resort, San Jose, CA

www.ingramcontent.com/pod-product-compliance
Lightning Source LLC
LaVergne TN
LVHW051110080426
835510LV00018B/1980